INTERNATIONAL LAW DOCUMENTS

THE TREATY OF PEACE WITH GERMANY
JUNE 28, 1919

WITH NOTE AND INDEX

▽

1919

WASHINGTON
GOVERNMENT PRINTING OFFICE
1920

PREFACE.

Since 1915 it has seemed advisable that the Naval War College publications on international law should present the material with which officers might be concerned. Following this precedent the treaty of peace with Germany of June 28, 1919, would naturally be made the volume for 1919. In publishing this treaty the text submitted to the Senate of the United States on July 10, 1919, has been used. An index has been added in order that the provisions of the treaty may easily be consulted. Although the treaty has not been ratified by the United States, its provisions are of importance to officers because the treaty is already operative as regards certain States in their relations with one another and with Germany.

The discussions upon international law at the Naval War College have been conducted by George Grafton Wilson, LL. D., professor of international law in Harvard University, and have given special attention to problems arising under the treaty of peace.

WM. S. SIMS,
Rear Admiral, United States Navy,
President Naval War College,
Newport, R. I.

DECEMBER 31, 1919.

II

6296

TABLE OF CONTENTS.

TREATY OF PEACE WITH GERMANY.

PRELIMINARY NOTE.

The Austrian declaration of war against Serbia on July 28, 1914, was followed by many other declarations.[1]

The United States declared war against Germany April 6, 1917. An armistice between Germany and the allied and associated powers was agreed upon on November 11, 1918. The representatives of the allied and associated powers assembled at Paris on January 18, 1919, for drawing up a treaty of peace. This treaty was handed to the German representatives on May 7, 1919. The treaty was signed at Versailles on June 28, 1919. The treaty was submitted to the Senate of the United States on July 10, 1919. The "advice and consent" of the Senate was necessary for putting the treaty into operation. After long debate this advice and consent was not given and accordingly for the United States the treaty was not operative.

According to the provisions of Article 440 of the treaty—

A first procès-verbal of the deposit of ratification will be drawn up as soon as the treaty has been ratified by Germany on the one hand, and by three of the principal allied and associated powers on the other hand.

From the date of this first procès-verbal the treaty will come into force between the high contracting parties who have ratified it. For the determination of all periods of time provided for in the present treaty this date will be the date of the coming into force of the treaty.

In all other respects the treaty will enter into force for each power at the date of the deposit of its ratification.

Under the provisions of the treaty (Art. 5) the first meeting of the Council of the League of Nations was held at Paris, January 16, 1920, and representatives of the following members of the League of Nations were present: Belgium, Brazil, the British Empire, France, Greece, Italy, Japan, Spain. The following States had also adhered to the League of Nations Covenant: The Argentine Republic, July 18, 1919; Paraguay, October 29, 1919; Chile, November 14, 1919; Persia, November 21, 1919.

---

[1] See Naval War College, International Law Documents, 1917, p. 15, and 1918, p. 11.

TREATY OF PEACE WITH GERMANY.

THE UNITED STATES OF AMERICA, THE BRITISH EM-
PIRE, FRANCE, ITALY and JAPAN,
These Powers being described in the present Treaty as the Prin-
cipal Allied and Associated Powers,
BELGIUM, BOLIVIA, BRAZIL, CHINA, CUBA, ECUADOR,
GREECE, GUATEMALA, HAITI, THE HEDJAZ, HON-
DURAS, LIBERIA, NICARAGUA, PANAMA, PERU, PO-
LAND, PORTUGAL, ROUMANIA, THE SERB-CROAT-SLO-
VENE STATE, SIAM, CZECHO-SLOVAKIA and URUGUAY,
These Powers constituting with the Principal Powers mentioned
above the Allied and Associated Powers,

of the one part;

And GERMANY,

of the other part;

Bearing in mind that on the request of the Imperial German Government an Armistice was granted on November 11, 1918, to Germany by the Principal Allied and Associated Powers in order that a
Treaty of Peace might be concluded with her, and
The Allied and Associated Powers being equally desirous that the
war in which they were successively involved directly or indirectly
and which originated in the declaration of war by Austria-Hungary
on July 28, 1914, against Serbia, the declaration of war by Germany
against Russia on August 1, 1914, and against France on August 3,
1914, and in the invasion of Belgium, should be replaced by a firm,
just and durable Peace,
For this purpose the HIGH CONTRACTING PARTIES represented as follows:

THE PRESIDENT OF THE UNITED STATES OF AMERICA,
by:

> The Honourable Woodrow WILSON, PRESIDENT OF THE UNITED
> STATES, acting in his own name and by his own proper
> authority;
> The Honourable Robert LANSING, Secretary of State;
> The Honourable Henry WHITE, formerly Ambassador Ex-
> traordinary and Plenipotentiary of the United States at
> Rome and Paris;
> The Honourable Edward M. HOUSE;
> General Tasker H. BLISS, Military Representative of the
> United States on the Supreme War Council;

3

HIS MAJESTY THE KING OF THE UNITED KINGDOM
OF GREAT BRITAIN AND IRELAND AND OF THE BRIT-
ISH DOMINIONS BEYOND THE SEAS, EMPEROR OF
INDIA, by:

> The Right Honourable David LLOYD GEORGE, M. P., First
> Lord of His Treasury and Prime Minister;
> The Right Honourable Andrew BONAR LAW, M. P., His Lord
> Privy Seal;
> The Right Honourable Viscount MILNER, G. C. B., G. C.
> M. G., His Secretary of State for the Colonies;
> The Right Honourable Arthur James BALFOUR, O. M., M. P.,
> His Secretary of State for Foreign Affairs;
> The Right Honourable George Nicoll BARNES, M. P., Minister
> without portfolio;

And

for the DOMINION of CANADA, by:

> The Honourable Charles Joseph DOHERTY, Minister of Jus-
> tice;
> The Honourable Arthur Lewis SIFTON, Minister of Customs;

for the COMMONWEALTH of AUSTRALIA, by:

> The Right Honourable William Morris HUGHES, Attorney
> General and Prime Minister;
> The Right Honourable Sir Joseph COOK, G. C. M. G., Minister
> for the Navy;

for the UNION OF SOUTH AFRICA, by:

> General the Right Honourable Louis BOTHA, Minister of Na-
> tive Affairs and Prime Minister;
> Lieutenant-General the Right Honourable Jan Christiaan
> SMUTS, K. C., Minister of Defence;

for the DOMINION of NEW ZEALAND, by:

> The Right Honourable William Ferguson MASSEY, Minister of
> Labour and Prime Minister;

for INDIA, by:

> The Right Honourable Edwin Samuel MONTAGU, M. P., His
> Secretary of State for India;
> Major-General His Highness Maharaja Sir Ganga Singh
> Bahadur, Maharaja of BIKANER, G. C. S. I., G. C. I. E.,
> G. C. V. O., K. C. B., A. D. C.;

THE PRESIDENT OF THE FRENCH REPUBLIC, by:

> Mr. Georges CLEMENCEAU, President of the Council, Minister
> of War;
> Mr. Stephen PICHON, Minister for Foreign Affairs;
> Mr. Louis-Lucien KLOTZ, Minister of Finance;
> Mr. André TARDIEU, Commissary General for Franco-Ameri-
> can Military Affairs;
> Mr. Jules CAMBON, Ambassador of France;

HIS MAJESTY THE KING OF ITALY, by:

Baron S. Sonnino, Deputy;

Marquis G. Imperiali, Senator, Ambassador of His Majesty the King of Italy at London;

Mr. S. Crespi, Deputy;

HIS MAJESTY THE EMPEROR OF JAPAN, by:

Marquis Saïonzi, formerly President of the Council of Ministers;

Baron Makino, formerly Minister for Foreign Affairs, Member of the Diplomatic Council;

Viscount Chinda, Ambassador Extraordinary and Plenipotentiary of H. M. the Emperor of Japan at London;

Mr. K. Matsui, Ambassador Extraordinary and Plenipotentiary of H. M. the Emperor of Japan at Paris;

Mr. H. Ijuin, Ambassador Extraordinary and Plenipotentiary of H. M. the Emperor of Japan at Rome;

HIS MAJESTY THE KING OF THE BELGIANS, by:

Mr. Paul Hymans, Minister for Foreign Affairs, Minister of State;

Mr. Jules van den Heuvel, Envoy Extraordinary and Minister Plenipotentiary, Minister of State;

Mr. Emile Vandervelde, Minister of Justice, Minister of State;

THE PRESIDENT OF THE REPUBLIC OF BOLIVIA, by:

Mr. Ismael Montes, Envoy Extraordinary and Minister Plenipotentiary of Bolivia at Paris;

THE PRESIDENT OF THE REPUBLIC OF BRAZIL, by:

Mr. João Pandiá Calogeras, Deputy, formerly Minister of Finance;

Mr. Raul Fernandes, Deputy;

Mr. Rodrigo Octavio de L. Menezes, Professor of International Law of Rio de Janeiro;

THE PRESIDENT OF THE CHINESE REPUBLIC, by:

Mr. Lou Tseng-Tsiang, Minister for Foreign Affiairs;

Mr. Chengting Thomas Wang, formerly Minister of Agriculture and Commerce;

THE PRESIDENT OF THE CUBAN REPUBLIC, by:

Mr. Antonio Sánchez de Bustamante, Dean of the Faculty of Law in the University of Havana, President of the Cuban Society of International Law;

THE PRESIDENT OF THE REPUBLIC OF ECUADOR, by:

Mr. Enrique Dorn y de Alsúa, Envoy Extraordinary and Minister Plenipotentiary of Ecuador at Paris;

HIS MAJESTY THE KING OF THE HELLENES, by:

Mr. Eleftherios K. Venisélos, President of the Council of Ministers;

Mr. Nicolas Politis, Minister for Foreign Affairs;

THE PRESIDENT OF THE REPUBLIC OF GUATEMALA, by:

    Mr. Joaquin MÉNDEZ, formerly Minister of State for Public Works and Public Instruction, Envoy Extraordinary and Minister Plenipotentiary of Guatemala at Washington, Envoy Extraordinary and Minister Plenipotentiary on special mission at Paris;

THE PRESIDENT OF THE REPUBLIC OF HAITI, by:

    Mr. Tertullien GUILBAUD, Envoy Extraordinary and Minister Plenipotentiary of Haiti at Paris;

HIS MAJESTY THE KING OF THE HEDJAZ, by:

    Mr. Rustem HAÏDAR;
    Mr. Abdul Hadi AOUNI;

THE PRESIDENT OF THE REPUBLIC OF HONDURAS, by:

    Dr. Policarpo BONILLA, on special mission to Washington, formerly President of the Republic of Honduras, Envoy Extraordinary and Minister Plenipotentiary;

THE PRESIDENT OF THE REPUBLIC OF LIBERIA, by:

    The Honourable Charles Dunbar Burgess KING, Secretary of State;

THE PRESIDENT OF THE REPUBLIC OF NICARAGUA, by:

    Mr. Salvador CHAMORRO, President of the Chamber of Deputies;

THE PRESIDENT OF THE REPUBLIC OF PANAMA, by:

    Mr. Antonio BURGOS, Envoy Extraordinary and Minister Plenipotentiary of Panama at Madrid;

THE PRESIDENT OF THE REPUBLIC OF PERU, by:

    Mr. Carlos G. CANDAMO, Envoy Extraordinary and Minister Plenipotentiary of Peru at Paris;

THE PRESIDENT OF THE POLISH REPUBLIC, by:

    Mr. Ignace J. PADEREWSKI, President of the Council of Ministers, Minister for Foreign Affairs;
    Mr. Roman DMOWSKI, President of the Polish National Committee;

THE PRESIDENT OF THE PORTUGUESE REPUBLIC, by:

    Dr. Affonso Augusto DA COSTA, formerly President of the Council of Ministers;
    Dr. Augusto Luiz Vieira SOARES, formerly Minister for Foreign Affairs;

HIS MAJESTY THE KING OF ROUMANIA, by:

    Mr. Ion I. C. BRATIANO, President of the Council of Ministers, Minister for Foreign Affairs;
    General Constantin COANDA, Corps Commander, A. D. C. to the King, formerly President of the Council of Ministers;

HIS MAJESTY THE KING OF THE SERBS, THE CROATS, AND THE SLOVENES, by:

Mr. Nicolas P. PACHITCH, formerly President of the Council of Ministers;

Mr. Ante TRUMBIC, Minister for Foreign Affairs;

Mr. Milenko VESNITCH, Envoy Extraordinary and Minister Plenipotentiary of H. M. the King of the Serbs, the Croats and the Slovenes at Paris;

HIS MAJESTY THE KING OF SIAM, by:

His Highness Prince CHAROON, Envoy Extraordinary and Minister Plenipotentiary of H. M. the King of Siam at Paris;

His Serene Highness Prince Traidos PRABANDHU, Under Secretary of State for Foreign Affairs;

THE PRESIDENT OF THE CZECHO-SLOVAK REPUB-LIC, by:

Mr. Karel KRAMÁŘ, President of the Council of Ministers;

Mr. Eduard BENEŠ, Minister for Foreign Affairs;

THE PRESIDENT OF THE REPUBLIC OF URUGUAY, by:

Mr. Juan Antonio BUERO, Minister for Foreign Affairs, formerly Minister of Industry;

GERMANY, by:

Mr. Hermann MÜLLER, Minister for Foreign Affairs of the Empire;

Dr. BELL, Minister of the Empire;

Acting in the name of the German Empire and of each and every component State,

WHO having communicated their full powers found in good and due form have AGREED AS FOLLOWS:

From the coming into force of the present Treaty the state of war will terminate. From that moment and subject to the provisions of this Treaty official relations with Germany, and with any of the German States, will be resumed by the Allied and Associated Powers.

PART I.

THE COVENANT OF THE LEAGUE OF NATIONS.

THE HIGH CONTRACTING PARTIES,

In order to promote international co-operation and to achieve international peace and security

by the acceptance of obligations not to resort to war,

by the prescription of open, just and honourable relations between nations,

by the firm establishment of the understandings of international law as the actual rule of conduct among Governments, and

by the maintenance of justice and a scrupulous respect for all treaty obligations in the dealings of organised peoples with one another,

Agree to this Covenant of the League of Nations.

ARTICLE 1.

The original Members of the League of Nations shall be those of the Signatories which are named in the Annex to this Covenant and also such of those other States named in the Annex as shall accede without reservation to this Covenant. Such accession shall be effected by a Declaration deposited with the Secretariat within two months of the coming into force of the Covenant. Notice thereof shall be sent to all other Members of the League.

Any fully self-governing State, Dominion or Colony not named in the Annex may become a Member of the League if its admission is agreed to by two-thirds of the Assembly, provided that it shall give effective guarantees of its sincere intention to observe its international obligations, and shall accept such regulations as may be prescribed by the League in regard to its military, naval and air forces and armaments.

Any Member of the League may, after two years' notice of its intention so to do, withdraw from the League, provided that all its international obligations and all its obligations under this Covenant shall have been fulfilled at the time of its withdrawal.

ARTICLE 2.

The action of the League under this Covenant shall be effected through the instrumentality of an Assembly and of a Council, with a permanent Secretariat,

ARTICLE 3.

The Assembly shall consist of Representatives of the Members of the League.

The Assembly shall meet at stated intervals and from time to time as occasion may require at the Seat of the League or at such other place as may be decided upon.

The Assembly may deal at its meetings with any matter within the sphere of action of the League or affecting the peace of the world.

At meetings of the Assembly each Member of the League shall have one vote, and may have not more than three Representatives.

ARTICLE 4.

The Council shall consist of Representatives of the Principal Allied and Associated Powers, together with Representatives of four other Members of the League. These four Members of the League shall be selected by the Assembly from time to time in its discretion. Until the appointment of the Representatives of the four Members of the League first selected by the Assembly, Representatives of Belgium, Brazil, Spain and Greece shall be members of the Council.

With the approval of the majority of the Assembly, the Council may name additional Members of the League whose Representatives shall always be members of the Council; the Council with like approval may increase the number of Members of the League to be selected by the Assembly for representation on the Council.

The Council shall meet from time to time as occasion may require, and at least once a year, at the Seat of the League, or at such other place as may be decided upon.

The Council may deal at its meetings with any matter within the sphere of action of the League or affecting the peace of the world.

Any Member of the League not represented on the Council shall be invited to send a Representative to sit as a member at any meeting of the Council during the consideration of matters specially effecting the interests of that Member of the League.

At meetings of the Council, each Member of the League represented on the Council shall have one vote, and may have not more than one Representative.

ARTICLE 5.

Except where otherwise expressly provided in this Covenant or by the terms of the present Treaty, decisions at any meeting of the Assembly or of the Council shall require the agreement of all the Members of the League represented at the meeting.

All matters of procedure at meetings of the Assembly or of the Council, including the appointment of Committees to investigate particular matters, shall be regulated by the Assembly or by the Council and may be decided by a majority of the Members of the League represented at the meeting.

The first meeting of the Assembly and the first meeting of the Council shall be summoned by the President of the United States of America.

ARTICLE 6.

The permanent Secretariat shall be established at the Seat of the League. The Secretariat shall comprise a Secretary General and such secretaries and staff as may be required.

The first Secretary General shall be the person named in the Annex; thereafter the Secretary General shall be appointed by the Council with the approval of the majority of the Assembly.

The secretaries and staff of the Secretariat shall be appointed by the Secretary General with the approval of the Council.

The Secretary General shall act in that capacity at all meetings of the Assembly and of the Council.

The expenses of the Secretariat shall be borne by the Members of the League in accordance with the apportionment of the expenses of the International Bureau of the Universal Postal Union.

ARTICLE 7.

The Seat of the League is established at Geneva.

The Council may at any time decide that the Seat of the League shall be established elsewhere.

All positions under or in connection with the League, including the Secretariat, shall be open equally to men and women.

Representatives of the Members of the League and officials of the League when engaged on the business of the League shall enjoy diplomatic privileges and immunities.

The buildings and other property occupied by the League or its officials or by Representatives attending its meetings shall be inviolable.

ARTICLE 8.

The Members of the League recognise that the maintenance of peace requires the reduction of national armaments to the lowest point consistent with national safety and the enforcement by common action of international obligations.

The Council, taking account of the geographical situation and circumstances of each State, shall formulate plans for such reduction for the consideration and action of the several Governments.

Such plans shall be subject to reconsideration and revision at least every ten years.

After these plans shall have been adopted by the several Governments, the limits of armaments therein fixed shall not be exceeded without the concurrence of the Council.

The Members of the League agree that the manufacture by private enterprise of munitions and implements of war is open to grave objections. The Council shall advise how the evil effects attendant upon such manufacture can be prevented, due regard being had to the necessities of those Members of the League which are not able to manufacture the munitions and implements of war necessary for their safety.

The Members of the League undertake to interchange full and frank information as to the scale of their armaments, their military, naval and air programmes and the condition of such of their industries as are adaptable to war-like purposes.

ARTICLE 9.

A permanent Commission shall be constituted to advise the Council on the execution of the provisions of Articles 1 and 8 and on military, naval and air questions generally.

ARTICLE 10.

The Members of the League undertake to respect and preserve as against external aggression the territorial integrity and existing political independence of all Members of the League. In case of any such aggression or in case of any threat or danger of such aggression the Council shall advise upon the means by which this obligation shall be fulfilled.

ARTICLE 11.

Any war or threat of war, whether immediately affecting any of the Members of the League or not, is hereby declared a matter of concern to the whole League, and the League shall take any action that may be deemed wise and effectual to safeguard the peace of nations. In case any such emergency should arise the Secretary General shall on the request of any Member of the League forthwith summon a meeting of the Council.

It is also declared to be the friendly right of each Member of the League to bring to the attention of the Assembly or of the Council any circumstance whatever affecting international relations which threatens to disturb international peace or the good understanding between nations upon which peace depends.

ARTICLE 12.

The Members of the League agree that if there should arise between them any dispute likely to lead to a rupture, they will submit the matter either to arbitration or to inquiry by the Council, and they agree in no case to resort to war until three months after the award by the arbitrators or the report by the Council.

In any case under this Article the award of the arbitrators shall be made within a reasonable time, and the report of the Council shall be made within six months after the submission of the dispute.

ARTICLE 13.

The Members of the League agree that whenever any dispute shall arise between them which they recognise to be suitable for submission to arbitration and which cannot be satisfactorily settled by diplomacy, they will submit the whole subject-matter to arbitration.

Disputes as to the interpretation of a treaty, as to any question of international law, as to the existence of any fact which if established would constitute a breach of any international obligation, or as to the extent and nature of the reparation to be made for any such breach, are declared to be among those which are generally suitable for submission to arbitration.

For the consideration of any such dispute the court of arbitration to which the case is referred shall be the Court agreed on by the parties to the dispute or stipulated in any convention existing between them.

The Members of the League agree that they will carry out in full good faith any award that may be rendered, and that they will not resort to war against a Member of the League which complies therewith. In the event of any failure to carry out such an award, the Council shall propose what steps should be taken to give effect thereto.

ARTICLE 14.

The Council shall formulate and submit to the Members of the League for adoption plans for the establishment of a Permanent Court of International Justice. The Court shall be competent to hear and determine any dispute of an international character which the parties thereto submit to it. The Court may also give an advisory opinion upon any dispute or question referred to it by the Council or by the Assembly.

ARTICLE 15.

If there should arise between Members of the League any dispute likely to lead to a rupture, which is not submitted to arbitration in accordance with Article 13, the Members of the League agree that they will submit the matter to the Council. Any party to the dispute may effect such submission by giving notice of the existence of the dispute to the Secretary General, who will make all necessary arrangements for a full investigation and consideration thereof.

For this purpose the parties to the dispute will communicate to the Secretary General, as promptly as possible, statements of their case with all the relevant facts and papers, and the Council may forthwith direct the publication thereof.

The Council shall endeavour to effect a settlement of the dispute, and if such efforts are successful, a statement shall be made public giving such facts and explanations regarding the dispute and the terms of settlement thereof as the Council may deem appropriate.

If the dispute is not thus settled, the Council either unanimously or by a majority vote shall make and publish a report containing a statement of the facts of the dispute and the recommendations which are deemed just and proper in regard thereto.

Any Member of the League represented on the Council may make public a statement of the facts of the dispute and of its conclusions regarding the same.

If a report by the Council is unanimously agreed to by the members thereof other than the Representatives of one or more of the parties to the dispute, the Members of the League agree that they will not go to war with any party to the dispute which complies with the recommendations of the report.

If the Council fails to reach a report which is unanimously agreed to by the members thereof, other than the Representatives of one or more of the parties to the dispute, the Members of the League reserve to themselves the right to take such action as they shall consider necessary for the maintenance of right and justice.

If the dispute between the parties is claimed by one of them, and is found by the Council, to arise out of a matter which by international law is solely within the domestic jurisdiction of that party, the Council shall so report, and shall make no recommendation as to its settlement.

The Council may in any case under this Article refer the dispute to the Assembly. The dispute shall be so referred at the request of either party to the dispute, provided that such request be made within fourteen days after the submission of the dispute to the Council.

In any case referred to the Assembly, all the provisions of this Article and of Article 12 relating to the action and powers of the Council shall apply to the action and powers of the Assembly, provided that a report made by the Assembly, if concurred in by the Representatives of those Members of the League represented on the Council and of a majority of the other Members of the League, exclusive in each case of the Representatives of the parties to the dispute, shall have the same force as a report by the Council concurred in by all the members thereof other than the Representatives of one or more of the parties to the dispute.

ARTICLE 16.

Should any Member of the League resort to war in disregard of its covenants under Articles 12, 13 or 15, it shall *ipso facto* be deemed to have committed an act of war against all other Members of the League, which hereby undertake immediately to subject it to the severance of all trade or financial relations, the prohibition of all intercourse between their nationals and the nationals of the covenant-breaking State, and the prevention of all financial, commercial or personal intercourse between the nationals of the covenant-breaking State and the nationals of any other State, whether a Member of the League or not.

It shall be the duty of the Council in such case to recommend to the several Governments concerned what effective military, naval or air force the Members of the League shall severally contribute to the armed forces to be used to protect the covenants of the League.

The Members of the League agree, further, that they will mutually support one another in the financial and economic measures which are taken under this Article, in order to minimise the loss and inconvenience resulting from the above measures, and that they will mutually support one another in resisting any special measures aimed at one of their number by the covenant-breaking State, and that they will take the necessary steps to afford passage through their territory to the forces of any of the Members of the League which are co-operating to protect the covenants of the League.

Any Member of the League which has violated any covenant of the League may be declared to be no longer a Member of the League by a vote of the Council concurred in by the Representatives of all the other Members of the League represented thereon.

ARTICLE 17.

In the event of a dispute between a Member of the League and a State which is not a Member of the League, or between States not Members of the League, the State or States not Members of the League shall be invited to accept the obligations of membership in the League for the purposes of such dispute, upon such conditions as the Council may deem just. If such invitation is accepted, the provisions of Articles 12 to 16 inclusive shall be applied with such modifications as may be deemed necessary by the Council.

7405°—20——2

Upon such invitation being given the Council shall immediately institute an inquiry into the circumstances of the dispute and recommend such action as may seem best and most effectual in the circumstances.

If a State so invited shall refuse to accept the obligations of membership in the League for the purposes of such dispute, and shall resort to war against a Member of the League, the provisions of Article 16 shall be applicable as against the State taking such action.

If both parties to the dispute when so invited refuse to accept the obligations of membership in the League for the purposes of such dispute, the Council may take such measures and make such recommendations as will prevent hostilities and will result in the settlement of the dispute.

ARTICLE 18.

Every treaty or international engagement entered into hereafter by any Member of the League shall be forthwith registered with the Secretariat and shall as soon as possible be published by it. No such treaty or international engagement shall be binding until so registered.

ARTICLE 19.

The Assembly may from time to time advise the reconsideration by Members of the League of treaties which have become inapplicable and the consideration of international conditions whose continuance might endanger the peace of the world.

ARTICLE 20.

The Members of the League severally agree that this Covenant is accepted as abrogating all obligations or understandings *inter se* which are inconsistent with the terms thereof, and solemnly undertake that they will not hereafter enter into any engagements inconsistent with the terms thereof.

In case any Member of the League shall, before becoming a Member of the League, have undertaken any obligations inconsistent with the terms of this Covenant, it shall be the duty of such Member to take immediate steps to procure its release from such obligations.

ARTICLE 21.

Nothing in this Covenant shall be deemed to affect the validity of international engagements, such as treaties of arbitration or regional understandings like the Monroe doctrine, for securing the maintenance of peace.

ARTICLE 22.

To those colonies and territories which as a consequence of the late war have ceased to be under the sovereignty of the States which formerly governed them and which are inhabited by peoples not yet able to stand by themselves under the strenuous conditions of the modern world, there should be applied the principle that the well-being and development of such peoples form a sacred trust of civilisation and that securities for the performance of this trust should be embodied in this Covenant.

The best method of giving practical effect to this principle is that the tutelage of such peoples should be entrusted to advanced nations who by reason of their resources, their experience or their geographical position can best undertake this responsibility, and who are willing to accept it, and that this tutelage should be exercised by them as Mandatories on behalf of the League.

The character of the mandate must differ according to the stage of the development of the people, the geographical situation of the territory, its economic conditions and other similar circumstances.

Certain communities formerly belonging to the Turkish Empire have reached a stage of development where their existence as independent nations can be provisionally recognised subject to the rendering of administrative advice and assistance by a Mandatory until such time as they are able to stand alone. The wishes of these communities must be a principal consideration in the selection of the Mandatory.

Other peoples, especially those of Central Africa, are at such a stage that the Mandatory must be responsible for the administration of the territory under conditions which will guarantee freedom of conscience and religion, subject only to the maintenance of public order and morals, the prohibition of abuses such as the slave trade, the arms traffic and the liquor traffic, and the prevention of the establishment of fortifications or military and naval bases and of military training of the natives for other than police purposes and the defence of territory, and will also secure equal opportunities for the trade and commerce of other Members of the League.

There are territories, such as South-West Africa and certain of the South Pacific Islands, which, owing to the sparseness of their population, or their small size, or their remoteness from the centres of civilisation, or their geographical contiguity to the territory of the Mandatory, and other circumstances, can be best administered under the laws of the Mandatory as integral portions of its territory, subject to the safeguards above mentioned in the interests of the indigenous population.

In every case of mandate, the Mandatory shall render to the Council an annual report in reference to the territory committed to its charge.

The degree of authority, control, or administration to be exercised by the Mandatory shall, if not previously agreed upon by the Members of the League, be explicitly defined in each case by the Council.

A permanent Commission shall be constituted to receive and examine the annual reports of the Mandatories and to advise the Council on all matters relating to the observance of the mandates.

ARTICLE 23.

Subject to and in accordance with the provisions of international conventions existing or hereafter to be agreed upon, the Members of the League:

(a) will endeavour to secure and maintain fair and humane conditions of labour for men, women, and children, both in their own countries and in all countries to which their commercial and industrial relations extend, and for that purpose will establish and maintain the necessary international organisations;

(b) undertake to secure just treatment of the native inhabitants of territories under their control;

(c) will entrust the League with the general supervision over the execution of agreements with regard to the traffic in women and children, and the traffic in opium and other dangerous drugs;

(d) will entrust the League with the general supervision of the trade in arms and ammunition with the countries in which the control of this traffic is necessary in the common interest;

(e) will make provision to secure and maintain freedom of communications and of transit and equitable treatment for the commerce of all Members of the League. In this connection, the special necessities of the regions devastated during the war of 1914–1918 shall be borne in mind;

(f) will endeavour to take steps in matters of international concern for the prevention and control of disease.

ARTICLE 24.

There shall be placed under the direction of the League all international bureaux already established by general treaties if the parties to such treaties consent. All such international bureaux and all commissions for the regulation of matters of international interest hereafter constituted shall be placed under the direction of the League.

In all matters of international interest which are regulated by general conventions but which are not placed under the control of international bureaux or commissions, the Secretariat of the League shall, subject to the consent of the Council and if desired by the parties, collect and distribute all relevant information and shall render any other assistance which may be necessary or desirable.

The Council may include as part of the expenses of the Secretariat the expenses of any bureau or commission which is placed under the direction of the League.

ARTICLE 25.

The Members of the League agree to encourge and promote the establishment and co-operation of duly authorised voluntary national Red Cross organizations having as purposes the improvement of health, the prevention of disease and the mitigation of suffering throughout the world.

ARTICLE 26.

Amendments to this Covenant will take effect when ratified by the Members of the League whose Representatives compose the Council and by a majority of the Members of the League whose Representatives compose the Assembly.

No such amendment shall bind any Member of the League which signifies its dissent therefrom, but in that case it shall cease to be a Member of the League.

ANNEX.

I. ORIGINAL MEMBERS OF THE LEAGUE OF NATIONS SIGNATORIES OF THE TREATY OF PEACE.

UNITED STATES OF AMERICA.
BELGIUM.
BOLIVIA.
BRAZIL.
BRITISH EMPIRE.
  CANADA.
  AUSTRALIA.
  SOUTH AFRICA.
  NEW ZEALAND.
  INDIA.
CHINA.
CUBA.
ECUADOR.
FRANCE.
GREECE.
GUATEMALA.

HAITI.
HEDJAZ.
HONDURAS.
ITALY.
JAPAN.
LIBERIA.
NICARAGUA.
PANAMA.
PERU.
POLAND.
PORTUGAL.
ROUMANIA.
SERB-CROAT-SLOVENE STATE.
SIAM.
CZECHO-SLOVAKIA.
URUGUAY.

STATES INVITED TO ACCEDE TO THE COVENANT.

ARGENTINE REPUBLIC.
CHILI.
COLOMBIA.
DENMARK.
NETHERLANDS.
NORWAY.
PARAGUAY.

PERSIA.
SALVADOR.
SPAIN.
SWEDEN.
SWITZERLAND.
VENEZUELA.

II. FIRST SECRETARY GENERAL OF THE LEAGUE OF NATIONS.

The Honourable Sir James Eric DRUMMOND, K. C. M. G., C. B.

PART II.

BOUNDARIES OF GERMANY.

ARTICLE 27.

The boundaries of Germany will be determined as follows:

1. *With Belgium:*

From the point common to the three frontiers of Belgium, Holland and Germany and in a southerly direction:

the north-eastern boundary of the former territory of *neutral Moresnet*, then the eastern boundary of the *Kreis* of Eupen, then the frontier between Belgium and the *Kreis* of Montjoie, then the north-eastern and eastern boundary of the *Kreis* of Malmédy to its junction with the frontier of Luxemburg.

2. *With Luxemburg:*

The frontier of August 3, 1914, to its junction with the frontier of France of the 18th July, 1870.

3. *With France:*

The frontier of July 18, 1870, from Luxemburg to Switzerland with the reservations made in Article 48 of Section IV (Saar Basin) of Part III.

4. *With Switzerland:*

The present frontier.

5. *With Austria:*

The frontier of August 3, 1914, from Switzerland to Czecho-Slovakia as hereinafter defined.

6. *With Czecho-Slovakia:*

The frontier of August 3, 1914, between Germany and Austria from its junction with the old administrative boundary separating Bohemia and the province of Upper Austria to the point north of the salient of the old province of Austrian Silesia situated at about 8 kilometres east of Neustadt.

7. *With Poland:*

From the point defined above to a point to be fixed on the ground about 2 kilometres east of Lorzendorf:

the frontier as it will be fixed in accordance with Article 88 of the present Treaty;

thence in a northerly direction to the point where the administrative boundary of Posnania crosses the river Bartsch:

a line to be fixed on the ground leaving the following places in Poland: Skorischau, Reichthal, Trembatschau, Kunzendorf, Schleise, Gross Kosel, Schreibersdorf, Rippin, Fürstlich-Niefken, Pawelau, Tscheschen, Konradau, Johannisdorf, Modzenowe, Bogdaj, and in Germany: Lorzendorf, Kaulwitz, Glausche, Dalbersdorf, Reesewitz, Stradam, Gross Wartenberg, Kraschen, Neu Mittelwalde, Domasla-witz, Wedelsdorf, Tscheschen Hammer;

thence the administrative boundary of Posnania north-westwards to the point where it cuts the Rawitsch-Herrnstadt railway;

thence to the point where the administrative boundary of Posnania cuts the Reisen-Tschirnau road:

a line to be fixed on the ground passing west of Triebusch and Gabel and east of Saborwitz;

thence the administrative boundary of Posnania to its junction with the eastern administrative boundary of the *Kreis* of Fraustadt;

thence in a north-westerly direction to a point to be chosen on the road between the villages of Unruhstadt and Kopnitz:

a line to be fixed on the ground passing west of Geyersdorf, Brenno, Fehlen, Altkloster, Klebel, and east of Ulbersdorf, Buchwald, Ilgen, Weine, Lupitze, Schwenten;

thence in a northerly direction to the northernmost point of Lake Chlop:

a line to be fixed on the ground following the median line of the lakes; the town and the station of Bentschen however (including the junction of the lines Schwiebus-Bentschen and Züllichau-Bentschen) remaining in Polish territory;

thence in a north-easterly direction to the point of junction of the boundaries of the *Kreise* of Schwerin, Birnbaum and Meseritz:

a line to be fixed on the ground passing east of Betsche;

thence in a northerly direction the boundary separating the *Kreise* of Schwerin and Birnbaum, then in an easterly direction the northern boundary of Posnania to the point where it cuts the river Netze;

thence upstream to its confluence with the Küddow:

the course of the Netze;

thence upstream to a point to be chosen about 6 kilometres south-east of Schneidemühl:

the course of the Küddow;

thence north-eastwards to the most southern point of the re-entant of the northern boundary of Posnania about 5 kilometres west of Stahren:

a line to be fixed on the ground leaving the Schneidemühl-Konitz railway in this area entirely in German territory;

thence the boundary of Posnania north-eastwards to the point of the salient it makes about 15 kilometres east of Flatow;

thence north-eastwards to the point where the river Kamionka meets the southern boundary of the *Kreis* of Konitz about 3 kilometres north-east of Grunau:

a line to be fixed on the ground leaving the following places to Poland: Jasdrowo, Gr. Lutau, Kl. Lutau, Wittkau, and to Germany: Gr. Butzig, Cziskowo, Battrow, Böck, Grunau;

thence in a northerly direction the boundary between the *Kreise* of Konitz and Schlochau to the point where this boundary cuts the river Brahe;

thence to a point on the boundary of Pomerania 15 kilometres east of Rummelsburg:

a line to be fixed on the ground leaving the following places in Poland: Konarzin, Kelpin, Adl. Briesen, and in Germany: Sampohl, Neuguth, Steinfort, Gr. Peterkau;

then the boundary of Pomerania in an easterly direction to its junction with the boundary between the *Kreise* of Konitz and Schlochau;

thence northwards the boundary between Pomerania and West Prussia to the point on the river Rheda about 3 kilometres north-west of Gohra where that river is joined by a tributary from the north-west;

thence to a point to be selected in the bend of the Piasnitz river about 1½ kilometres north-west of Warschkau:

a line to be fixed on the ground;

thence this river downstream, then the median line of Lake Zarnowitz, then the old boundary of West Prussia to the Baltic Sea.

8. *With Denmark:*

The frontier as it will be fixed in accordance with Articles 109 to 111 of Part III, Section XII (Schleswig).

ARTICLE 28.

The boundaries of East Prussia, with the reservations made in Section IX (East Prussia) of Part III, will be determined as follows:

from a point on the coast of the Baltic Sea about 1½ kilometres north of Pröbbernau church in a direction of about 159° East from true North:

a line to be fixed on the ground for about 2 kilometres;

thence in a straight line to the light at the bend of the Elbing Channel in approximately latitude 54° 19½′ North, longitude 19° 26′ East of Greenwich;

thence to the easternmost mouth of the Nogat River at a bearing of approximately 209° East from true North;

thence up the course of the Nogat River to the point where the latter leaves the Vistula (Weichsel);

thence up the principal channel of navigation of the Vistula, then the southern boundary of the *Kreis* of Marienwerder, then that of the *Kreis* of Rosenberg eastwards to the point where it meets the old boundary of East Prussia.

thence the old boundary between East and West Prussia, then the boundary between the *Kreise* of Osterode and Neidenburg, then the course of the river Skottau downstream, then the course of the Neide upstream to a point situated about 5 kilometres west of Bialutten being the nearest point to the old frontier of Russia;

thence in an easterly direction to a point immediately south of the intersection of the road Neidenburg-Mlava with the old frontier of Russia:

a line to be fixed on the ground passing north of Bialutten;

thence the old frontier of Russia to a point east of Schmalleningken, then the principal channel of navigation of the Niemen (Memel) downstream, then the Skierwieth arm of the delta to the Kurisches Haff;

thence a straight line to the point where the eastern shore of the Kurische Nehrung meets the administrative boundary about 4 kilometres south-west of Nidden;

thence this administrative boundary to the western shore of the Kurische Nehrung.

Article 29.

The boundaries as described above are drawn in red on a one-in-a-million map which is annexed to the present Treaty (Map No 1.)

In the case of any discrepancies between the text of the Treaty and this map or any other map which may be annexed, the text will be final.

Article 30.

In the case of boundaries which are defined by a waterway, the terms "course" and "channel" used in the present Treaty signify: in the case of non-navigable rivers, the median line of the waterway or of its principal arm, and, in the case of navigable rivers, the median line of the principal channel of navigation. It will rest with the Boundary Commissions provided by the present Treaty to specify in each case whether the frontier line shall follow any changes of the course or channel which may take place or whether it shall be definitely fixed by the position of the course or channel at the time when the present Treaty comes into force.

PART III.

POLITICAL CLAUSES FOR EUROPE.

Section I.

BELGIUM.

Article 31.

Germany, recognizing that the Treaties of April 19, 1839, which established the status of Belgium before the war, no longer conform to the requirements of the situation, consents to the abrogation of the said Treaties and undertakes immediately to recognize and to observe whatever conventions may be entered into by the Principal Allied and Associated Powers, or by any of them, in concert with the Governments of Belgium and of the Netherlands, to replace the said Treaties of 1839. If her formal adhesion should be required to such conventions or to any of their stipulations, Germany undertakes immediately to give it.

Article 32.

Germany recognizes the full sovereignty of Belgium over the whole of the contested territory of Moresnet (called *Moresnet neutre*).

Article 33.

Germany renounces in favour of Belgium all rights and title over the territory of Prussian Moresnet situated on the west of the road from Liége to Aix-la-Chapelle; the road will belong to Belgium where it bounds this territory.

ARTICLE 34.

Germany renounces in favour of Belgium all rights and title over the territory comprising the whole of the *Kreise* of Eupen and of Malmédy.

During the six months after the coming into force of this Treaty, registers will be opened by the Belgian authority at Eupen and Malmédy in which the inhabitants of the above territory will be entitled to record in writing a desire to see the whole or part of it remain under German sovereignty.

The results of this public expression of opinion will be communicated by the Belgian Government to the League of Nations, and Belgium undertakes to accept the decision of the League.

ARTICLE 35.

A Commission of seven persons, five of whom will be appointed by the Principal Allied and Associated Powers, one by Germany and one by Belgium, will be set up fifteen days after the coming into force of the present Treaty to settle on the spot the new frontier line between Belgium and Germany, taking into account the economic factors and the means of communication.

Decisions will be taken by a majority and will be binding on the parties concerned.

ARTICLE 36.

When the transfer of the sovereignty over the territories referred to above has become definite, German nationals habitually resident in the territories will definitively acquire Belgian nationality *ipso facto*, and will lose their German nationality.

Nevertheless, German nationals who became resident in the territories after August 1, 1914, shall not obtain Belgian nationality without a permit from the Belgian Government.

ARTICLE 37.

Within the two years following the definitive transfer of the sovereignty over the territories assigned to Belgium under the present Treaty, German nationals over 18 years of age habitually resident in those territories will be entitled to opt for German nationality.

Option by a husband will cover his wife, and option by parents will cover their children under 18 years of age.

Persons who have exercised the above right to opt must within the ensuing twelve months transfer their place of residence to Germany.

They will be entitled to retain their immovable property in the territories acquired by Belgium. They may carry with them their movable property of every description. No export or import duties may be imposed upon them in connection with the removal of such property.

ARTICLE 38.

The German Government will hand over without delay to the Belgian Government the archives, registers, plans, title deeds and documents of every kind concerning the civil, military, financial, judicial or other administrations in the territory transferred to Belgian sovereignty.

The German Government will likewise restore to the Belgian Government the archives and documents of every kind carried off during the war by the German authorities from the Belgian public administrations, in particular from the Ministry of Foreign Affairs at Brussels.

ARTICLE 39.

The proportion and nature of the financial liabilities of Germany and of Prussia which Belgium will have to bear on account of the territories ceded to her shall be fixed in conformity with Articles 254 and 256 of Part IX (Financial Clauses) of the present Treaty.

SECTION II.

LUXEMBURG.

ARTICLE 40.

With regard to the Grand Duchy of Luxemburg, Germany renounces the benefit of all the provisions inserted in her favour in the Treaties of February 8, 1842, April 2, 1847, October 20–25, 1865, August 18, 1866, February 21 and May 11, 1867, May 10, 1871, June 11, 1872, and November 11, 1902, and in all Conventions consequent upon such Treaties.

Germany recognizes that the Grand Duchy of Luxemburg ceased to form part of the German Zollverein as from January 1, 1919, renounces all rights to the exploitation of the railways, adheres to the termination of the régime of neutrality of the Grand Duchy, and accepts in advance all international arrangements which may be concluded by the Allied and Associated Powers relating to the Grand Duchy.

ARTICLE 41.

Germany undertakes to grant to the Grand Duchy of Luxemburg, when a demand to that effect is made to her by the Principal Allied and Associated Powers, the rights and advantages stipulated in favour of such Powers or their nationals in the present Treaty with regard to economic questions, to questions relative to transport and to aerial navigation.

SECTION III.

LEFT BANK OF THE RHINE.

ARTICLE 42.

Germany is forbidden to maintain or construct any fortifications either on the left bank of the Rhine or on the right bank to the west of a line drawn 50 kilometres to the East of the Rhine.

Article 43.

In the area defined above the maintenance and the assembly of armed forces, either permanently or temporarily, and military manœuvres of any kind, as well as the upkeep of all permanent works for mobilization, are in the same way forbidden.

Article 44.

In case Germany violates in any manner whatever the provisions of Articles 42 and 43, she shall be regarded as committing a hostile act against the Powers signatory of the present Treaty and as calculated to disturb the peace of the world.

Section IV.

SAAR BASIN.

Article 45.

As compensation for the destruction of the coal-mines in the north of France and as part payment towards the total reparation due from Germany for the damage resulting from the war, Germany cedes to France in full and absolute possession, with exclusive rights of exploitation, unencumbered and free from all debts and charges of any kind, the coal-mines situated in the Saar Basin as defined in Article 48.

Article 46.

In order to assure the rights and welfare of the population and to guarantee to France complete freedom in working the mines, Germany agrees to the provisions of Chapters I and II of the Annex hereto.

Article 47.

In order to make in due time permanent provision for the government of the Saar Basin in accordance with the wishes of the populations, France and Germany agree to the provisions of Chapter III of the Annex hereto.

Article 48.

The boundaries of the territory of the Saar Basin, as dealt with in the present stipulations, will be fixed as follows:

On the south and south-west: by the frontier of France as fixed by the present Treaty.

On the north-west and north: by a line following the northern administrative boundary of the *Kreis* of Merzig from the point where it leaves the French frontier to the point where it meets the administrative boundary separating the commune of Saarhölzbach from the commune of Britten; following this communal boundary southwards and reaching the administrative boundary of the canton of Merzig so as to include in the territory of the Saar Basin the canton of Mettlach, with the exception of the commune of Britten; following successively the northern administrative boundaries of the cantons of Merzig and Haustadt, which are incorporated in the aforesaid Saar Basin, then successively the administrative boundaries separating the *Kreise* of Sarrelouis, Ottweiler and Saint-Wendel from the *Kreise* of Merzig, Trèves (Trier) and the Principality of Birkenfeld as far as a point situated about 500 metres north of the village of Furschweiler (viz., the highest point of the Metzelberg).

On the north-east and east: from the last point defined above to a point about 3½ kilometres east-north-east of Saint-Wendel:

a line to be fixed on the ground passing east of Furschweiler, west of Roschberg, east of points 418, 329 (south of Roschberg), west of Leitersweiler, north-east of point 464, and following the line of the crest southwards to its junction with the administrative boundary of the *Kreis* of Kusel;

thence in a southerly direction the boundary of the *Kreis* of Kusel, then the boundary of the *Kreis* of Homburg towards the south-south-east to a point situated about 1000 metres west of Dunzweiler;

thence to a point about 1 kilometre south of Hornbach:

a line to be fixed on the ground passing through point 424 (about 1000 metres south-east of Dunzweiler), point 363 (Fuchs-Berg), point 322 (south-west of Waldmohr), then east of Jägersburg and Erbach, then encircling Homburg, passing through the points 361 (about 2½ kilometres north-east by east of that town), 342 (about 2 kilometres south-east of that town), 347 (Schreiners-Berg), 356, 350 (about 1½ kilometres south-east of Schwarzenbach), then passing east of Einöd, south-east of points 322 and 333, about 2 kilometres east of Weben-heim, about 2 kilometres east of Mimbach, passing east of the plateau which is traversed by the road from Mimbach to Böckweiler (so as to include this road in the territory of the Saar Basin), passing immediately north of the junction of the roads from Böckweiler and Altheim situated about 2 kilometres north of Altheim, then passing south of Ringweilerhof and north of point 322, rejoining the frontier of France at the angle which it makes about 1 kilometre south of Hornbach (see Map No. 2 scale 1/100,000 annexed to the present Treaty).

A Commission composed of five members, one appointed by France, one by Germany, and three by the Council of the League of Nations, which will select nationals of other Powers, will be constituted within fifteen days from the coming into force of the present Treaty, to trace on the spot the frontier line described above.

In those parts of the preceding line which do not coincide with administrative boundaries, the Commission will endeavour to keep to the line indicated, while taking into consideration, so far as is possible, local economic interests and existing communal boundaries.

The decisions of this Commission will be taken by a majority, and will be binding on the parties concerned.

ARTICLE 49.

Germany renounces in favour of the League of Nations, in the capacity of trustee, the government of the territory defined above.

At the end of fifteen years from the coming into force of the present Treaty the inhabitants of the said territory shall be called upon to indicate the sovereignty under which they desire to be placed.

ARTICLE 50.

The stipulations under which the cession of the mines in the Saar Basin shall be carried out, together with the measures intended to guarantee the rights and the well-being of the inhabitants and the government of the territory, as well as the conditions in accordance with which the plebiscite hereinbefore provided for is to be made, are laid down in the Annex hereto. This Annex shall be considered as an integral part of the present Treaty, and Germany declares her adherence to it.

ANNEX.

In accordance with the provisions of Articles 45 to 50 of the present Treaty, the stipulations under which the cession by Germany to France of the mines of the Saar Basin will be effected, as well as the measures intended to ensure respect for the rights and well-being of the population and the government of the territory, and the conditions in which the inhabitants will be called upon to indicate the sovereignty under which they may wish to be placed, have been laid down as follows:

CHAPTER I.

CESSION AND EXPLOITATION OF MINING PROPERTY.

1.

From the date of the coming into force of the present Treaty, all the deposits of coal situated within the Saar Basin as defined in Article 48 of the said Treaty, become the complete and absolute property of the French State.

The French State will have the right of working or not working the said mines, or of transferring to a third party the right of working them, without having to obtain any previous authorisation or to fulfil any formalities.

The French State may always require that the German mining laws and regulations referred to below shall be applied in order to ensure the determination of its rights.

2.

The right of ownership of the French State will apply not only to the deposits which are free and for which concessions have not yet been granted, but also to the deposits for which concessions have already been granted, whoever may be the present proprietors, irrespective of whether they belong to the Prussian State, to the Bavarian State, to other States or bodies, to companies or to individuals, whether they have been worked or not, or whether a right of exploitation distinct from the right of the owners of the surface of the soil has or has not been recognized.

As far as concerns the mines which are being worked, the transfer of the ownership to the French State will apply to all the accessories and subsidiaries of the said mines, in particular to their plant and equipment both on and below the surface, to their extracting machinery, their plants for transforming coal into electric power, coke and by-products, their workshops, means of communication, electric lines, plant for catching and distributing water, land, buildings such as offices, managers', employees' and workmen's dwellings, schools, hospitals and dispensaries, their stocks and supplies of every description, their archives and plans, and in general everything which those who own or exploit the mines possess or enjoy for the purpose of exploiting the mines and their accessories and subsidiaries.

The transfer will apply also to the debts owing for products delivered before the entry into possession by the French State, and after the signature of the present Treaty, and to deposits of money made by customers, whose rights will be guaranteed by the French State.

4.

The French State will acquire the property free and clear of all debts and charges. Nevertheless, the rights acquired, or in course of being acquired, by the employees of the mines and their accessories and subsidiaries at the date of the coming into force of the present Treaty, in connection with pensions for old age or disability, will not be affected. In return, Germany must pay over to the French State a sum representing the actuarial amounts to which the said employees are entitled.

5.

The value of the property thus ceded to the French State will be determined by the Reparation Commission referred to in Article 233 of Part VIII (Reparation) of the present Treaty.

This value shall be credited to Germany in part payment of the amount due for reparation.

It will be for Germany to indemnify the proprietors or parties concerned, whoever they may be.

6.

No tariff shall be established on the German railways and canals which may directly or indirectly discriminate to the prejudice of the transport of the personnel or products of the mines and their accessories or subsidiaries, or of the material necessary to their exploitation. Such transport shall enjoy all the rights and privileges which any international railway conventions may guarantee to similar products of French origin.

7.

The equipment and personnel necessary to ensure the despatch and transport of the products of the mines and their accessories and subsidiaries, as well as the carriage of workmen and employees, will be provided by the local railway administration of the Basin.

8.

No obstacle shall be placed in the way of such improvements of railways or waterways as the French State may judge necessary to assure the despatch and the transport of the products of the mines and their accessories and subsidiaries, such as double trackage, enlargement of stations, and construction of yards and appurtenances. The distribution of expenses will, in the event of disagreement, be submitted to arbitration.

The French State may also establish any new means of communication, such as roads, electric lines and telephone connections which it may consider necessary for the exploitation of the mines.

It may exploit freely and without any restrictions the means of communication of which it may become the owner, particularly those connecting the mines and their accessories and subsidiaries with the means of communication situated in French territory.

9.

The French State shall always be entitled to demand the application of the German mining laws and regulations in force on November 11, 1918, excepting provisions adopted exclusively in view of the state of war, with a view to the acquisition of such land as it may judge necessary for the exploitation of the mines and their accessories and subsidiaries.

The payment for damage caused to immovable property by the working of the said mines and their accessories and subsidiaries shall be made in accordance with the German mining laws and regulations above referred to.

10.

Every person whom the French State may substitute for itself as regards the whole or part of its rights to the exploitation of the mines and their accessories and subsidiaries shall enjoy the benefit of the privileges provided in this Annex.

11.

The mines and other immovable property which become the property of the French State may never be made the subject of measures of forfeiture, forced sale, expropriation or requisition, nor of any other measure affecting the right of property.

The personnel and the plant connected with the exploitation of these mines or their accessories and subsidiaries, as well as the product extracted from the mines or manufactured in their accessories and subsidiaries, may not at any time be made the subject of any measures of requisition.

The exploitation of the mines and their accessories and subsidiaries, which become the property of the French State, will continue, subject to the provisions of paragraph 23 below, to be subject to the régime established by the German laws and regulations in force on November 11, 1918, excepting provisions adopted exclusively in view of the state of war.

The rights of the workmen shall similarly be maintained, subject to the provisions of the said paragraph 23, as established on November 11, 1918, by the German laws and regulations above referred to.

No impediment shall be placed in the way of the introduction or employment in the mines and their accessories and subsidiaries of workmen from without the Basin.

The employees and workmen of French nationality shall have the right to belong to French labour unions.

13.

The amount contributed by the mines and their accessories and subsidiaries, either to the local budget of the territory of the Saar Basin or to the communal funds, shall be fixed with due regard to the ratio of the value of the mines to the total taxable wealth of the Basin.

14.

The French State shall always have the right of establishing and maintaining, as incidental to the mines, primary or technical schools for its employees and their children, and of causing instruction therein to be given in the French language, in accordance with such curriculum and by such teachers as it may select.

It shall also have the right to establish and maintain hospitals, dispensaries, workmen's houses and gardens and other charitable and social institutions.

15.

The French State shall enjoy complete liberty with respect to the distribution, dispatch and sale prices of the products of the mines and their accessories and subsidiaries.

Nevertheless, whatever may be the total product of the mines, the French Government undertakes that the requirements of local consumption for industrial and domestic purposes shall always be satisfied in the proportion existing in 1913 between the amount consumed locally and the total output of the Saar Basin.

Chapter II.

GOVERNMENT OF THE TERRITORY OF THE SAAR BASIN.

16.

The Government of the territory of the Saar Basin shall be entrusted to a Commission representing the League of Nations. This Commission shall sit in the territory of the Saar Basin.

17.

The Governing Commission provided for by paragraph 16 shall consist of five members chosen by the Council of the League of Nations, and will include one citizen of France, one native inhabitant of the Saar Basin, not a citizen of France, and three members belonging to three countries other than France or Germany.

The members of the Governing Commission shall be appointed for one year and may be re-appointed. They can be removed by the Council of the League of Nations, which will provide for their replacement.

The members of the Governing Commission will be entitled to a salary which will be fixed by the Council of the League of Nations, and charged on the local revenues.

18.

The Chairman of the Governing Commission shall be appointed for one year from among the members of the Commission by the Council of the League of Nations and may be re-appointed.

The Chairman will act as the executive of the Commission.

19.

Within the territory of the Saar Basin the Governing Commission shall have all the powers of government hitherto belonging to the German Empire, Prussia, or Bavaria, including the appointment and dismissal of officials, and the creation of such administrative and representative bodies as it may deem necessary.

It shall have full powers to administer and operate the railways, canals and the different public services.

Its decisions shall be taken by a majority.

20.

Germany will place at the disposal of the Governing Commission all official documents and archives under the control of Germany, of any German State, or of any local authority, which relate to the territory of the Saar Basin or to the rights of the inhabitants thereof.

21.

It will be the duty of the Governing Commission to ensure, by such means and under such conditions as it may deem suitable, the protection abroad of the interests of the inhabitants of the territory of the Saar Basin.

22.

The Governing Commission shall have the full right of user of all property, other than mines, belonging, either in public or in private domain, to the Government of the German Empire, or the Government of any German State, in the territory of the Saar Basin.

As regards the railways an equitable apportionment of rolling stock shall be made by a mixed Commission on which the Government of the territory of the Saar Basin and the German railways will be represented.

Persons, goods, vessels, carriages, wagons and mails coming from or going to the Saar Basin shall enjoy all the rights and privileges relating to transit and transport which are specified in the provisions of Part XII (Ports, Waterways and Railways) of the present Treaty.

23.

The laws and regulations in force on November 11, 1918, in the territory of the Saar Basin (except those enacted in consequence of the state of war) shall continue to apply.

If, for general reasons or to bring these laws and regulations into accord with the provisions of the present Treaty, it is necessary to introduce modifications, these shall be decided on, and put into effect by the Governing Commission, after consultation with the elected representatives of the inhabitants in such a manner as the Commission may determine.

No modification may be made in the legal régime for the exploitation of the mines, provided for in paragraph 12, without the French State being previously consulted, unless such modification results from a general regulation respecting labour adopted by the League of Nations.

In fixing the conditions and hours of labour for men, women and children, the Governing Commission is to take into consideration the wishes expressed by the local labour organisations, as well as the principles adopted by the League of Nations.

24.

Subject to the provisions of paragraph 4, no rights of the inhabitants of the Saar Basin acquired or in process of acquisition at the date of the coming into force of this Treaty, in respect of any insurance system of Germany or in respect of any pension of any kind, are affected by any of the provisions of the present Treaty.

Germany and the Government of the territory of the Saar Basin will preserve and continue all of the aforesaid rights.

25.

The civil and criminal courts existing in the territory of the Saar Basin shall continue.

A civil and criminal court will be established by the Governing Commission to hear appeals from the decisions of the said courts and to decide matters for which these courts are not competent.

The Governing Commission will be responsible for settling the organisation and jurisdiction of the said court.

Justice will be rendered in the name of the Governing Commission.

26.

The Governing Commission will alone have the power of levying taxes and dues in the territory of Saar Basin.

These taxes and dues will be exclusively applied to the needs of the territory.

The fiscal system existing on November 11, 1918, will be maintained as far as possible, and no new tax except customs duties may be imposed without previously consulting the elected representatives of the inhabitants.

27.

The present stipulations will not affect the existing nationality of the inhabitants of the territory of the Saar Basin.

No hindrance shall be placed in the way of those who wish to acquire a different nationality, but in such case the acquisition of the new nationality will involve the loss of any other.

28.

Under the control of the Governing Commission the inhabitants will retain their local assemblies, their religious liberties, their schools and their language.

The right of voting will not be exercised for any assemblies other than the local assemblies, and will belong to every inhabitant over the age of twenty years, without distinction of sex.

29.

Any of the inhabitants of the Saar Basin who may desire to leave the territory will have full liberty to retain in it their immovable property or to sell it at fair prices, and to remove their movable property free of any charges.

30.

There will be no military service, whether compulsory or voluntary, in the territory of the Saar Basin, and the construction of fortifications therein is forbidden.

Only a local gendarmerie for the maintenance of order may be established.

It will be the duty of the Governing Commission to provide in all cases for the protection of persons and property in the Saar Basin.

31.

The territory of the Saar Basin as defined by Article 48 of the present Treaty shall be subjected to the French customs régime. The receipts from the customs duties on goods intended for local consumption shall be included in the budget of the said territory after deduction of all costs of collection.

No export tax shall be imposed upon metallurgical products or coal exported from the said territory to Germany, nor upon German exports for the use of the industries of the territory of the Saar Basin.

Natural or manufactured products originating in the Basin in transit over German territory and, similarly, German products in transit over the territory of the Basin shall be free of all customs duties.

Products which both originate in and pass from the Basin into Germany shall be free of import duties for a period of five years from the date of the coming into force of the present Treaty, and during the same period articles imported from Germany into the territory of the Basin for local consumption shall likewise be free of import duties.

During these five years the French Government reserves to itself the right of limiting to the annual average of the quantities imported into Alsace-Lorraine and France in the years 1911 to 1913 the quantities which may be sent into France of all articles coming from the Basin which include raw materials and semi-manufactured goods imported duty free from Germany. Such average shall be determined after reference to all available official information and statistics.

32.

No prohibition or restriction shall be imposed upon the circulation of French money in the territory of the Saar Basin.

The French State shall have the right to use French money in all purchases, payments and contracts connected with the exploitation of the mines or their accessories and subsidiaries.

33.

The Governing Commission shall have power to decide all questions arising from the interpretation of the preceding provisions.

France and Germany agree that any dispute involving a difference of opinion as to the interpretation of the said provisions shall in the same way be submitted to the Governing Commission, and the decision of a majority of the Commission shall be binding on both countries.

CHAPTER III.

PLEBISCITE.

34.

At the termination of a period of fifteen years from the coming into force of the present Treaty, the population of the territory of the Saar Basin will be called upon to indicate their desires in the following manner:

A vote will take place by communes or districts, on the three following alternatives: (*a*) maintenance of the régime established by the present Treaty and by this Annex; (*b*) union with France; (*c*) union with Germany.

All persons without distinction of sex, more than twenty years old at the date of the voting, resident in the territory at the date of the signature of the present Treaty, will have the right to vote.

The other conditions, methods and the date of the voting shall be fixed by the Council of the League of Nations in such a way as to secure the freedom, secrecy and trustworthiness of the voting.

35.

The League of Nations shall decide on the sovereignty under which the territory is to be placed, taking into account the wishes of the inhabitants as expressed by the voting:

(*a*) If, for the whole or part of the territory, the League of Nations decides in favour of the maintenance of the régime established by the present Treaty and this Annex, Germany hereby agrees to make such renunciation of her sovereignty in favour of the League of Nations as the latter shall deem necessary. It will be the duty of the League of Nations to take appropriate steps to adapt the régime definitively adopted to the permanent welfare of the territory and the general interest;

(*b*) If, for the whole or part of the territory, the League of Nations decides in favour of union with France, Germany hereby agrees to cede to France in accordance with the decision of the League of Nations all rights and title over the territory specified by the League;

(c) If, for the whole or part of the territory, the League of Nations decides in favour of union with Germany, it will be the duty of the League of Nations to cause the German Government to be re-established in the government of the territory specified by the League.

36.

If the League of Nations decides in favour of the union of the whole or part of the territory of the Saar Basin with Germany, France's rights of ownership in the mines situated in such part of the territory will be repurchased by Germany in their entirety at a price payable in gold. The price to be paid will be fixed by three experts, one nominated by Germany, one by France, and one, who shall be neither a Frenchman nor a German, by the Council of the League of Nations; the decision of the experts will be given by a majority.

The obligation of Germany to make such payment shall be taken into account by the Reparation Commission, and for the purpose of this payment Germany may create a prior charge upon her assets or revenues upon such detailed terms as shall be agreed to by the Reparation Commission.

If, nevertheless, Germany after a period of one year from the date on which the payment becomes due shall not have effected the said payment, the Reparation Commission shall do so in accordance with such instructions as may be given by the League of Nations, and, if necessary, by liquidating that part of the mines which is in question.

37.

If, in consequence of the repurchase provided for in paragraph 36, the ownership of the mines or any part of them is transferred to Germany, the French State and French nationals shall have the right to purchase such amount of coal of the Saar Basin as their industrial and domestic needs are found at that time to require. An equitable arrangement regarding amounts of coal, duration of contract, and prices will be fixed in due time by the Council of the League of Nations.

38.

It is understood that France and Germany may, by special agreements concluded before the time fixed for the payment of the price for the repurchase of the mines, modify the provisions of paragraphs 36 and 37.

39.

The Council of the League of Nations shall make such provisions as may be necessary for the establishment of the régime which is to take effect after the decisions of the League of Nations mentioned in paragraph 35 have become operative, including an equitable apportionment of any obligations of the Government of the territory of the Saar Basin arising from loans raised by the Commission or from other causes.

From the coming into force of the new régime, the powers of the Governing Commission will terminate, except in the case provided for in paragraph 35 (a).

40.

In all matters dealt with in the present Annex, the decisions of the Council of the League of Nations will be taken by a majority.

Section V.

ALSACE-LORRAINE.   6296

The HIGH CONTRACTING PARTIES, recognising the moral obligation to redress the wrong done by Germany in 1871 both to the rights of France and to the wishes of the population of Alsace and Lorraine, which were separated from their country in spite of the solemn protest of their representatives at the Assembly of Bordeaux,

Agree upon the following Articles:

ARTICLE 51.

The territories which were ceded to Germany in accordance with the Preliminaries of Peace signed at Versailles on February 26, 1871, and the Treaty of Frankfort of May 10, 1871, are restored to French sovereignty as from the date of the Armistice of November 11, 1918.

The provisions of the Treaties establishing the delimitation of the frontiers before 1871 shall be restored.

ARTICLE 52.

The German Government shall hand over without delay to the French Government all archives, registers, plans, titles and documents of every kind concerning the civil, military, financial, judicial or other administrations of the territories restored to French sovereignty. If any of these documents, archives, registers, titles or plans have been misplaced, they will be restored by the German Government on the demand of the French Government.

ARTICLE 53.

Separate agreements shall be made between France and Germany dealing with the interests of the inhabitants of the territories referred to in Article 51, particularly as regards their civil rights, their business and the exercise of their professions, it being understood that Germany undertakes as from the present date to recognise and accept the regulations laid down in the Annex hereto regarding the nationality of the inhabitants or natives of the said territories, not to claim at any time or in any place whatsoever as German nationals those who shall have been declared on any ground to be French, to receive all others in her territory, and to conform, as regards the property of German nationals in the territories indicated in Article 51, with the provisions of Article 297 and the Annex to Section IV of Part X (Economic Clauses) of the present Treaty.

Those German nationals who without acquiring French nationality shall receive permission from the French Government to reside in the said territories shall not be subjected to the provisions of the said Article.

ARTICLE 54.

Those persons who have regained French nationality in virtue of paragraph 1 of the Annex hereto will be held to be Alsace-Lorrainers for the purposes of the present Section.

The persons referred to in paragraph 2 of the said Annex will from the day on which they have claimed French nationality be held to be Alsace-Lorrainers with retroactive effect as from November 11, 1918. For those whose application is rejected, the privilege will terminate at the date of the refusal.

Such juridical persons will also have the status of Alsace-Lorrainers as shall have been recognised as possessing this quality, whether by the French administrative authorities or by a judicial decision.

ARTICLE 55.

The territories referred to in Article 51 shall return to France free and quit of all public debts under the conditions laid down in Article 255 of Part IX (Financial Clauses) of the present Treaty.

ARTICLE 56.

In conformity with the provisions of Article 256 of Part IX (Financial Clauses) of the present Treaty, France shall enter into possession of all property and estate, within the territories referred to in Article 51, which belong to the German Empire or German States, without any payment or credit on this account to any of the States ceding the territories.

This provision applies to all movable or immovable property of public or private domain together with all rights whatsoever belonging to the German Empire or German States or to their administrative areas.

Crown property and the property of the former Emperor or other German sovereigns shall be assimilated to property of the public domain.

ARTICLE 57.

Germany shall not take any action, either by means of stamping or by any other legal or administrative measures not applying equally to the rest of her territory, which may be to the detriment of the legal value or redeemability of German monetary instruments or monies which, at the date of the signature of the present Treaty, are legally current, and at that date are in the possession of the French Government.

ARTICLE 58.

A special Convention will determine the conditions for repayment in marks of the exceptional war expenditure advanced during the course of the war by Alsace-Lorraine or by the public bodies in Alsace-

Lorraine on account of the Empire in accordance with German law, such as payment to the families of persons mobilised, requisitions, billeting of troops, and assistance to persons who have been evacuated.

In fixing the amount of these sums Germany shall be credited with that portion which Alsace-Lorraine would have contributed to the Empire to meet the expenses resulting from these payments, this contribution being calculated according to the proportion of the Imperial revenues derived from Alsace-Lorraine in 1913.

ARTICLE 59.

The French Government will collect for its own account the Imperial taxes, duties and dues of every kind leviable in the territories referred to in Article 51 and not collected at the time of the Armistice of November 11, 1918.

ARTICLE 60.

The German Government shall without delay restore to Alsace-Lorrainers (individuals, juridical persons and public institutions) all property, rights and interests belonging to them on November 11, 1918, in so far as these are situated in German territory.

ARTICLE 61.

The German Government undertakes to continue and complete without delay the execution of the financial clauses regarding Alsace-Lorraine contained in the Armistice Conventions.

ARTICLE 62.

The German Government undertakes to bear the expense of all civil and military pensions which had been earned in Alsace-Lorraine on date of November 11, 1918, and the maintenance of which was a charge on the budget of the German Empire.

The German Government shall furnish each year the funds necessary for the payment in francs, at the average rate of exchange for that year, of the sums in marks to which persons resident in Alsace-Lorraine would have been entitled if Alsace-Lorraine had remained under German jurisdiction.

ARTICLE 63.

For the purposes of the obligation assumed by Germany in Part VIII (Reparation) of the present Treaty to give compensation for damages caused to the civil populations of the Allied and Associated countries in the form of fines, the inhabitants of the territories referred to in Article 51 shall be assimilated to the above-mentioned populations.

ARTICLE 64.

The regulations concerning the control of the Rhine and of the Moselle are laid down in Part XII (Ports, Waterways and Railways) of the present Treaty.

ARTICLE 65.

Within a period of three weeks after the coming into force of the present Treaty, the port of Strasburg and the port of Kehl shall be constituted, for a period of seven years, a single unit from the point of view of exploitation.

The administration of this single unit will be carried on by a manager named by the Central Rhine Commission, which shall also have power to remove him.

This manager shall be of French nationality.

He will reside in Strasburg and will be subject to the supervision of the Central Rhine Commission.

There will be established in the two ports free zones in conformity with Part XII (Ports, Waterways and Railways) of the present Treaty.

A special Convention between France and Germany, which shall be submitted to the approval of the Central Rhine Commission, will fix the details of this organisation, particularly as regards finance.

It is understood that for the purpose of the present Article the port of Kehl includes the whole of the area necessary for the movements of the port and the trains which serve it, including the harbour, quays and railroads, platforms, cranes, sheds and warehouses, silos, elevators and hydro-electric plants, which make up the equipment of the port.

The German Government undertakes to carry out all measures which shall be required of it in order to assure that all the making-up and switching of trains arriving at or departing from Kehl, whether for the right bank or the left bank of the Rhine, shall be carried on in the best conditions possible.

All property rights shall be safeguarded. In particular the administration of the ports shall not prejudice any property rights of the French or Baden railroads.

Equality of treatment as respects traffic shall be assured in both ports to the nationals, vessels and goods of every country.

In case at the end of the sixth year France shall consider that the progress made in the improvement of the port of Strasburg still requires a prolongation of this temporary régime, she may ask for such prolongation from the Central Rhine Commission, which may grant an extension for a period not exceeding three years.

Throughout the whole period of any such extension the free zones above provided for shall be maintained.

Pending appointment of the first manager by the Central Rhine Commission a provisional manager who shall be of French nationality may be appointed by the Principal Allied and Associated Powers subject to the foregoing provisions.

For all purposes of the present Article the Central Rhine Commission will decide by a majority of votes.

ARTICLE 66.

The railway and other bridges across the Rhine now existing within the limits of Alsace-Lorraine shall, as to all their parts and their whole length, be the property of the French State, which shall ensure their upkeep.

ARTICLE 67.

The French Government is substituted in all the rights of the German Empire over all the railways which were administered by the Imperial railway administration and which are actually working or under construction.

The same shall apply to the rights of the Empire with regard to railway and tramway concessions within the territories referred to in Article 51.

This substitution shall not entail any payment on the part of the French State.

The frontier railway stations shall be established by a subsequent agreement, it being stipulated in advance that on the Rhine frontier they shall be situated on the right bank.

ARTICLE 68.

In accordance with the provisions of Article 268 of Chapter I of Section I of Part X (Economic Clauses) of the present Treaty, for a period of five years from the coming into force of the present Treaty, natural or manufactured products originating in and coming from the territories referred to in Article 51 shall, on importation into German customs territory, be exempt from all customs duty.

The French Government may fix each year, by decree communicated to the German Government, the nature and amount of the products which shall enjoy this exemption.

The amount of each product which may be thus sent annually into Germany shall not exceed the average of the amounts sent annually in the years 1911–1913.

Further, during the period of five years above mentioned, the German Government shall allow the free export from Germany and the free reimportation into Germany, exempt from all customs duties and other charges (including internal charges), of yarns, tissues, and other textile materials or textile products of any kind and in any condition, sent from Germany into the territories referred to in Article 51, to be subjected there to any finishing process, such as bleaching, dyeing, printing, mercerization, gassing, twisting or dressing.

ARTICLE 69.

During a period of ten years from the coming into force of the present Treaty, central electric supply works situated in German territory and formerly furnishing electric power to the territories referred to in Article 51 or to any establishment the working of which passes permanently or temporarily from Germany to France, shall be required to continue such supply up to the amount of consumption corresponding to the undertakings and contracts current on November 11, 1918.

Such supply shall be furnished according to the contracts in force and at a rate which shall not be higher than that paid to the said works by German nationals.

ARTICLE 70.

It is understood that the French Government preserves its right to prohibit in the future in the territories referred to in Article 51 all new German participation:

(1) In the management or exploitation of the public domain and of public services, such as railways, navigable waterways, water works, gas works, electric power, etc.;

(2) In the ownership of mines and quarries of every kind and in enterprises connected therewith;

(3) In metallurgical establishments, even though their working may not be connected with that of any mine.

ARTICLE 71.

As regards the territories referred to in Article 51, Germany renounces on behalf of herself and her nationals as from November 11, 1918, all rights under the law of May 25, 1910, regarding the trade in potash salts, and generally under any stipulations for the intervention of German organisations in the working of the potash mines. Similarly, she renounces on behalf of herself and her nationals all rights under any agreements, stipulations or laws which may exist to her benefit with regard to other products of the aforesaid territories.

ARTICLE 72.

The settlement of the questions relating to debts contracted before November 11, 1918, between the German Empire and the German States or their nationals residing in Germany on the one part and Alsace-Lorrainers residing in Alsace-Lorraine on the other part shall be effected in accordance with the provisions of Section III of Part X (Economic Clauses) of the present Treaty, the expression "before the war" therein being replaced by the expression "before November 11, 1918". The rate of exchange applicable in the case of such settlement shall be the average rate quoted on the Geneva Exchange during the month preceding November 11, 1918.

There may be established in the territories referred to in Article 51, for the settlement of the aforesaid debts under the conditions laid down in Section III of Part X (Economic Clauses) of the present Treaty, a special clearing office, it being understood that this office shall be regarded as a "central office" under the provisions of paragraph 1 of the Annex to the said Section.

ARTICLE 73.

The private property, rights and interests of Alsace-Lorrainers in Germany will be regulated by the stipulations of Section IV of Part X (Economic Clauses) of the present Treaty.

ARTICLE 74.

The French Government reserves the right to retain and liquidate all the property, rights and interests which German nationals or societies controlled by Germany possessed in the territories referred to in Article 51 on November 11, 1918, subject to the conditions laid down in the last paragraph of Article 53 above.

Germany will directly compensate her nationals who may have been dispossessed by the aforesaid liquidations.

The product of these liquidations shall be applied in accordance with the stipulations of Sections III and IV of Part X (Economic Clauses) of the present Treaty.

ARTICLE 75.

Notwithstanding the stipulations of Section V of Part X (Economic Clauses) of the present Treaty, all contracts made before the date of the promulgation in Alsace-Lorraine of the French decree of November 30, 1918, between Alsace-Lorrainers whether individuals or juridical persons) or others resident in Alsace-Lorraine on the one part and the German Empire or German States and their nationals resident in Germany on the other part, the execution of which has been suspended by the Armistice or by subsequent French legislation, shall be maintained.

Nevertheless, any contract of which the French Government shall notify the cancellation to Germany in the general interest within a period of six months from the date of the coming into force of the present Treaty, shall be annulled except in respect of any debt or other pecuniary obligation arising out of any act done or money paid thereunder before November 11, 1918. If this dissolution would cause one of the parties substantial prejudice, equitable compensation, calculated solely on the capital employed without taking account of loss of profits, shall be accorded to the prejudiced party.

With regard to prescriptions, limitations and forfeitures in Alsace-Lorraine, the provisions of Articles 300 and 301 of Section V of Part X (Economic Clauses) shall be applied with the substitution for the expression " outbreak of war " of the expression " November 11, 1918 ", and for the expression " duration of the war " of the expression "period from November 11, 1918, to the date of the coming into force of the present Treaty ".

ARTICLE 76.

Questions concerning rights in industrial, literary or artistic property of Alsace-Lorrainers shall be regulated in accordance with the general stipulations of Section VII of Part X (Economic Clauses) of the present Treaty, it being understood that Alsace-Lorrainers holding rights of this nature under German legislation will preserve full and entire enjoyment of those rights on German territory.

ARTICLE 77.

The German Government undertakes to pay over to the French Government such proportion of all reserves accumulated by the Empire or by public or private bodies dependent upon it, for the purposes of disability and old age insurance, as would fall to the disability and old age insurance fund at Strasburg.

The same shall apply in respect of the capital and reserves accumulated in Germany falling legitimately to other social insurance, funds, to miners' superannuation funds, to the fund of the railways of

Alsace-Loraine, to other superannuation organisations established for the benefit of the personnel of public administrations and institutions operating in Alsace-Loraine, and also in respect of the capital and reserves due by the insurance fund of private employees at Berlin, by reason of engagements entered into for the benefit of insured persons of that category resident in Alsace-Lorraine.

A special Convention shall determine the conditions and procedure of these transfers.

ARTICLE 78.

With regard to the execution of judgments, appeals and prosecutions, the following rules shall be applied:

(1) All civil and commercial judgments which shall have been given since August 3, 1914, by the Courts of Alsace-Lorraine between Alsace-Lorrainers, or between Alsace-Lorrainers and foreigners, or between foreigners, and which shall not have been appealed from before November 11, 1918, shall be regarded as final and susceptible of immediate execution without further formality.

When the judgment has been given between Alsace-Lorrainers and Germans or between Alsace-Lorrainers and subjects of the allies of Germany, it shall only be capable of execution after the issue of an *exequatur* by the corresponding new tribunal in the restored territory referred to in Article 51.

(2) All judgments given by German Courts since August 3, 1914, against Alsace-Lorrainers for political crimes or misdemeanors shall be regarded as null and void.

(3) All sentences passed since November 11, 1918, by the Court of the Empire at Leipzig on appeals against the decisions of the Courts of Alsace-Lorraine shall be regarded as null and void and shall be so pronounced. The papers in regard to the cases in which such sentences have been given shall be returned to the Courts of Alsace-Lorraine concerned.

All appeals to the Court of the Empire against decisions of the Courts of Alsace-Lorraine shall be suspended. The papers shall be returned under the aforesaid conditions for transfer without delay to the French Cour de Cassation, which shall be competent to decide them.

(4) All prosecutions in Alsace-Lorraine for offences committed during the period between November 11, 1918, and the coming into force of the present Treaty will be conducted under German law except in so far as this has been modified by decrees duly published on the spot by the French authorities.

(5) All other questions as to competence, procedure or administration of justice shall be determined by a special Convention between France and Germany.

ARTICLE 79.

The stipulations as to nationality contained in the Annex hereto shall be considered as of equal force with the provisions of the present Section.

All other questions concerning Alsace-Lorraine which are not regulated by the present Section and the Annex thereto or by the general provisions of the present Treaty will form the subject of further conventions between France and Germany.

ANNEX.

1.

As from November 11, 1918, the following persons are *ipso facto* reinstated in French nationality:

(1) Persons who lost French nationality by the application of the Franco-German Treaty of May 10, 1871, and who have not since that date acquired any nationality other than German;

(2) The legitimate or natural descendants of the persons referred to in the immediately preceding paragraph, with the exception of those whose ascendants in the paternal line include a German who migrated into Alsace-Lorraine after July 15, 1870;

(3) All persons born in Alsace-Lorraine of unknown parents, or whose nationality is unknown.

2.

Within the period of one year from the coming into force of the present Treaty, persons included in any of the following categories may claim French nationality:

(1) All persons not restored to French nationality under paragraph 1 above, whose ascendants include a Frenchman or Frenchwoman who lost French nationality under the conditions referred to in the said paragraph;

(2) All foreigners, not nationals of a German State, who acquired the status of a citizen of Alsace-Loraine before August 3, 1914;

(3) All Germans domiciled in Alsace-Lorraine, if they have been so domiciled since a date previous to July 15, 1870, or if one of their ascendants was at that date domiciled in Alsace-Lorraine;

(4) All Germans born or domiciled in Alsace-Lorraine who have served in the Allied or Associated armies during the present war, and their descendants;

(5) All persons born in Alsace-Lorraine before May 10, 1871, of foreign parents, and the descendants of such persons;

(6) The husband or wife of any person whose French nationality may have been restored under paragraph 1, or who may have claimed and obtained French nationality in accordance with the preceding provisions.

The legal representative of a minor may exercise, on behalf of that minor, the right to claim French nationality; and if that right has not been exercised, the minor may claim French nationality within the year following his majority.

Except in the cases provided for in No. (6) of the present paragraph, the French authorities reserve to themselves the right, in individual cases, to reject the claim to French nationality.

3.

Subject to the provisions of paragraph 2, Germans born or domiciled in Alsace-Lorraine shall not acquire French nationality by reason of the restoration of Alsace-Lorraine to France, even though they may have the status of citizens of Alsace-Lorraine.

They may acquire French nationality only by naturalisation, on condition of having been domiciled in Alsace-Lorraine from a date previous to August 3, 1914, and of submitting proof of unbroken residence within the restored territory for a period of three years from November 11, 1918.

France will be solely responsible for their diplomatic and consular protection from the date of their application for French naturalisation.

The French Government shall determine the procedure by which reinstatement in French nationality as of right shall be effected, and the conditions under which decisions shall be given upon claims to such nationality and applications for naturalisation, as provided by the present Annex.

Section VI.

AUSTRIA.

Article 80.

Germany acknowledges and will respect strictly the independence of Austria, within the frontiers which may be fixed in a Treaty between that State and the Principal Allied and Associated Powers; she agrees that this independence shall be inalienable, except with the consent of the Council of the League of Nations.

Section VII.

CZECHO-SLOVAK STATE.

Article 81.

Germany, in conformity with the action already taken by the Allied and Associated Powers, recognizes the complete independence of the Czecho-Slovak State which will include the autonomous territory of the Ruthenians to the south of the Carpathians. Germany hereby recognizes the frontiers of this State as determined by the Principal Allied and Associated Powers and the other interested States.

Article 82.

The old frontier as it existed on August 3, 1914, between Austria-Hungary and the German Empire will constitute the frontier between Germany and the Czecho-Slovak State.

Article 83.

Germany renounces in favour of the Czecho-Slovak State all rights and title over the portion of Silesian territory defined as follows:

starting from a point about 2 kilometres south-east of Katscher, on the boundary between the *Kreise* of Leobschütz and Ratibor:

the boundary between the two *Kreise*;

then, the former boundary between Germany and Austria-Hungary up to a point on the Oder immediately to the south of the Ratibor-Oderberg railway;

thence, towards the north-west and up to a point about 2 kilometres to the south-east of Katscher:

a line to be fixed on the spot passing to the west of Kranowitz.

A Commission composed of seven members, five nominated by the Principal Allied and Associated Powers, one by Poland and one by the Czecho-Slovak State, will be appointed fifteen days after the coming into force of the present Treaty to trace on the spot the frontier line between Poland and the Czecho-Slovak State.

The decisions of this Commission will be taken by a majority and shall be binding on the parties concerned.

Germany hereby agrees to renounce in favour of the Czecho-Slovak State all rights and title over the part of the *Kreis* of Leobschütz comprised within the following boundaries in case after the determination of the frontier between Germany and Poland the said part of that *Kreis* should become isolated from Germany:

from the south-eastern extremity of the salient of the former Austrian frontier at about 5 kilometres to the west of Leobschütz southwards and up to the point of junction with the boundary between the *Kreise* of Leobschütz and Ratibor:

the former frontier between Germany and Austria-Hungary;

then, northwards, the administrative boundary between the *Kreise* of Leobschütz and Ratibor up to a point situated about 2 kilometres to the south-east of Katscher;

thence, north-westwards and up to the starting-point of this definition:

a line to be fixed on the spot passing to the east of Katscher.

ARTICLE 84.

German nationals habitually resident in any of the territories recognized as forming part of the Czecho-Slovak State will obtain Czecho-Slovak nationality *ipso facto* and lose their German nationality.

ARTICLE 85.

Within a period of two years from the coming into force of the present Treaty, German nationals over eighteen years of age habitually resident in any of the territories recognized as forming part of the Czecho-Slovak State will be entitled to opt for German nationality. Czecho-Slovaks who are German nationals and are habitually resident in Germany will have a similar right to opt for Czecho-Slovak nationality.

Option by a husband will cover his wife and option by parents will cover their children under eighteen years of age.

Persons who have exercised the above right to opt must within the succeeding twelve months transfer their place of residence to the State for which they have opted.

They will be entitled to retain their landed property in the territory of the other State where they had their place of residence before exercising the right to opt. They may carry with them their moveable property of every description. No export or import duties may be imposed upon them in connection with the removal of such property.

Within the same period Czecho-Slovaks who are German nationals and are in a foreign country will be entitled, in the absence of any provisions to the contrary in the foreign law, and if they have not acquired the foreign nationality, to obtain Czecho-Slovak nationality and lose their German nationality by complying with the requirements laid down by the Czecho-Slovak State.

ARTICLE 86.

The Czecho-Slovak State accepts and agrees to embody in a Treaty with the Principal Allied and Associated Powers such provisions as may be deemed necessary by the said Powers to protect the interests of inhabitants of that State who differ from the majority of the population in race, language or religion.

The Czecho-Slovak State further accepts and agrees to embody in a Treaty with the said Powers such provisions as they may deem necessary to protect freedom of transit and equitable treatment of the commerce of other nations.

The proportion and nature of the financial obligations of Germany and Prussia which the Czecho-Slovak State will have to assume on account of the Silesian territory placed under its sovereignty will be determined in accordance with Article 254 of Part IX (Financial Clauses) of the present Treaty.

Subsequent agreements will decide all questions not decided by the present Treaty which may arise in consequence of the cession of the said territory.

SECTION VIII.

POLAND.

ARTICLE 87.

Germany, in conformity with the action already taken by the Allied and Associated Powers, recognizes the complete independence of Poland, and renounces in her favour all rights and title over the territory bounded by the Baltic Sea, the eastern frontier of Germany as laid down in Article 27 of Part II (Boundaries of Germany) of the present Treaty up to a point situated about 2 kilometres to the east of Lorzendorf, then a line to the acute angle which the northern boundary of Upper Silesia makes about 3 kilometres north-west of Simmenau, then the boundary of Upper Silesia to its meeting point with the old frontier between Germany and Russia, then this frontier to the point where it crosses the course of the Niemen, and then the northern frontier of East Prussia as laid down in Article 28 of Part II aforesaid.

The provisions of this Article do not, however, apply to the territories of East Prussia and the Free City of Danzig, as defined in

Article 28 of Part II (Boundaries of Germany) and in Article 100 of Section XI (Danzig) of this Part.

The boundaries of Poland not laid down in the present Treaty will be subsequently determined by the Principal Allied and Associated Powers.

A Commission consisting of seven members, five of whom shall be nominated by the Principal Allied and Associated Powers, one by Germany and one by Poland, shall be constituted fifteen days after the coming into force of the present Treaty to delimit on the spot the frontier line between Poland and Germany.

The decisions of the Commission will be taken by a majority of votes and shall be binding upon the parties concerned.

ARTICLE 88.

In the portion of Upper Silesia included within the boundaries described below, the inhabitants will be called upon to indicate by a vote whether they wish to be attached to Germany or to Poland:

starting from the northern point of the salient of the old province of Austrian Silesia situated about 8 kilometres east of Neustadt, the former frontier between Germany and Austria to its junction with the boundary between the *Kreise* of Leobschütz and Ratibor;

thence in a northerly direction to a point about 2 kilometres southeast of Katscher:

the boundary between the *Kreise* of Leobschütz and Ratibor;

thence in a south-easterly direction to a point on the course of the Oder immediately south of the Ratibor-Oderberg railway:

a line to be fixed on the ground passing south of Kranowitz;

thence the old boundary between Germany and Austria, then the old boundary between Germany and Russia to its junction with the administrative boundary between Posnania and Upper Silesia;

thence this administrative boundary to its junction with the administrative boundary between Upper and Middle Silesia;

thence westwards to the point where the administrative boundary turns in an acute angle to the south-east about 3 kilometres northwest of Simmenau:

the boundary between Upper and Middle Silesia;

then in a westerly direction to a point to be fixed on the ground about 2 kilometres east of Lorzendorf:

a line to be fixed on the ground passing north of Klein Hennersdorf:

thence southwards to the point where the boundary between Upper and Middle Silesia cuts the Städtel-Karlsruhe road:

a line to be fixed on the ground passing west of Hennersdorf, Polkowitz, Noldau, Steinersdorf and Dammer, and east of Strehlitz, Nassadel, Eckersdorf, Schwirz and Städtel;

thence the boundary between Upper and Middle Silesia to its junction with the eastern boundary of the *Kreis* of Falkenberg;

then the eastern boundary of the *Kreis* of Falkenberg to the point of the salient which is 3 kilometres east of Puschine;

thence to the northern point of the salient of the old province of Austrian Silesia situated about 8 kilometres east of Neustadt:

a line to be fixed on the ground passing east of Zülz.

The régime under which this plebiscite will be taken and given effect to is laid down in the Annex hereto.

The Polish and German Governments hereby respectively bind themselves to conduct no prosecutions on any part of their territory and to take no exceptional proceedings for any political action performed in Upper Silesia during the period of the régime laid down in the Annex hereto and up to the settlement of the final status of the country.

Germany hereby renounces in favour of Poland all rights and title over the portion of Upper Silesia lying beyond the frontier line fixed by the Principal Allied and Associated Powers as the result of the plebiscite.

ANNEX.

1.

Within fifteen days from the coming into force of the present Treaty the German troops and such officials as may be designated by the Commission set up under the provisions of paragraph 2 shall evacuate the plebiscite area. Up to the moment of the completion of the evacuation they shall refrain from any form of requisitioning in money or in kind and from all acts likely to prejudice the material interests of the country.

Within the same period the Workmen's and Soldiers' Councils which have been constituted in this area shall be dissolved. Members of such Councils who are natives of another region and are exercising their functions at the date of the coming into force of the present Treaty, or who have gone out of office since March 1, 1919, shall be evacuated.

All military and semi-military unions formed in the said area by inhabitants of the district shall be immediately disbanded. All members of such military organizations who are not domiciled in the said area shall be required to leave it.

2.

The plebiscite area shall be immediately placed under the authority of an International Commission of four members to be designated by the following Powers; the United States of America, France, the British Empire and Italy. It shall be occupied by troops belonging to the Allied and Associated Powers, and the German Government undertakes to give facilities for the transference of these troops to Upper Silesia.

3.

The Commission shall enjoy all the powers exercised by the German or the Prussian Government, except those of legislation or taxation. It shall also be substituted for the Government of the province and the *Regierungsbezirk*.

It shall be within the competence of the Commission to interpret the powers hereby conferred upon it and to determine to what extent it shall exercise them, and to what extent they shall be left in the hands of the existing authorities.

Changes in the existing laws and the existing taxation shall only be brought into force with the consent of the Commission.

The Commission will maintain order with the help of the troops which will be at its disposal, and, to the extent which it may deem necessary, by means of gendarmerie recruited among the inhabitants of the country.

The Commission shall provide immediately for the replacement of the evacuated German officials and, if occasion arises, shall itself order the evacuation of such authorities and proceed to the replacement of such local authorities as may be required.

It shall take all steps which it thinks proper to ensure the freedom, fairness and secrecy of the vote. In particular, it shall have the right to order the expulsion of any person who may in any way have attempted to distort the result of the plebiscite by methods of corruption or intimidation.

The Commission shall have full power to settle all questions arising from the execution of the present clauses. It shall be assisted by technical advisers chosen by it from among the local population.

The decisions of the Commission shall be taken by a majority vote.

4.

The vote shall take place at such date as may be determined by the Principal Allied and Associated Powers, but not sooner than six months or later than eighteen months after the establishment of the Commission in the area.

The right to vote shall be given to all persons without distinction of sex who:

(a) Have completed their twentieth year on the 1st January of the year in which the plebiscite takes place;

(b) Were born in the plebiscite area or have been domiciled there since a date to be determined by the Commission, which shall not be subsequent to January 1, 1919, or who have been expelled by the German authorities and have not retained their domicile there.

Persons convicted of political offences shall be enabled to exercise their right of voting.

Every person will vote in the commune where he is domiciled or in which he was born, if he has not retained his domicile in the area.

The result of the vote will be determined by communes according to the majority of votes in each commune.

5.

On the conclusion of the voting, the number of votes cast in each commune will be communicated by the Commission to the Principal Allied and Associated Powers, with a full report as to the taking of the vote and a recommendation as to the line which ought to be adopted as the frontier of Germany in Upper Silesia. In this recommendation regard will be paid to the wishes of the inhabitants as shown by the vote, and to the geographical and economic conditions of the locality.

6.

As soon as the frontier has been fixed by the Principal Allied and Associated Powers, the German authorities will be notified by the International Commission that they are free to take over the administration of the territory which it is recognised should be German; the said authorities must proceed to do so within one month of such notification and in the manner prescribed by the Commission.

Within the same period and in the manner prescribed by the Commission, the Polish Government must proceed to take over the administration of the territory which it is recognised should be Polish.

When the administration of the territory has been provided for by the German and Polish authorities respectively, the powers of the Commission will terminate.

The cost of the army of occupation and expenditure by the Commission, whether in discharge of its own functions or in the administration of the territory, will be a charge on the area.

Article. 89.

Poland undertakes to accord freedom of transit to persons, goods, vessels, carriages, wagons and mails in transit between East Prussia and the rest of Germany over Polish territory, including territorial waters, and to treat them at least as favourably as the persons, goods, vessels, carriages, wagons and mails respectively of Polish or of any other more favoured nationality, origin, importation, starting point, or ownerships as regards facilities, restrictions and all other matters.

Goods in transit shall be exempt from all customs or other similar duties.

Freedom of transit will extend to telegraphic and telephonic services under the conditions laid down by the conventions referred to in Article 98.

Article 90.

Poland undertakes to permit for a period of fifteen years the exportation to Germany of the products of the mines in any part of Upper Silesia transferred to Poland in accordance with the present Treaty.

Such products shall be free from all export duties or other charges or restrictions on exportation.

Poland agrees to take such steps as may be necessary to secure that any such products shall be available for sale to purchasers in Germany on terms as favourable as are applicable to like products sold under similar conditions to purchasers in Poland or in any other country.

Article 91.

German nationals habitually resident in territories recognised as forming part of Poland will acquire Polish nationality *ipso facto* and will lose their German nationality.

German nationals, however, or their descendants who became resident in these territories after January 1, 1908, will not acquire Polish nationality without a special authorisation from the Polish State.

Within a period of two years after the coming into force of the present Treaty, German nationals over 18 years of age habitually resident in any of the territories recognised as forming part of Poland will be entitled to opt for German nationality.

Poles who are German nationals over 18 years of age and habitually resident in Germany will have a similar right to opt for Polish nationality.

Option by a husband will cover his wife and option by parents will cover their children under 18 years of age.

Persons who have exercised the above right to opt may within the succeeding twelve months transfer their place of residence to the State for which they have opted.

They will be entitled to retain their immovable property in the territory of the other State where they had their place of residence before exercising the right to opt.

They may carry with them their movable property of every description. No export or import duties or charges may be imposed upon them in connection with the removal of such property.

Within the same period Poles who are German nationals and are in a foreign country will be entitled, in the absence of any provisions to the contrary in the foreign law, and if they have not acquired the foreign nationality, to obtain Polish nationality and to lose their German nationality by complying with the requirements laid down by the Polish State.

In the portion of Upper Silesia submitted to a plebiscite the provisions of this Article shall only come into force as from the definitive attribution of the territory.

ARTICLE 92.

The proportion and the nature of the financial liabilities of Germany and Prussia which are to be borne by Poland will be determined in accordance with Article 254 of Part IX (Financial Clauses) of the present Treaty.

There shall be excluded from the share of such financial liabilities assumed by Poland that portion of the debt which, according to the finding of the Reparation Commission referred to in the above-mentioned Article, arises from measures adopted by the German and Prussian Governments with a view to German colonisation in Poland.

In fixing under Article 256 of the present Treaty the value of the property and possessions belonging to the German Empire and to the German States which pass to Poland with the territory transferred above, the Reparation Commission shall exclude from the valuation buildings, forests and other State property which belonged to the former Kingdom of Poland; Poland shall acquire these properties free of all costs and charges.

In all the German territory transferred in accordance with the present Treaty and recognised as forming definitively part of Poland, the property, rights and interests of German nationals shall not be liquidated under Article 297 by the Polish Government except in accordance with the following provisions:

(1) The proceeds of the liquidation shall be paid direct to the owner;

(2) If on his application the Mixed Arbitral Tribunal provided for by Section VI of Part X (Economic Clauses) of the present Treaty, or an arbitrator appointed by that Tribunal, is satisfied that the conditions of the sale or measures taken by the Polish Government outside its general legislation were unfairly prejudicial to the price obtained, they shall have discretion to award to the owner equitable compensation to be paid by the Polish Government.

Further agreements will regulate all questions arising out of the cession of the above territory which are not regulated by the present Treaty.

ARTICLE 93.

Poland accepts and agrees to embody in a Treaty with the Principal Allied and Associated Powers such provisions as may be deemed necessary by the said Powers to protect the interests of inhabitants of Poland who differ from the majority of the population in race, language or religion.

Poland further accepts and agrees to embody in a Treaty with the said Powers such provisions as they may deem necessary to protect freedom of transit and equitable treatment of the commerce of other nations.

SECTION IX.

EAST PRUSSIA.

ARTICLE 94.

In the area between the southern frontier of East Prussia, as described in Article 28 of Part II (Boundaries of Germany) of the present Treaty, and the line described below, the inhabitants will be called upon to indicate by a vote the State to which they wish to belong:

The western and northern boundary of *Regierungsbezirk* Allenstein to its junction with the boundary between the *Kreise* of Oletsko and Angerburg; thence, the northern boundary of the *Kreis* of Oletsko to its junction with the old frontier of East Prussia.

ARTICLE 95.

The German troops and authorities will be withdrawn from the area defined above within a period not exceeding fifteen days after the coming into force of the present Treaty. Until the evacuation is completed they will abstain from all requisitions in money or in kind and from all measures injurious to the economic interests of the country.

On the expiration of the above-mentioned period the said area will be placed under the authority of an International Commission of five members appointed by the Principal Allied and Associated Powers. This Commission will have general powers of administration and, in particular, will be charged with the duty of arranging for the vote and of taking such measures as it may deem necessary to ensure its freedom, fairness and secrecy. The Commission will have all necessary authority to decide any questions to which the execution of these provisions may give rise. The Commission will make such arrangements as may be necessary for assistance in the exercise of its functions by officials chosen by itself from the local population. Its decisions will be taken by a majority.

Every person, irrespective of sex, will be entitled to vote who:

(a) Is 20 years of age at the date of the coming into force of the present Treaty, and

(b) Was born within the area where the vote will take place or has been habitually resident there from a date to be fixed by the Commission.

Every person will vote in the commune where he is habitually resident or, if not habitually resident in the area, in the commune where he was born.

The result of the vote will be determined by communes (*Gemeinde*) according to the majority of the votes in each commune.

On the conclusion of the voting the number of votes cast in each commune will be communicated by the Commission to the Principal Allied and Associated Powers, with a full report as to the taking of the vote and a recommendation as to the line which ought to be adopted as the boundary of East Prussia in this region. In this recommendation regard will be paid to the wishes of the inhabitants as shown by the vote and to the geographical and economic conditions of the locality. The Principal Allied and Associated Powers will then fix the frontier between East Prussia and Poland in this region.

If the line fixed by the Principal Allied and Associated Powers is such as to exclude from East Prussia any part of the territory defined in Article 94, the renunciation of its rights by Germany in favour of Poland, as provided in Article 87 above, will extend to the territories so excluded.

As soon as the line has been fixed by the Principal Allied and Associated Powers, the authorities administering East Prussia will be notified by the International Commission that they are free to take over the administration of the territory to the north of the line so fixed, which they shall proceed to do within one month of such notification and in the manner prescribed by the Commission. Within the same period and as prescribed by the Commission, the Polish Government must proceed to take over the administration of the territory to the south of the line. When the administration of the territory by the East Prussian and Polish authorities respectively has been provided for, the powers of the Commission will terminate.

Expenditure by the Commission, whether in the discharge of its own functions or in the administration of the territory, will be borne by the local revenues. East Prussia will be required to bear such proportion of any deficit as may be fixed by the Principal Allied and Associated Powers.

ARTICLE 96.

In the area comprising the *Kreise* of Stuhm and Rosenberg and the portion of the *Kreis* of Marienburg which is situated east of the

Nogat and that of Marienwerder east of the Vistula, the inhabitants will be called upon to indicate by a vote, to be taken in each commune (*Gemeinde*), whether they desire the various communes situated in this territory to belong to Poland or to East Prussia.

ARTICLE 97.

The German troops and authorities will be withdrawn from the area defined in Article 96 within a period not exceeding fifteen days after the coming into force of the present Treaty. Until the evacuation is completed they will abstain from all requisitions in money or in kind and from all measures injurious to the economic interests of the country.

On the expiration of the above-mentioned period, the said area will be placed under the authority of an International Commission of five members appointed by the Principal Allied and Associated Powers. This Commission, supported if occasion arises by the necessary forces, will have general powers of administration and in particular will be charged with the duty of arranging for the vote and of taking such measures as it may deem necessary to ensure its freedom, fairness and secrecy. The Commission will conform as far as possible to the provisions of the present Treaty relating to the plebiscite in the Allenstein area; its decisions will be taken by a majority.

Expenditure by the Commission, whether in the discharge of its own functions or in the administration of the territory, will be borne by the local revenues.

On the conclusion of the voting the number of votes cast in each commune will be communicated by the Commission to the Principal Allied and Associated Powers with a full report as to the taking of the vote and a recommendation as to the line which ought to be adopted as the boundary of East Prussia in this region. In this recommendation regard will be paid to the wishes of the inhabitants as shown by the vote and to the geographical and economic conditions of the locality. The Principal Allied and Associated Powers will then fix the frontier between East Prussia and Poland in this region, leaving in any case to Poland for the whole of the section bordering on the Vistula full and complete control of the river including the east bank as far east of the river as may be necessary for its regulation and improvement. Germany agrees that in any portion of the said territory which remains German, no fortifications shall at any time be erected.

The Principal Allied and Associated Powers will at the same time draw up regulations for assuring to the population of East Prussia to the fullest extent and under equitable conditions access to the Vistula and the use of it for themselves, their commerce and their boats.

The determination of the frontier and the foregoing regulations shall be binding upon all the parties concerned.

When the administration of the territory has been taken over by the East Prussian and Polish authorities respectively, the powers of the Commission will terminate.

ARTICLE 98.

Germany and Poland undertake, within one year of the coming into force of this Treaty, to enter into conventions of which the terms, in case of difference, shall be settled by the Council of the League of Nations, with the object of securing, on the one hand to Germany full and adequate railroad, telegraphic and telephonic facilities for communication between the rest of Germany and East Prussia over the intervening Polish territory, and on the other hand to Poland full and adequate railroad, telegraphic and telephonic facilities for communication between Poland and the Free City of Danzig over any German territory that may, on the right bank of the Vistula, intervene between Poland and the Free City of Danzig.

SECTION X.

MEMEL.

ARTICLE 99.

Germany renounces in favour of the Principal Allied and Associated Powers all rights and title over the territories included between the Baltic, the north eastern frontier of East Prussia as defined in Article 28 of Part II (Boundaries of Germany) of the present Treaty and the former frontier between Germany and Russia.

Germany undertakes to accept the settlement made by the Principal Allied and Associated Powers in regard to these territories, particularly in so far as concerns the nationality of the inhabitants.

SECTION XI.

FREE CITY OF DANZIG.

ARTICLE 100.

Germany renounces in favour of the Principal Allied and Associated Powers all rights and title over the territory comprised within the following limits:

from the Baltic Sea southwards to the point where the principal channels of navigation of the Nogat and the Vistula (Weichsel) meet:

the boundary of East Prussia as described in Article 28 of Part II (Boundaries of Germany) of the present Treaty;

thence the principal channel of navigation of the Vistula downstream to a point about $6\frac{1}{2}$ kilometres north of the bridge of Dirschau;

thence north-west to point 5, $1\frac{1}{2}$ kilometres south-east of the church of Güttland:

a line to be fixed on the ground;

thence in a general westerly direction to the salient made by the boundary of the *Kreis* of Berent $8\frac{1}{2}$ kilometres north-east of Schöneck:

a line to be fixed on the ground passing between Mühlbanz on the south and Rambeltsch on the north;

thence the boundary of the *Kreis* of Berent westwards to the re-entrant which it forms 6 kilometres north-north-west of Schöneck;

thence to a point on the median line of Lonkener See:

a line to be fixed on the ground passing north of Neu Fietz and Schatarpi and south of Barenhütte and Lonken;

thence the median line of Lonkener See to its northernmost point;

thence to the southern end of Pollenziner See:

a line to be fixed on the ground;

thence the median line of Pollenziner See to its northernmost point;

thence in a north-easterly direction to a point about 1 kilometre south of Koliebken church, where the Danzig-Neustadt railway crosses a stream:

a line to be fixed on the ground passing south-east of Kamehlen, Krissau, Fidlin, Sulmin (Richthof), Mattern, Schäferei, and to the north-west of Neuendorf, Marschau, Czapielken, Hoch- and Klein-Kelpin, Pulvermühl, Renneberg and the towns of Oliva and Zoppot;

thence the course of the stream mentioned above to the Baltic Sea.

The boundaries described above are drawn on a German, map scale 1/100,000, attached to the present Treaty (Map No. 3).

ARTICLE 101.

A Commission composed of three members appointed by the Principal Allied and Associated Powers, including a High Commissioner as President, one member appointed by Germany and one member appointed by Poland, shall be constituted within fifteen days of the coming into force of the present Treaty for the purpose of delimiting on the spot the frontier of the territory as described above, taking into account as far as possible the existing communal boundaries.

ARTICLE 102.

The Principal Allied and Associated Powers undertake to establish the town of Danzig, together with the rest of the territory described in Article 100, as a Free City. It will be placed under the protection of the League of Nations.

ARTICLE 103.

A constitution for the Free City of Danzig shall be drawn up by the duly appointed representatives of the Free City in agreement with a High Commissioner to be appointed by the League of Nations. This constitution shall be placed under the guarantee of the League of Nations.

The High Commissioner will also be entrusted with the duty of dealing in the first instance with all differences arising between Poland and the Free City of Danzig in regard to this Treaty or any arrangements or agreements made thereunder.

The High Commissioner shall reside at Danzig.

ARTICLE 104.

The Principal Allied and Associated Powers undertake to negotiate a Treaty between the Polish Government and the Free City of Danzig, which shall come into force at the same time as the establishment of the said Free City, with the following objects:

(1) To effect the inclusion of the Free City of Danzig within the Polish Customs frontiers, and to establish a free area in the port;

(2) To ensure to Poland without any restriction the free use and service of all waterways, docks, basins, wharves and other works within the territory of the Free City necessary for Polish imports and exports;

(3) To ensure to Poland the control and administration of the Vistula and of the whole railway system within the Free City, except such street and other railways as serve primarily the needs of the Free City, and of postal, telegraphic and telephonic communication between Poland and the port of Danzig;

(4) To ensure to Poland the right to develop and improve the waterways, docks, basins, wharves, railways and other works and means of communication mentioned in this Article, as well as to lease or purchase through appropriate processes such land and other property as may be necessary for these purposes;

(5) To provide against any discrimination within the Free City of Danzig to the detriment of citizens of Poland and other persons of Polish origin or speech;

(6) To provide that the Polish Government shall undertake the conduct of the foreign relations of the Free City of Danzig as well as the diplomatic protection of citizens of that city when abroad.

ARTICLE 105.

On the coming into force of the present Treaty German nationals ordinarily resident in the territory described in Article 100 will *ipso facto* lose their German nationality in order to become nationals of the Free City of Danzig.

ARTICLE 106.

Within a period of two years from the coming into force of the present Treaty, German nationals over 18 years of age ordinarily resident in the territory described in Article 100 will have the right to opt for German nationality.

Option by a husband will cover his wife and option by parents will cover their children less than 18 years of age.

All persons who exercise the right of option referred to above must during the ensuing twelve months transfer their place of residence to Germany.

These persons will be entitled to preserve the immovable property possessed by them in the territory of the Free City of Danzig. They may carry with them their movable property of every description. No export or import duties shall be imposed upon them in this connection.

ARTICLE 107.

All property situated within the territory of the Free City of Danzig belonging to the German Empire or to any German State shall pass to the Principal Allied and Associated Powers for transfer to the Free City of Danzig or to the Polish State as they may consider equitable.

ARTICLE 108.

The proportion and nature of the financial liabilities of Germany and of Prussia to be borne by the Free City of Danzig shall be fixed in accordance with Article 254 of Part IX (Financial Clauses) of the present Treaty.

All other questions which may arise from the cession of the territory referred to in Article 100 shall be settled by further agreements.

SECTION XII.

SCHLESWIG.

ARTICLE 109.

The frontier between Germany and Denmark shall be fixed in conformity with the wishes of the population.

For this purpose, the population inhabiting the territories of the former German Empire situated to the north of a line, from East to West, (shown by a brown line on the map No. 4, annexed to the present Treaty):

leaving the Baltic Sea about 13 kilometres east-north-east of Flensburg,

running

south-west so as to pass south-east of: Sygum, Ringsberg, Munkbrarup, Adelby, Tastrup, Jarplund, Oversee, and north-west of: Langballigholz, Langballig, Bönstrup, Rüllschau, Weseby, Kleinwolstrup, Gross-Solt,

thence westwards passing south of Frörup and north of Wanderup,

thence in a south-westerly direction passing south-east of Oxlund, Stieglund and Ostenau and north-west of the villages on the Wanderup-Kollund road,

thence in a north-westerly direction passing south-west of Löwenstedt, Joldelund, Goldelund, and north-east of Kolkerheide and Högel to the bend of the Soholmer Au, about 1 kilometre east of Soholm, where it meets the southern boundary of the *Kreis* of Tondern,

following this boundary to the North Sea,

passing south of the islands of Fohr and Amrum and north of the islands of Oland and Langeness,

shall be called upon to pronounce by a vote which will be taken under the following conditions:

(1) Within a period not exceeding ten days from the coming into force of the present Treaty, the German troops and authorities (including the *Oberpräsidenten*, *Regierungs-präsidenten*, *Landräthe*,

Amtsvorsteher, Oberbürgermeister) shall evacuate the zone lying to the north of the line above fixed.

Within the same period the Workmen's and Soldiers' Councils which have been constituted in this zone shall be dissolved; members of such Councils who are natives of another region and are exercising their functions at the date of the coming into force of the present Treaty, or who have gone out of office since March 1, 1919, shall also be evacuated.

The said zone shall immediately be placed under the authority of an International Commission, composed of five members, of whom three will be designated by the Principal Allied and Associated Powers; the Norwegian and Swedish Governments will each be requested to designate a member; in the event of their failing to do so, these two members will be chosen by the Principal Allied and Associated Powers.

The Commission, assisted in case of need by the necessary forces, shall have general powers of administration. In particular, it shall at once provide for filling the places of the evacuated German authorities, and if necessary shall itself give orders for their evacuation, and proceed to fill the places of such local authorities as may be required. It shall take all steps which it thinks proper to ensure the freedom, fairness, and secrecy of the vote. It shall be assisted by German and Danish technical advisers chosen by it from among the local population. Its decisions will be taken by a majority.

One half of the expenses of the Commission and of the expenditure occasioned by the plebiscite shall be paid by Germany.

(2). The right to vote shall be given to all persons, without distinction of sex, who:

(*a*) Have completed their twentieth year at the date of the coming into force of the present Treaty; and

(*b*) Were born in the zone in which the plebiscite is taken, or have been domiciled there since a date before January 1, 1900, or had been expelled by the German authorities without having retained their domicile there.

Every person will vote in the commune (*Gemeinde*) where he is domiciled or of which he is a native.

Military persons, officers, non-commissioned officers and soldiers of the German army, who are natives of the zone of Schleswig in which the plebiscite is taken, shall be given the opportunity to return to their native place in order to take part in the voting there.

(3). In the section of the evacuated zone lying to the north of a line, from East to West (shown by a red line on map No. 4 which is annexed to the present Treaty):

passing south of the island of Alsen and following the median line of Flensburg Fjord,

leaving the fjord about 6 kilometres north of Flensburg and following the course of the stream flowing past Kupfermühle upstream to a point north of Niehuus,

passing north of Pattburg and Ellund and south of Fröslee to meet the eastern boundary of the *Kreis* of Tondern at its junction with the boundary between the old jurisdictions of Slogs and Kjær (*Slogs Herred* and *Kjær Herred*),

following the latter boundary to where it meets the Scheidebek, following the course of the Scheidebek (Alte Au), Süder Au and Wied Au downstream successively to the point where the latter bends northwards about 1,500 metres west of Ruttebüll,

thence, in a west-north-westerly direction to meet the North Sea north of Sieltoft,

thence, passing north of the island of Sylt,

the vote above provided for shall be taken within a period not exceeding three weeks after the evacuation of the country by the German troops and authorities.

The result will be determined by the majority of votes cast in the whole of this section. This result will be immediately communicated by the Commission to the Principal Allied and Associated Powers and proclaimed.

If the vote results in favour of the reincorporation of this territory in the Kingdom of Denmark, the Danish Government in agreement with the Commission will be entitled to effect its occupation with their military and administrative authorities immediately after the proclamation.

(4) In the section of the evacuated zone situated to the south of the preceding section and to the north of the line which starts from the Baltic Sea 13 kilometres from Flensburg and ends north of the islands of Oland and Langeness, the vote will be taken within a period not exceeding five weeks after the plebiscite shall have been held in the first section.

The result will be determined by communes (*Gemeinden*), in accordance with the majority of the votes cast in each commune (*Gemeinde*).

ARTICLE 110.

Pending a delimitation on the spot, a frontier line will be fixed by the Principal Allied and Associated Powers according to a line based on the result of the voting, and proposed by the International Commission, and taking into account the particular geographical and economic conditions of the localities in question.

From that time the Danish Government may effect the occupation of these territories with the Danish civil and military authorities, and the German Government may reinstate up to the said frontier line the German civil and military authorities whom it has evacuated.

Germany hereby renounces definitely in favour of the Principal Allied and Associated Powers all rights of sovereignty over the territories situated to the north of the frontier line fixed in accordance with the above provisions. The Principal Allied and Associated Powers will hand over the said territories to Denmark.

ARTICLE 111.

A Commission composed of seven members, five of whom shall be nominated by the Principal Allied and Associated Powers, one by Denmark, and one by Germany, shall be constituted within fifteen days from the date when the final result of the vote is known, to trace the frontier line on the spot.

The decisions of the Commission will taken by a majority of votes and shall be binding on the parties concerned.

ARTICLE 112.

All the inhabitants of the territory which is returned to Denmark will acquire Danish nationality *ipso facto*, and will lose their German nationality.

Persons, however, who had become habitually resident in this territory after October 1, 1918, will not be able to acquire Danish nationality without permission from the Danish Government.

ARTICLE 113.

Within two years from the date on which the sovereignty over the whole or part of the territory of Schleswig subjected to the plebiscite is restored to Denmark:

Any person over 18 years of age, born in the territory restored to Denmark, not habitually resident in this region, and possessing German nationality, will be entitled to opt for Denmark;

Any person over 18 years of age habitually resident in the territory restored to Denmark will be entitled to opt for Germany.

Option by a husband will cover his wife and option by parents will cover their children less than 18 years of age.

Persons who have exercised the above right to opt must within the ensuing twelve months transfer their place of residence to the State in favour of which they have opted.

They will be entitled to retain the immovable property which they own in the territory of the other State in which they were habitually resident before opting. They may carry with them their movable property of every description. No export or import duties may be imposed upon them in connection with the removal of such property.

ARTICLE 114.

The proportion and nature of the financial or other obligations of Germany and Prussia which are to be assumed by Denmark will be fixed in accordance with Article 254 of Part IX (Financial Clauses) of the present Treaty.

Further stipulations will determine any other questions arising out of the transfer to Denmark of the whole or part of the territory of which she was deprived by the Treaty of October 30, 1864.

SECTION XIII.

HELIGOLAND.

ARTICLE 115.

The fortifications, military establishments, and harbours of the Islands of Heligoland and Dune shall be destroyed under the supervision of the Principal Allied Governments by German labour and at the expense of Germany within a period to be determined by the said Governments.

The term "harbours" shall include the north-east mole, the west wall, the outer and inner breakwaters and reclaimed land within them, and all naval and military works, fortifications and buildings, constructed or under construction, between lines connecting the following positions taken from the British Admiralty chart No. 126 of April 19, 1918.

(*a*) lat. 54° 10′ 49″ N.; long. 7° 53′ 39″ E.;
(*b*) — 54° 10′ 35″ N.; — 7° 54′ 18″ E.;
(*c*) — 54° 10′ 14″ N.; — 7° 54′ 00″ E.;
(*d*) — 54° 10′ 17″ N.; — 7° 53′ 37″ E.;
(*e*) — 54° 10′ 44″ N.; — 7° 53′ 26″ E.

These fortifications, military establishments and harbours shall not be reconstructed nor shall any similar works be constructed in future.

Section XIV.

RUSSIA AND RUSSIAN STATES.

Article 116.

Germany acknowledges and agrees to respect as permanent and inalienable the independence of all the territories which were part of the former Russian Empire on August 1, 1914.

In accordance with the provisions of Article 259 of Part IX (Financial Clauses) and Article 292 of Part X (Economic Clauses) Germany accepts definitely the abrogation of the Brest-Litovsk Treaties and of all other treaties, conventions and agreements entered into by her with the Maximalist Government in Russia.

The Allied and Associated Powers formally reserve the rights of Russia to obtain from Germany restitution and reparation based on the principles of the present Treaty.

Article 117.

Germany undertakes to recognize the full force of all treaties or agreements which may be entered into by the Allied and Associated Powers with States now existing or coming into existence in future in the whole or part of the former Empire of Russia as it existed on August 1, 1914, and to recognize the frontiers of any such States as determined therein.

PART IV.

GERMAN RIGHTS AND INTERESTS OUTSIDE GERMANY.

Article 118.

In territory outside her European frontiers as fixed by the present Treaty, Germany renounces all rights, titles and privileges whatever in or over territory which belonged to her or to her allies, and all rights, titles and privileges whatever their origin which she held as against the Allied and Associated Powers.

Germany hereby undertakes to recognize and to conform to the measures which may be taken now or in the future by the Principal Allied and Associated Powers, in agreement where necessary with third Powers, in order to carry the above stipulation into effect.

In particular Germany declares her acceptance of the following Articles relating to certain special subjects.

Section I.

GERMAN COLONIES.

Article 119.

Germany renounces in favour of the Principal Allied and Associated Powers all her rights and titles over her oversea possessions.

Article 120.

All movable and immovable property in such territories belonging to the German Empire or to any German State shall pass to the Government exercising authority over such territories, on the terms laid down in Article 257 of Part IX (Financial Clauses) of the present Treaty. The decision of the local courts in any dispute as to the nature of such property shall be final.

Article 121.

The provisions of Sections I and IV of Part X (Economic Clauses) of the present Treaty shall apply in the case of these territories whatever be the form of Government adopted for them.

Article 122.

The Government exercising authority over such territories may make such provisions as it thinks fit with reference to the repatriation from them of German nationals and to the conditions upon which German subjects of European origin shall, or shall not, be allowed to reside, hold property, trade or exercise a profession in them.

Article 123.

The provisions of Article 260 of Part IX (Financial Clauses) of the present Treaty shall apply in the case of all agreements concluded with German nationals for the construction or exploitation of public works in the German oversea possessions, as well as any sub-concessions or contracts resulting therefrom which may have been made to or with such nationals.

Article 124.

Germany hereby undertakes to pay, in accordance with the estimate to be presented by the French Government and approved by the Reparation Commission, reparation for damage suffered by French nationals in the Cameroons or the frontier zone by reason of the acts of the German civil and military authorities and of German private individuals during the period from January 1, 1900, to August 1, 1914.

ARTICLE 125.

Germany renounces all rights under the Conventions and Agreements with France of November 4, 1911, and September 28, 1912, relating to Equatorial Africa. She undertakes to pay to the French Government, in accordance with the estimate to be presented by that Government and approved by the Reparation Commission, all the deposits, credits, advances, etc., effected by virtue of these instruments in favour of Germany.

ARTICLE 126.

Germany undertakes to accept and observe the agreements made or to be made by the Allied and Associated Powers or some of them with any other Power with regard to the trade in arms and spirits, and to the matters dealt with in the General Act of Berlin of February 26, 1885, the General Act of Brussels of July 2, 1890, and the conventions completing or modifying the same.

ARTICLE 127.

The native inhabitants of the former German oversea possessions shall be entitled to the diplomatic protection of the Governments exercising authority over those territories.

SECTION II.

CHINA.

ARTICLE 128.

Germany renounces in favour of China all benefits and privileges resulting from the provisions of the final Protocol signed at Peking on September 7, 1901, and from all annexes, notes and documents supplementary thereto. She likewise renounces in favour of China any claim to indemnities accruing thereunder subsequent to March 14, 1917.

ARTICLE 129.

From the coming into force of the present Treaty the High Contracting Parties shall apply, in so far as concerns them respectively:
(1) The Arrangement of August 29, 1902, regarding the new Chinese customs tariff;
(2) The Arrangement of September 27, 1905, regarding Whang-Poo, and the provisional supplementary Arrangement of April 4, 1912.

China, however, will no longer be bound to grant to Germany the advantages or privileges which she allowed Germany under these Arrangements.

ARTICLE 130.

Subject to the provisions of Section VIII of this Part, Germany cedes to China all the buildings, wharves and pontoons, barracks, forts, arms and munitions of war, vessels of all kinds, wireless telegraphy installations and other public property belonging to the German Government, which are situated or may be in the German Concessions at Tientsin and Hankow or elsewhere in Chinese territory.

It is understood, however, that premises used as diplomatic or consular residences or offices are not included in the above cession, and, furthermore, that no steps shall be taken by the Chinese Government to dispose of the German public and private property situated within the so-called Legation Quarter at Peking without the consent of the Diplomatic Representatives of the Powers which, on the coming into force of the present Treaty, remain Parties to the Final Protocol of September 7, 1901.

ARTICLE 131.

Germany undertakes to restore to China within twelve months from the coming into force of the present Treaty all the astronomical instruments which her troops in 1900–1901 carried away from China, and to defray all expenses which may be incurred in effecting such restoration, including the expenses of dismounting, packing, transporting, insurance and installation in Peking.

ARTICLE 132.

Germany agrees to the abrogation of the leases from the Chinese Government under which the German Concessions at Hankow and Tientsin are now held.

China, restored to the full exercise of her sovereign rights in the above areas, declares her intention of opening them to international residence and trade. She further declares that the abrogation of the leases under which these concessions are now held shall not affect the property rights of nationals of Allied and Associated Powers who are holders of lots in these concessions.

ARTICLE 133.

Germany waives all claims against the Chinese Government or against any Allied or Associated Government arising out of the internment of German nationals in China and their repatriation. She equally renounces all claims arising out of the capture and condemnation of German ships in China, or the liquidation, sequestration or control of German properties, rights and interests in that country since August 14, 1917. This provision, however, shall not affect the rights of the parties interested in the proceeds of any such liquidation, which shall be governed by the provisions of Part X (Economic Clauses) of the present Treaty.

ARTICLE 134.

Germany renounces in favour of the Government of His Britannic Majesty the German State property in the British Concession at

Shameen at Canton. She renounces in favour of the French and Chinese Governments conjointly the property of the German school situated in the French Concession at Shanghai.

Section III.

SIAM.

Article 135.

Germany recognises that all treaties, conventions and agreements between her and Siam, and all rights, title and privileges derived therefrom, including all rights of extraterritorial jurisdiction, terminated as from July 22, 1917.

Article 136.

All goods and property in Siam belonging to the German Empire or to any German State, with the exception of premises used as diplomatic or consular residences or offices, pass *ipso facto* and without compensation to the Siamese Government.

The goods, property and private rights of German nationals in Siam shall be dealt with in accordance with the provisions of Part X (Economic Clauses) of the present Treaty.

Article 137.

Germany waives all claims against the Siamese Government on behalf of herself or her nationals arising out of the seizure or condemnation of German ships, the liquidation of German property, or the internment of German nationals in Siam. This provision shall not affect the rights of the parties interested in the proceeds of any such liquidation, which shall be governed by the provisions of Part X (Economic Clauses) of the present Treaty.

Section IV.

LIBERIA.

Article 138.

Germany renounces all rights and privileges arising from the arrangements of 1911 and 1912 regarding Liberia, and particularly the right to nominate a German Receiver of Customs in Liberia.

She further renounces all claim to participate in any measures whatsoever which may be adopted for the rehabilitation of Liberia.

Article 139.

Germany recognizes that all treaties and arrangements between her and Liberia terminated as from August 4, 1917.

ARTICLE 140.

The property, rights and interests of Germans in Liberia shall be dealt with in accordance with Part X (Economic Clauses) of the present Treaty.

SECTION V.

MOROCCO.

ARTICLE 141.

Germany renounces all rights, titles and privileges conferred on her by the General Act of Algeciras of April 7, 1906, and by the Franco-German Agreements of February 9, 1909, and November 4, 1911. All treaties, agreements, arrangements and contracts concluded by her with the Sherifian Empire are regarded as abrogated as from August 3, 1914.

In no case can Germany take advantage of these instruments and she undertakes not to intervene in any way in negotiations relating to Morocco which may take place between France and the other Powers.

ARTICLE 142.

Germany having recognized the French Protectorate in Morocco, hereby accepts all the consequences of its establishment, and she renounces the régime of the capitulations therein.

This renunciation shall take effect as from August 3, 1914.

ARTICLE 143.

The Sherifian Government shall have complete liberty of action in regulating the status of German nationals in Morocco and the conditions in which they may establish themselves there.

German protected persons, semsars and "associés agricoles" shall be considered as having ceased, as from August 3, 1914, to enjoy the privileges attached to their status and shall be subject to the ordinary law.

ARTICLE 144.

All property and possessions in the Sherifian Empire of the German Empire and the German States pass to the Maghzen without payment.

For this purpose, the property and possessions of the German Empire and States shall be deemed to include all the property of the Crown, the Empire or the States, and the private property of the former German Emperor and other Royal personages.

All movable and immovable property in the Sherifian Empire belonging to German nationals shall be dealt with in accordance with Sections III and IV of Part X (Economic Clauses) of the present Treaty.

Mining rights which may be recognised as belonging to German nationals by the Court of Arbitration set up under the Moroccan Mining Regulations shall form the subject of a valuation, which the arbitrators shall be requested to make, and these rights shall then be treated in the same way as property in Morocco belonging to German nationals.

ARTICLE 145.

The German Government shall ensure the transfer to a person nominated by the French Government of the shares representing Germany's portion of the capital of the State Bank of Morocco. The value of these shares, as assessed by the Reparation Commission, shall be paid to the Reparation Commission for the credit of Germany on account of the sums due for reparation. The German Government shall be responsible for indemnifying its nationals so dispossessed.

This transfer will take place without prejudice to the repayment of debts which German nationals may have contracted towards the State Bank of Morocco.

ARTICLE 146.

Moroccan goods entering Germany shall enjoy the treatment accorded to French goods.

SECTION VI.

EGYPT.

ARTICLE 147.

Germany declares that she recognises the Protectorate proclaimed over Egypt by Great Britain on December 18, 1914, and that she renounces the régime of the Capitulations in Egypt.

This renunciation shall take effect as from August 4, 1914.

ARTICLE 148.

All treaties, agreements, arrangements and contracts concluded by Germany with Egypt are regarded as abrogated as from August 4, 1914.

In no case can Germany avail herself of these instruments and she undertakes not to intervene in any way in negotiations relating to Egypt which may take place between Great Britain and the other Powers.

ARTICLE 149.

Until an Egyptian law of judicial organization establishing courts with universal jurisdiction comes into force, provision shall be made, by means of decrees issued by His Highness the Sultan, for the exercise of jurisdiction over German nationals and property by the British Consular Tribunals.

ARTICLE 150.

The Egyptian Government shall have complete liberty of action in regulating the status of German nationals and the conditions under which they may establish themselves in Egypt.

ARTICLE 151.

Germany consents to the abrogation of the decree issued by His Highness the Khedive on November 28, 1904, relating to the Commission of the Egyptian Public Debt, or to such changes as the Egyptian Government may think it desirable to make therein.

ARTICLE 152.

Germany consents, in so far as she is concerned, to the transfer to His Britannic Majesty's Government of the powers conferred on His Imperial Majesty the Sultan by the Convention signed at Constantinople on October 29, 1888, relating to the free navigation of the Suez Canal.

She renounces all participation in the Sanitary, Maritime, and Quarantine Board of Egypt and consents, in so far as she is concerned, to the transfer to the Egyptian Authorities of the powers of that Board.

ARTICLE 153.

All property and possessions in Egypt of the German Empire and the German States pass to the Egyptian Government without payment.

For this purpose, the property and possessions of the German Empire and States shall be deemed to include all the property of the Crown, the Empire or the States, and the private property of the former German Emperor and other Royal personages.

All movable and immovable property in Egypt belonging to German nationals shall be dealt with in accordance with Sections III and IV of Part X (Economic Clauses) of the present Treaty.

ARTICLE 154.

Egyptian goods entering Germany shall enjoy the treatment accorded to British goods.

SECTION VII.

TURKEY AND BULGARIA.

ARTICLE 155.

Germany undertakes to recognise and accept all arrangements which the Allied and Associated Powers may make with Turkey and Bulgaria with reference to any rights, interests and privileges whatever which might be claimed by Germany or her nationals in Turkey and Bulgaria and which are not dealt with in the provisions of the present Treaty.

Section VIII.

SHANTUNG.

Article 156.

Germany renounces, in favour of Japan, all her rights, title and privileges—particularly those concerning the territory of Kiaochow, railways, mines and submarine cables—which she acquired in virtue of the Treaty concluded by her with China on March 6, 1898, and of all other arrangements relative to the Province of Shantung.

All German rights in the Tsingtao-Tsinanfu Railway, including its branch lines, together with its subsidiary property of all kinds, stations, shops, fixed and rolling stock, mines, plant and material for the exploitation of the mines, are and remain acquired by Japan, together with all rights and privileges attaching thereto.

The German State submarine cables from Tsingtao to Shanghai and from Tsingtao to Chefoo, with all the rights, privileges and properties attaching thereto, are similarly acquired by Japan, free and clear of all charges and encumbrances.

Article 157.

The movable and immovable property owned by the German State in the territory of Kiaochow, as well as all the rights which Germany might claim in consequence of the works or improvements made or of the expenses incurred by her, directly or indirectly, in connection with this territory, are and remain acquired by Japan, free and clear of all charges and encumbrances.

Article 158.

Germany shall hand over to Japan within three months from the coming into force of the present Treaty the archives, registers, plans, title-deeds and documents of every kind, wherever they may be, relating to the administration, whether civil, military, financial, judicial or other, of the territory of Kiaochow.

Within the same period Germany shall give particulars to Japan of all treaties, arrangements or agreements relating to the rights, title or privileges referred to in the two preceding Articles.

PART V.

MILITARY, NAVAL AND AIR CLAUSES.

In order to render possible the initiation of a general limitation of the armaments of all nations, Germany undertakes strictly to observe the military, naval and air clauses which follow.

SECTION I.

MILITARY CLAUSES.

CHAPTER I.

EFFECTIVES AND CADRES OF THE GERMAN ARMY.

ARTICLE 159.

The German military forces shall be demobilized and reduced as prescribed hereinafter.

ARTICLE 160.

(1) By a date which must not be later than March 31, 1920, the German Army must not comprise more than seven divisions of infantry and three divisions of cavalry.

After that date the total number of effectives in the Army of the States constituting Germany must not exceed one hundred thousand men, including officers and establishments of depots. The Army shall be devoted exclusively to the maintenance of order within the territory and to the control of the frontiers.

The total effective strength of officers, including the personnel of staffs, whatever their composition, must not exceed four thousand.

(2) Divisions and Army Corps headquarters staffs shall be organised in accordance with Table No. I annexed to this Section.

The number and strengths of the units of infantry, artillery, engineers, technical services and troops laid down in the aforesaid Table constitute maxima which must not be exceeded.

The following units may each have their own depot:

An Infantry regiment;
A Cavalry regiment;
A regiment of Field Artillery;
A battalion of Pioneers.

(3) The divisions must not be grouped under more than two army corps headquarters staffs.

The maintenance or formation of forces differently grouped or of other organisations for the command of troops or for preparation for war is forbidden.

The Great German General Staff and all similar organisations shall be dissolved and may not be reconstituted in any form.

The officers, or persons in the position of officers, in the Ministries of War in the different States in Germany and in the Administrations attached to them, must not exceed three hundred in number and are included in the maximum strength of four thousand laid down in the third sub-paragraph of paragraph (1) of this Article.

ARTICLE 161.

Army administrative services consisting of civilian personnel not included in the number of effectives prescribed by the present Treaty will have such personnel reduced in each class to one-tenth of that laid down in the Budget of 1913.

ARTICLE 162.

The number of employees or officials of the German States, such as customs officers, forest guards and coastguards, shall not exceed that of the employees or officials functioning in these capacities in 1913.

The number of gendarmes and employees or officials of the local or municipal police may only be increased to an extent corresponding to the increase of population since 1913 in the districts or municipalities in which they are employed.

These employees and officials may not be assembled for military training.

ARTICLE 163.

The reduction of the strength of the German military forces as provided for in Article 160 may be effected gradually in the following manner:

Within three months from the coming into force of the present Treaty the total number of effectives must be reduced to 200,000 and the number of units must not exceed twice the number of those laid down in Article 160.

At the expiration of this period, and at the end of each subsequent period of three months, a Conference of military experts of the Principal Allied and Associated Powers will fix the reductions to be made in the ensuing three months, so that by March 31, 1920, at the latest the total number of German effectives does not exceed the maximum number of 100,000 men laid down in Article 160. In these successive reductions the same ratio between the number of officers and of men, and between the various kinds of units, shall be maintained as is laid down in that Article.

CHAPTER II.

ARMAMENT, MUNITIONS AND MATERIAL.

ARTICLE 164.

Up till the time at which Germany is admitted as a member of the League of Nations the German Army must not possess an armament greater than the amounts fixed in Table No. II annexed to this Section, with the exception of an optional increase not exceeding one-twentyfifth part for small arms and one-fiftieth part for guns, which shall be exclusively used to provide for such eventual replacements as may be necessary.

Germany agrees that after she has become a member of the League of Nations the armaments fixed in the said Table shall remain in force until they are modified by the Council of the League. Furthermore she hereby agrees strictly to observe the decisions of the Council of the League on this subject.

ARTICLE 165.

The maximum number of guns, machine guns, trench-mortars, rifles and the amount of ammunition and equipment which Germany is allowed to maintain during the period between the coming into force of the present Treaty and the date of March 31, 1920, referred to in Article 160, shall bear the same proportion to the amount authorized in Table No III annexed to this Section as the strength of the German Army as reduced from time to time in accordance with Article 163 bears to the strength permitted under Article 160.

ARTICLE 166.

At the date of March 31, 1920, the stock of munitions which the German Army may have at its disposal shall not exceed the amounts fixed in Table No. III annexed to this Section.

Within the same period the German Government will store these stocks at points to be notified to the Governments of the Principal Allied and Associated Powers. The German Government is forbidden to establish any other stocks, depots or reserves of munitions.

ARTICLE 167.

The number and calibre of the guns constituting at the date of the coming into force of the present Treaty the armament of the fortified works, fortresses, and any land or coast forts which Germany is allowed to retain must be notified immediately by the German Government to the Governments of the Principal Allied and Associated Powers, and will constitute maximum amounts which may not be exceeded.

Within two months from the coming into force of the present Treaty, the maximum stock of ammunition for these guns will be reduced to, and maintained at, the following uniform rates:—fifteen hundred rounds per piece for those the calibre of which is 10.5 cm. and under: five hundred rounds per piece for those of higher calibre.

ARTICLE 168.

The manufacture of arms, munitions, or any war material, shall only be carried out in factories or works the location of which shall be communicated to and approved by the Governments of the Principal Allied and Associated Powers, and the number of which they retain the right to restrict.

Within three months from the coming into force of the present Treaty, all other establishments for the manufacture, preparation, storage or design of arms, munitions, or any war material whatever shall be closed down. The same applies to all arsenals except those used as depots for the authorised stocks of munitions. Within the same period the personnel of these arsenals will be dismissed.

ARTICLE 169.

Within two months from the coming into force of the present Treaty German arms, munitions and war material, including anti-aircraft material, existing in Germany in excess of the quantities allowed, must be surrendered to the Governments of the Principal Allied and Associated Powers to be destroyed or rendered useless.

This will also apply to any special plant intended for the manufacture of military material, except such as may be recognised as necessary for equipping the authorised strength of the German army.

The surrender in question willl be effected at such points in German territory as may be selected by the said Governments.

Within the same period arms, munitions and war material, including anti-aircraft material, of origin other than German, in whatever state they may be, will be delivered to the said Governments, who will decide as to their disposal.

Arms and munitions which on account of the successive reductions in the strength of the German army become in excess of the amounts authorized by Tables II and III annexed to this Section must be handed over in the manner laid down above within such periods as may be decided by the Conferences referred to in Article 163.

ARTICLE 170.

Importation into Germany of arms, munitions and war material of every kind shall be strictly prohibited.

The same applies to the manufacture for, and export to, foreign countries of arms, munitions and war material of every kind.

ARTICLE 171.

The use of asphyxiating, poisonous or other gases and all analogous liquids, materials or devices being prohibited, their manufacture and importation are strictly forbidden in Germany.

The same applies to materials specially intended for the manufacture, storage and use of the said products or devices.

The manufacture and the importation into Germany of armoured cars, tanks and all similar constructions suitable for use in war are also prohibited.

ARTICLE 172.

Within a period of three months from the coming into force of the present Treaty, the German Government will disclose to the Governments of the Principal Allied and Associated Powers the nature and mode of manufacture of all explosives, toxic substances or other like chemical preparations used by them in the war or prepared by them for the purpose of being so used.

CHAPTER III.

RECRUITING AND MILITARY TRAINING.

ARTICLE 173.

Universal compulsory military service shall be abolished in Germany.

The German Army may only be constituted and recruited by means of voluntary enlistment.

ARTICLE 174.

The period of enlistment for non-commissioned officers and privates must be twelve consecutive years.

The number of men discharged for any reason before the expiration of their term of enlistment must not exceed in any year five per cent. of the total effectives fixed by the second sub-paragraph of paragraph (1) of Article 160 of the present Treaty.

ARTICLE 175.

The officers who are retained in the Army must undertake the obligation to serve in it up to the age of forty-five years at least.

Officers newly appointed must undertake to serve on the active list for twenty-five consecutive years at least.

Officers who have previously belonged to any formations whatever of the Army, and who are not retained in the units allowed to be maintained, must not take part in any military exercise whether theoretical or practical, and will not be under any military obligations whatever.

The number of officers discharged for any reason before the expiration of their term of service must not exceed in any year five per cent. of the total effectives of officers provided for in the third sub-paragraph (1) of Article 160 of the present Treaty.

ARTICLE 176.

On the expiration of two months from the coming into force of the present Treaty there must only exist in Germany the number of military schools which is absolutely indispensable for the recruitment of the officers of the units allowed. These schools will be exclusively intended for the recruitment of officers of each arm, in the proportion of one school per arm.

The number of students admitted to attend the courses of the said schools will be strictly in proportion to the vacancies to be filled in the cadres of officers. The students and the cadres will be reckoned in the effectives fixed by the second and third sub-paragraphs of paragraph (1) of Article 160 of the present Treaty.

Consequently, and during the period fixed above, all military academies or similar institutions in Germany, as well as the different military schools for officers, student officers (*Aspiranten*), cadets, non-commissioned officers or student non-commissioned officers (*Aspiranten*), other than the schools above provided for, will be abolished.

ARTICLE 177.

Educational establishments, the universities, societies of discharged soldiers, shooting or touring clubs and, generally speaking, associations of every description, whatever be the age of their members, must not occupy themselves with any military matters.

In particular they will be forbidden to instruct or exercise their members, or to allow them to be instructed or exercised, in the profession or use of arms.

These societies, associations, educational establishments and universities must have no connection with the Ministries of War or any other military authority.

ARTICLE 178.

All measures of mobilization or appertaining to mobilization are forbidden.

In no case must formations, administrative services or General Staffs include supplementary cadres.

ARTICLE 179.

Germany agrees, from the coming into force of the present Treaty, not to accredit nor to send to any foreign country any military, naval or air mission, nor to allow any such mission to leave her territory, and Germany further agrees to take appropriate measures to prevent German nationals from leaving her territory to become enrolled in the Army, Navy or Air service of any foreign Power, or to be attached to such Army, Navy or Air service for the purpose of assisting in the military, naval or air training thereof, or otherwise for the purpose of giving military, naval or air instruction in any foreign country.

The Allied and Associated Powers agree, so far as they are concerned, from the coming into force of the present Treaty, not to enrol in nor to attach to their armies or naval or air forces any German national for the purpose of assisting in the military training of such armies or naval or air forces, or otherwise to employ any such German national as military, naval or aeronautic instructor.

The present provision does not, however, affect the right of France to recruit for the Foreign Legion in accordance with French military laws and regulations.

CHAPTER IV.

FORTIFICATIONS.

ARTICLE 180.

All fortified works, fortresses and field works situated in German territory to the west of a line drawn fifty kilometres to the east of the Rhine shall be disarmed and dismantled.

Within a period of two months from the coming into force of the present Treaty such of the above fortified works, fortresses and field works as are situated in territory not occupied by Allied and Associated troops shall be disarmed, and within a further period of four months they shall be dismantled. Those which are situated in territory occupied by Allied and Associated troops shall be disarmed and dismantled within such periods as may be fixed by the Allied High Command.

The construction of any new fortification, whatever its nature and importance, is forbidden in the zone referred to in the first paragraph above.

The system of fortified works of the southern and eastern frontiers of Germany shall be maintained in its existing state.

TABLE No. I.

STATE AND ESTABLISHMENT OF ARMY CORPS HEADQUARTERS STAFFS AND OF INFAN-
TRY AND CAVALRY DIVISIONS.

These tabular statements do not form a fixed establishment to be imposed on Germany, but the figures contained in them (number of units and strengths) represent maximum figures, which should not in any case be exceeded.

I.—ARMY CORPS HEADQUARTERS STAFFS.

Unit.	Maximum No. authorised.	Maximum strengths of each unit.	
		Officers.	N.C.O.'s and Men.
Army Corps Headquarters Staff	2	30	150
Total for Headquarters Staffs		60	300

II. ESTABLISHMENT OF AN INFANTRY DIVISION.

Unit.	Maximum No. of such units in a single division.	Maximum strengths of each unit.	
		Officers.	N.C.O.'s and men.
Headquarters of an infantry division	1	25	70
Headquarters of divisional infantry	1	4	30
Headquarters of divisional artillery	1	4	30
Regiment of infantry	3	70	2,300
(Each regiment comprises 3 battalions of infantry. Each battalion comprises 3 companies of infantry and 1 machine-gun company.)			
Trench mortar company	3	6	150
Divisional squadron	1	6	150
Field artillery regiment	1	85	1,300
(Each regiment comprises 3 groups of artillery. Each group comprises 3 batteries.)			
Pioneer battalion	1	12	400
(This battalion comprises 2 companies of pioneers, 1 pontoon detachment, 1 searchlight section.)			
Signal detachment	1	12	300
(This detachment comprises 1 telephone detachment, 1 listening section, 1 carrier pigeon section.)			
Divisional medical service	1	20	400
Parks and convoys		14	800
Total for infantry division		410	10,830

III. ESTABLISHMENT OF A CAVALRY DIVISION.

Unit.	Maximum No. of such units in a single division.	Maximum strengths of each unit.	
		Officers.	N.C.O.'s and men.
Headquarters of a cavalry division	1	15	50
Cavalry regiment	6	40	800
(Each regiment comprises 4 squadrons.)			
Horse artillery group (3 batteries)	1	20	400
Total for cavalry division		275	5,250

Table No. II.

TABULAR STATEMENT OF ARMAMENT ESTABLISHMENT FOR A MAXIMUM OF SEVEN INFANTRY DIVISIONS, THREE CAVALRY DIVISIONS, AND TWO ARMY CORPS HEADQUARTERS STAFFS.

Material.	Infantry division. (1)	For 7 infantry divisions. (2)	Cavalry division. (3)	For 3 cavalry divisions. (4)	Two army corps headquarters staffs. (5)	Total of columns 2, 4, and 5. (6)
Rifles	12,000	84,000			This establishment must be drawn from the increased armaments of the divisional infantry.	84,000
Carbines			6,000	18,000		18,000
Heavy machine guns	108	756	12	36		792
Light machine guns	162	1,134				1,134
Medium trench mortars	9	63				63
Light trench mortars	27	189				189
7.7-cm. guns	24	168	12	36		204
10.5-cm. howitzers	12	84				84

Table No. III.

MAXIMUM STOCKS AUTHORISED.

Material.	Maximum number of Arms authorised.	Establishment, per unit.	Maximum, totals.
		Rounds.	Rounds.
Rifles	84,000	400	40,800,000
Carbines	18,000		
Heavy machine guns	792	8,000	15,408,000
Light machine guns	1,134		
Medium trench mortars	63	400	25,200
Light trench mortars	189	800	151,200
Field artillery:			
7.7 cm. guns	204	1,000	204,000
10.5 cm. howitzers	84	800	67,200

Section II.

NAVAL CLAUSES.

Article 181.

After the expiration of a period of two months from the coming into force of the present Treaty the German naval forces in commission must not exceed:

6 battleships of the *Deutschland* or *Lothringen* type,
6 light cruisers,
12 destroyers,
12 torpedo boats,

or an equal number of ships constructed to replace them as provided in Article 190.

No submarines are to be included.

All other warships, except where there is provision to the contrary in the present Treaty, must be placed in reserve or devoted to commercial purposes.

Article 182.

Until the completion of the minesweeping prescribed by Article 193 Germany will keep in commission such number of minesweeping vessels as may be fixed by the Governments of the Principal Allied and Associated Powers.

Article 183.

After the expiration of a period of two months from the coming into force of the present Treaty the total personnel of the German Navy, including the manning of the fleet, coast defences, signal stations, administration and other land services, must not exceed fifteen thousand, including officers and men of all grades and corps.

The total strength of officers and warrant officers must not exceed fifteen hundred.

Within two months from the coming into force of the present Treaty the personnel in excess of the above strength shall be demobilized.

No naval or military corps or reserve force in connection with the Navy may be organised in Germany without being included in the above strength.

Article 184.

From the date of the coming into force of the present Treaty all the German surface warships which are not in German ports cease to belong to Germany, who renounces all rights over them.

Vessels which, in compliance with the Armistice of November 11, 1918, are now interned in the ports of the Allied and Associated Powers are declared to be finally surrendered.

Vessels which are now interned in neutral ports will be there surrendered to the Governments of the Principal Allied and Associated Powers. The German Government must address a notification to that effect to the neutral Powers on the coming into force of the present Treaty.

Article 185.

Within a period of two months from the coming into force of the present Treaty the German surface warships enumerated below will be surrendered to the Governments of the Principal Allied and Associated Powers in such Allied ports as the said Powers may direct.

These warships will have been disarmed as provided in Article XXIII of the Armistice of November 11, 1918. Nevertheless they must have all their guns on board.

BATTLESHIPS.

Oldenburg.	*Posen.*
Thuringen.	*Westfalen.*
Ostfriesland.	*Rheinland.*
Helgoland.	*Nassau.*

LIGHT CRUISERS.

Stettin.	*Stralsund.*
Danzig.	*Augsburg.*
München.	*Kolberg.*
Lübeck.	*Stuttgart.*

and, in addition, forty-two modern destroyers and fifty modern torpedo boats, as chosen by the Governments of the Principal Allied and Associated Powers.

ARTICLE 186.

On the coming into force of the present Treaty the German Government must undertake, under the supervision of the Governments of the Principal Allied and Associated Powers, the breaking-up of all the German surface warships now under construction.

ARTICLE 187.

The German auxiliary cruisers and fleet auxiliaries enumerated below will be disarmed and treated as merchant ships.

INTERRED IN NEUTRAL COUNTRIES:

Berlin.	*Seydlitz.*
Santa Fé.	*Yorck.*

IN GERMANY:

Ammon.	*Fürst Bülow.*
Answald.	*Gertrud.*
Bosnia.	*Kigoma.*
Cordoba.	*Rugia.*
Cassel.	*Santa Elena.*
Dania.	*Schleswig.*
Rio Negro.	*Möwe.*
Rio Pardo.	*Sierra Ventana.*
Santa Cruz.	*Chemnitz.*
Schwaben.	*Emil Georg von Strauss.*
Solingen.	*Habsburg.*
Steigerwald.	*Meteor.*
Franken.	*Waltraute.*
Gundomar.	*Scharnhorst.*

ARTICLE 188.

On the expiration of one month from the coming into force of the present Treaty all German submarines, submarine salvage vessels and docks for submarines, including the tubular dock, must have been handed over to the Governments of the Principal Allied and Associated Powers.

Such of these submarines, vessels and docks as are considered by the said Governments to be fit to proceed under their own power or to be towed shall be taken by the German Government into such Allied ports as have been indicated.

The remainder, and also those in course of construction, shall be broken up entirely by the German Government under the supervision of the said Governments. The breaking-up must be completed within three months at the most after the coming into force of the present Treaty.

ARTICLE 189.

Articles, machinery and material arising from the breaking-up of German warships of all kinds, whether surface vessels or submarines, may not be used except for purely industrial or commercial purposes.

They may not be sold or disposed of to foreign countries.

ARTICLE 190.

Germany is forbidden to construct or acquire any warships other than those intended to replace the units in commission provided for in Article 181 of the present Treaty.

The warships intended for replacement purposes as above shall not exceed the following displacement:

Armoured ships	10,000 tons,
Light cruisers	6,000 tons,
Destroyers	800 tons,
Torpedo boats	200 tons.

Except where a ship has been lost, units of the different classes shall only be replaced at the end of a period of twenty years in the case of battleships and cruisers, and fifteen years in the case of destroyers and torpedo boats, counting from the launching of the ship.

ARTICLE 191.

The construction or acquisition of any submarine, even for commercial purposes, shall be forbidden in Germany.

ARTICLE 192.

The warships in commission of the German fleet must have on board or in reserve only the allowance of arms, munitions and war material fixed by the Principal Allied and Associated Powers.

Within a month from the fixing of the quantities as above, arms, munitions and war material of all kinds, including mines and torpedoes, now in the hands of the German Government and in excess of the said quantities, shall be surrendered to the Governments of the said Powers at places to be indicated by them. Such arms, munitions and war material will be destroyed or rendered useless.

All other stocks, depots or reserves of arms, munitions or naval war material of all kinds are forbidden.

The manufacture of these articles in German territory for, and their export to, foreign countries shall be forbidden.

ARTICLE 193.

On the coming into force of the present Treaty Germany will forthwith sweep up the mines in the following areas in the North Sea to the eastward of longitude 4° 00′ E. of Greenwich:

(1) Between parallels of latitude 53° 00′ N. and 59° 00′ N.; (2) To the northward of latitude 60° 30′ N.

Germany must keep these areas free from mines.

Germany must also sweep and keep free from mines such areas in the Baltic as may ultimately be notified by the Governments of the Principal Allied and Associated Powers.

ARTICLE 194.

The personnel of the German Navy shall be recruited entirely by voluntary engagements entered into for a minimum period of twenty-five consecutive years for officers and warrant officers; twelve consecutive years for petty officers and men.

The number engaged to replace those discharged for any reason before the expiration of their term of service must not exceed five per cent. per annum of the totals laid down in this Section (Article 183).

The personnel discharged from the Navy must not receive any kind of naval or military training or undertake any further service in the Navy or Army.

Officers belonging to the German Navy and not demobilised must engage to serve till the age of forty-five, unless discharged for sufficient reasons.

No officer or man of the German mercantile marine shall receive any training in the Navy.

ARTICLE 195.

In order to ensure free passage into the Baltic to all nations, Germany shall not erect any fortifications in the area comprised between latitudes 55° 27′ N. and 54° 00′ N. and longitudes 9° 00′ E. and 16° 00′ E. of the meridian of Greenwich, nor instal any guns commanding the maritime routes between the North Sea and the Baltic. The fortifications now existing in this area shall be demolished and the guns removed under the supervisions of the Allied Governments and in periods to be fixed by them.

The German Government shall place at the disposal of the Governments of the Principal Allied and Associated Powers all hydrographical information now in its possession concerning the channels and adjoining waters between the Baltic and the North Sea.

ARTICLE 196.

All fortified works and fortifications, other than those mentioned in Section XIII (Heligoland) of Part III (Political Clauses for Europe) and in Article 195, now established within fifty kilometres of the German coast or on German islands off that coast shall be considered as of a defensive nature and may remain in their existing condition.

No new fortifications shall be constructed within these limits. The armament of these defences shall not exceed, as regards the number and calibre of guns, those in position at the date of the coming into force of the present Treaty. The German Government shall communicate forthwith particulars thereof to all the European Governments.

On the expiration of a period of two months from the coming into force of the present Treaty the stocks of ammunition for these guns shall be reduced to and maintained at a maximum figure of fifteen hundred rounds per piece for calibres of 4.1-inch and under, and five hundred rounds per piece for higher calibres.

ARTICLE 197.

During the three months following the coming into force of the present Treaty the German high-power wireless telegraphy stations at Nauen, Hanover and Berlin shall not be used for the transmission of messages concerning naval, military or political questions of interest to Germany or any State which has been allied to Germany in the war, without the assent of the Governments of the Principal Allied and Associated Powers. These stations may be used for commercial purposes, but only under the supervision of the said Governments, who will decide the wave-length to be used.

During the same period Germany shall not build any more high-power wireless telegraphy stations in her own territory or that of Austria, Hungary, Bulgaria or Turkey.

SECTION III.

AIR CLAUSES.

ARTICLE 198.

The armed forces of Germany must not include any military or naval air forces.

Germany may, during a period not extending beyond October 1, 1919, maintain a maximum number of one hundred seaplanes or flying boats, which shall be exclusively employed in searching for submarine mines, shall be furnished with the necessary equipment for this purpose, and shall in no case carry arms, munitions or bombs of any nature whatever.

In addition to the engines installed in the seaplanes or flying boats above mentioned, one spare engine may be provided for each engine of each of these craft.

No dirigible shall be kept.

ARTICLE 199.

Within two months from the coming into force of the present Treaty the personnel of air forces on the rolls of the German land

and sea forces shall be demobilised. Up to October 1, 1919, however, Germany may keep and maintain a total number of one thousand men, including officers, for the whole of the cadres and personnel, flying and non-flying, of all formations and establishments.

ARTICLE 200.

Until the complete evacuation of German territory by the Allied and Associated troops, the aircraft of the Allied and Associated Powers shall enjoy in Germany freedom of passage through the air, freedom of transit and of landing.

ARTICLE 201.

During the six months following the coming into force of the present Treaty, the manufacture and importation of aircraft, parts of aircraft, engines for aircraft, and parts of engines for aircraft, shall be forbidden in all German territory.

ARTICLE 202.

On the coming into force of the present Treaty, all military and naval aeronautical material, except the machines mentioned in the second and third paragraphs of Article 198, must be delivered to the Governments of the Principal Allied and Associated Powers.

Delivery must be effected at such places as the said Governments may select, and must be completed within three months.

In particular, this material will include all items under the following heads which are or have been in use or were designed for warlike purposes:

Complete aeroplanes and seaplanes, as well as those being manufactured, repaired or assembled.

Dirigibles able to take the air, being manufactured, repaired or assembled.

Plant for the manufacture of hydrogen.

Dirigible sheds and shelters of every kind for aircraft.

Pending their delivery, dirigibles will, at the expense of Germany, be maintained inflated with hydrogen; the plant for the manufacture of hydrogen, as well as the sheds for dirigibles, may, at the discretion of the said Powers, be left to Germany until the time when the dirigibles are handed over.

Engines for aircraft.

Nacelles and fuselages.

Armament (guns, machine guns, light machine guns, bomb-dropping apparatus, torpedo-dropping apparatus, synchronization apparatus, aiming apparatus).

Munitions (cartridges, shells, bombs loaded or unloaded, stocks of explosives or of material for their manufacture).

Instruments for use on aircraft.

Wireless apparatus and photographic or cinematograph apparatus for use on aircraft.

Component parts of any of the items under the preceding heads.

The material referred to above shall not be removed without special permission from the said Governments.

Section IV.

INTER-ALLIED COMMISSIONS OF CONTROL.

Article 203.

All the military, naval and air clauses contained in the present Treaty, for the execution of which a time-limit is prescribed, shall be executed by Germany under the control of Inter-Allied Commissions specially appointed for this purpose by the Principal Allied and Associated Powers.

Article 204.

The Inter-Allied Commissions of Control will be specially charged with the duty of seeing to the complete execution of the delivery, destruction, demolition and rendering things useless to be carried out at the expense of the German Government in accordance with the present Treaty.

They will communicate to the German authorities the decisions which the Principal Allied and Associated Powers have reserved the right to take, or which the execution of the military, naval and air clauses may necessitate.

Article 205.

The Inter-Allied Commissions of Control may establish their organisations at the seat of the central German Government.

They shall be entitled as often as they think desirable to proceed to any point whatever in German territory, or to send sub-commissions, or to authorize one or more of their members to go, to any such point.

Article 206.

The German Government must give all necessary facilities for the accomplishment of their missions to the Inter-Allied Commissions of Control and to their members.

It shall attach a qualified representative to each Inter-Allied Commission of Control for the purpose of receiving the communications which the Commission may have to address to the German Government and of supplying or procuring for the Commission all information or documents which may be required.

The German Government must in all cases furnish at its own cost all labour and material required to effect the deliveries and the works of destruction, dismantling, demolition, and of rendering things useless, provided for in the present Treaty.

Article 207.

The upkeep and cost of the Commissions of Control and the expenses involved by their work shall be borne by Germany.

Article 208.

The Military Inter-Allied Commission of Control will represent the Governments of the Principal Allied and Associated Powers in dealing with the German Government in all matters concerning the execution of the military clauses.

In particular it will be its duty to receive from the German Government the notifications relating to the location of the stocks and depots of munitions, the armament of the fortified works, fortresses and forts which Germany is allowed to retain, and the location of the works or factories for the production of arms, munitions and war material and their operations.

It will take delivery of the arms, munitions and war material, will select the points where such delivery is to be effected, and will supervise the works of destruction, demolition, and of rendering things useless, which are to be carried out in accordance with the present Treaty.

The German Government must furnish to the Military Inter-Allied Commission of Control all such information and documents as the latter may deem necessary to ensure the complete execution of the military clauses, and in particular all legislative and administrative documents and regulations.

ARTICLE 209.

The Naval Inter-Allied Commission of Control will represent the Governments of the Principal Allied and Associated Powers in dealing with the German Government in all matters concerning the execution of the naval clauses.

In particular it will be its duty to proceed to the building yards and to supervise the breaking-up of the ships which are under construction there, to take delivery of all surface ships or submarines, salvage ships, docks and the tubular docks, and to supervise the destruction and breaking-up provided for.

The German Government must furnish to the Naval Inter-Allied Commission of Control all such information and documents as the Commission may deem necessary to ensure the complete execution of the naval clauses, in particular the designs of the warships, the composition of their armaments, the details and models of the guns, munitions, torpedoes, mines, explosives, wireless telegraphic apparatus and, in general, everything relating to naval war material, as well as all legislative or administrative documents or regulations.

ARTICLE 210.

The Aeronautical Inter-Allied Commission of Control will represent the Governments of the Principal Allied and Associated Powers in dealing with the German Government in all matters concerning the execution of the air clauses.

In particular it will be its duty to make an inventory of the aeronautical material existing in German territory, to inspect aeroplane, balloon and motor manufactories, and factories producing arms, munitions and explosives capable of being used by aircraft, to visit all aerodromes, sheds, landing grounds, parks and depots, to authorise, where necessary, a removal of material and to take delivery of such material.

The German Government must furnish to the Aeronautical Inter-Allied Commission of Control all such information and legislative, administrative or other documents which the Commission may consider necessary to ensure the complete execution of the air clauses, and in particular a list of the personnel belonging to all the German Air Services, and of the existing material, as well as of that in process of manufacture or on order, and a list of all establishments working for aviation, of their positions, and of all sheds and landing grounds.

SECTION V.

GENERAL ARTICLES.

ARTICLE 211.

After the expiration of a period of three months from the coming into force of the present Treaty, the German laws must have been modified and shall be maintained by the German Government in conformity with this Part of the present Treaty.

Within the same period all the administrative or other measures relating to the execution of this Part of the Treaty must have been taken.

ARTICLE 212.

The following portions of the Armistice of November 11, 1918: Article VI, the first two and the sixth and seventh paragraphs of Article VII; Article IX; Clauses I, II and V of Annex n° 2, and the Protocol, dated April 4, 1919, supplementing the Armistice of November 11, 1918, remain in force so far as they are not inconsistent with the above stipulations.

ARTICLE 213.

So long as the present Treaty remains in force, Germany undertakes to give every facility for any investigation which the Council of the League of Nations, acting if need be by a majority vote, may consider necessary.

PART VI.

PRISONERS OF WAR AND GRAVES.

SECTION I.

PRISONERS OF WAR.

ARTICLE 214.

The repatriation of prisoners of war and interned civilians shall take place as soon as possible after the coming into force of the present Treaty and shall be carried out with the greatest rapidity.

ARTICLE 215.

The repatriation of German prisoners of war and interned civilians shall, in accordance with Article 214, be carried out by a Commission composed of representatives of the Allied and Associated Powers on the one part and of the German Government on the other part.

For each of the Allied and Associated Powers a Sub-Commission, composed exclusively of Representatives of the interested Power and of Delegates of the German Government, shall regulate the details of carrying into effect the repatriation of the prisoners of war.

ARTICLE 216.

From the time of their delivery into the hands of the German authorities the prisoners of war and interned civilians are to be returned without delay to their homes by the said authorities.

Those amongst them who before the war were habitually resident in territory occupied by the troops of the Allied and Associated Powers are likewise to be sent to their homes, subject to the consent and control of the military authorities of the Allied and Associated armies of occupation.

ARTICLE 217.

The whole cost of repatriation from the moment of starting shall be borne by the German Government who shall also provide the land and sea transport and staff considered necessary by the Commission referred to in Article 215.

ARTICLE 218.

Prisoners of war and interned civilians awaiting disposal or undergoing sentence for offences against discipline shall be repatriated irrespective of the completion of their sentence or of the proceedings pending against them.

This stipulation shall not apply to prisoners of war and interned civilians punished for offences committed subsequent to May 1, 1919.

During the period pending their repatriation all prisoners of war and interned civilians shall remain subject to the existing regulations, more especially as regards work and discipline.

ARTICLE 219.

Prisoners of war and interned civilians who are awaiting disposal or undergoing sentence for offences other than those against discipline may be detained.

ARTICLE 220.

The German Government undertakes to admit to its territory without distinction all persons liable to repatriation.

Prisoners of war or other German nationals who do not desire to be repatriated may be excluded from repatriation; but the Allied and Associated Governments reserve to themselves the right either to repatriate them or to take them to a neutral country or to allow them to reside in their own territories.

The German Government undertakes not to institute any exceptional proceedings against these persons or their families nor to take any repressive or vexatious measures of any kind whatsoever against them on this account.

ARTICLE 221.

The Allied and Associated Governments reserve the right to make the repatriation of German prisoners of war or German nationals in their hands conditional upon the immediate notification and release by the German Government of any prisoners of war who are nationals of the Allied and Associated Powers and may still be in Germany.

ARTICLE 222.

Germany undertakes:

(1) To give every facility to Commissions to enquire into the cases of those who cannot be traced; to furnish such Commissions with all necessary means of transport; to allow them access to camps, prisons, hospitals and all other places; and to place at their disposal all documents, whether public or private, which would facilitate their enquiries;

(2) To impose penalties upon any German officials or private persons who have concealed the presence of any nationals of any of the Allied and Associated Powers or have neglected to reveal the presence of any such after it had come to their knowledge.

ARTICLE 223.

Germany undertakes to restore without delay from the date of the coming into force of the present Treaty all articles, money, securities and documents which have belonged to nationals of the Allied and Associated Powers and which have been retained by the German authorities.

ARTICLE 224.

The High Contracting Parties waive reciprocally all repayment of sums due for the maintenance of prisoners of war in their respective territories.

SECTION II.

GRAVES.

ARTICLE 225.

The Allied and Associated Governments and the German Government will cause to be respected and maintained the graves of the soldiers and sailors buried in their respective territories.

They agree to recognise any Commission appointed by an Allied or Associated Government for the purpose of identifying, registering, caring for or erecting suitable memorials over the said graves and to facilitate the discharge of its duties.

Furthermore they agree to afford, so far as the provisions of their laws and the requirements of public health allow, every facility for giving effect to requests that the bodies of their soldiers and sailors may be transferred to their own country.

ARTICLE 226.

The graves of prisoners of war and interned civilians who are nationals of the different belligerent States and have died in captivity shall be properly maintained in accordance with Article 225 of the present Treaty.

The Allied and Associated Governments on the one part and the German Government on the other part reciprocally undertake also to furnish to each other:

(1) A complete list of those who have died, together with all information useful for identification;

(2) All information as to the number and position of the graves of all those who have been buried without identification.

PART VII.

PENALTIES.

ARTICLE 227.

The Allied and Associated Powers publicly arraign William II of Hohenzollern, formerly German Emperor, for a supreme offence against international morality and the sanctity of treaties.

A special tribunal will be constituted to try the accused, thereby assuring him the guarantees essential to the right of defence. It will be composed of five judges, one appointed by each of the following Powers: namely, the United States of America, Great Britain, France, Italy and Japan.

In its decision the tribunal will be guided by the highest motives of international policy, with a view to vindicating the solemn obligations of international undertakings and the validity of international morality. It will be its duty to fix the punishment which it considers should be imposed.

The Allied and Associated Powers will address a request to the Government of the Netherlands for the surrender to them of the ex-Emperor in order that he may be put on trial.

ARTICLE 228.

The German Government recognizes the right of the Allied and Associated Powers to bring before military tribunals persons accused of having committed acts in violation of the laws and customs of war. Such persons shall, if found guilty, be sentenced to punishments laid down by law. This provision will apply notwithstanding any proceedings or prosecution before a tribunal in Germany or in the territory of her allies.

The German Government shall hand over to the Allied and Associated Powers, or to such one of them as shall so request, all persons accused of having committed an act in violation of the laws and customs of war, who are specified either by name or by the rank, office or employment which they held under the German authorities.

ARTICLE 229.

Persons guilty of criminal acts against the nationals of one of the Allied and Associated Powers will be brought before the military tribunals of that Power.

Persons guilty of criminal acts against the nationals of more than one of the Allied and Associated Powers will be brought before military tribunals composed of members of the military tribunals of the Powers concerned.

In every case the accused will be entitled to name his own counsel.

ARTICLE 230.

The German Government undertakes to furnish all documents and information of every kind, the production of which may be considered necessary to ensure the full knowledge of the incriminating acts, the discovery of offenders and the just appreciation of responsibility.

PART VIII.

REPARATION.

SECTION I.

GENERAL PROVISIONS.

ARTICLE 231.

The Allied and Associated Governments affirm and Germany accepts the responsibility of Germany and her allies for causing all the loss and damage to which the Allied and Associated Governments and their nationals have been subjected as a consequence of the war imposed upon them by the aggression of Germany and her allies.

ARTICLE 232.

The Allied and Associated Governments recognize that the resources of Germany are not adequate, after taking into account permanent diminutions of such resources which will result from other provisions of the present Treaty, to make complete reparation for all such loss and damage.

The Allied and Associated Governments, however, require, and Germany undertakes, that she will make compensation for all damage done to the civilian population of the Allied and Associated Powers and to their property during the period of the belligerency of each as an Allied or Associated Power against Germany by such aggression by land, by sea and from the air. and in general all damage as defined in Annex I hereto.

In accordance with Germany's pledges, already given, as to complete restoration for Belgium, Germany undertakes, in addition to the compensation for damage elsewhere in this Part provided for, as a consequence of the violation of the Treaty of 1839, to make reimbursement of all sums which Belgium has borrowed from the Allied and Associated Governments up to November 11, 1918, together with interest at the rate of five per cent. (5%) per annum on such sums. This amount shall be determined by the Reparation Commission, and the German Government undertakes thereupon forthwith to make a special issue of bearer bonds to an equivalent amount payable in marks gold, on May 1, 1926, or, at the option of the German Government, on the 1st of May in any year up to 1926. Subject to the foregoing, the form of such bonds shall be determined by the Reparation Commission. Such bonds shall be handed over to the Reparation Commission, which has authority to take and acknowledge receipt thereof on behalf of Belgium.

ARTICLE 233.

The amount of the above damage for which compensation is to be made by Germany shall be determined by an Inter-Allied Commission, to be called the *Reparation Commission* and constituted in the form and with the powers set forth hereunder and in Annexes II to VII inclusive hereto.

This Commission shall consider the claims and give to the German Government a just opportunity to be heard.

The findings of the Commission as to the amount of damage defined as above shall be concluded and notified to the German Government on or before May 1, 1921, as representing the extent of that Government's obligations.

The Commission shall concurrently draw up a schedule of payments prescribing the time and manner for securing and discharging the entire obligation within a period of thirty years from May 1, 1921. If, however, within the period mentioned, Germany fails to discharge her obligations, any balance remaining unpaid may, within the discretion of the Commission, be postponed for settlement in subsequent years, or may be handled otherwise in such manner as the Allied and Associated Governments, acting in accordance with the procedure laid down in this Part of the present Treaty, shall determine.

ARTICLE 234.

The Reparation Commission shall after May 1, 1921, from time to time, consider the resources and capacity of Germany, and, after giving her representatives a just opportunity to be heard, shall have discretion to extend the date, and to modify the form of payments, such as are to be provided for in accordance with Article 233; but not to cancel any part, except with the specific authority of the several Governments represented upon the Commission.

ARTICLE 235.

In order to enable the Allied and Associated Powers to proceed at once to the restoration of their industrial and economic life, pending the full determination of their claims, Germany shall pay in such instalments and in such manner (whether in gold, commodities, ships, securities or otherwise) as the Reparation Commission may fix, during 1919, 1920 and the first four months of 1921, the equivalent of 20,000,000,000 gold marks. Out of this sum the expenses of the armies of occupation subsequent to the Armistice of November 11, 1918, shall first be met, and such supplies of food and raw materials as may be judged by the Governments of the Principal Allied and Associated Powers to be essential to enable Germany to meet her obligations for reparation may also, with the approval of the said Governments, be paid for out of the above sum. The balance shall be reckoned towards liquidation of the amounts due for reparation. Germany shall further deposit bonds as prescribed in paragraph 12 (c) of Annex II hereto.

ARTICLE 236.

Germany further agrees to the direct application of her economic resources to reparation as specified in Annexes, III, IV, V, and VI, relating respectively to merchant shipping, to physical restoration, to coal and derivatives of coal, and to dyestuffs and other chemical products; provided always that the value of the property transferred and any services rendered by her under these Annexes, assessed in the manner therein prescribed, shall be credited to her towards liquidation of her obligations under the above Articles.

ARTICLE 237.

The successive instalments, including the above sum, paid over by Germany in satisfaction of the above claims will be divided by the Allied and Associated Governments in proportions which have been determined upon by them in advance on a basis of general equity and of the rights of each.

For the purposes of this division the value of property transferred and services rendered under Article 243, and under Annexes III, IV, V, VI, and VII, shall be reckoned in the same manner as cash payments effected in that year.

ARTICLE 238.

In addition to the payments mentioned above Germany shall effect, in accordance with the procedure laid down by the Reparation Commission, restitution in cash of cash taken away, seized or sequestrated, and also restitution of animals, objects of every nature and securities taken away, seized or sequestrated, in the cases in which it proves possible to identify them in territory belonging to Germany or her allies.

Until this procedure is laid down, restitution will continue in accordance with the provisions of the Armistice of November 11, 1918, and its renewals and the Protocols thereto.

Article 239.

The German Government undertakes to make forthwith the restitution contemplated by Article 238 and to make the payments and deliveries contemplated by Articles 233, 234, 235 and 236.

Article 240.

The German Government recognizes the Commission provided for by Article 233 as the same may be constituted by the Allied and Associated Governments in accordance with Annex II, and agrees irrevocably to the possession and exercise by such Commission of the power and authority given to it under the present Treaty.

The German Government will supply to the Commission all the information which the Commission may require relative to the financial situation and operations and to the property, productive capacity, and stocks and current production of raw materials and manufactured articles of Germany and her nationals, and further any information relative to military operations which in the judgment of the Commission may be necessary for the assessment of Germany's liability for reparation as defined in Annex I.

The German Government will accord to the members of the Commission and its authorised agents the same rights and immunities as are enjoyed in Germany by duly accredited diplomatic agents of friendly Powers.

Germany further agrees to provide for the salaries and expenses of the Commission and of such staff as it may employ.

Article 241.

Germany undertakes to pass, issue and maintain in force any legislation, orders and decrees that may be necessary to give complete effect to these provisions.

Article 242.

The provisions of this Part of the present Treaty do not apply to the property, rights and interests referred to in Sections III and IV of Part X (Economic Clauses) of the present Treaty, nor to the product of their liquidation, except so far as concerns any final balance in favour of Germany under Article 243 (a).

Article 243.

The following shall be reckoned as credits to Germany in respect of her reparation obligations:

(a) Any final balance in favour of Germany under Section V (Alsace-Lorraine) of Part III (Political Clauses for Europe) and Sections III and IV of Part X (Economic Clauses) of the present Treaty;

(b) Amounts due to Germany in respect of transfers under Section IV (Saar Basin) of Part III (Political Clauses for Europe), Part IX (Financial Clauses), and Part XII (Ports, Waterways and Railways);

(c) Amounts which in the judgment of the Reparation Commission should be credited to Germany on account of any other transfers under the present Treaty of property, rights, concessions or other interests.

In no case however shall credit be given for property restored in accordance with Article 238 of the present Part.

ARTICLE 244.

The transfer of the German submarine cables which do not form the subject of particular provisions of the present Treaty is regulated by Annex VII hereto.

ANNEX I.

Compensation may be claimed from Germany under Article 232 above in respect of the total damage under the following categories:

(1) Damage to injured persons and to surviving dependents by personal injury to or death of civilians caused by acts of war, including bombardments or other attacks on land, on sea, or from the air, and all the direct consequences thereof, and of all operations of war by the two groups of belligerents wherever arising.

(2) Damage caused by Germany or her allies to civilian victims of acts of cruelty, violence or maltreatment (including injuries to life or health as a consequence of imprisonment, deportation, internment or evacuation, of exposure at sea or of being forced to labour), wherever arising, and to the surviving dependents of such victims.

(3) Damage caused by Germany or her allies in their own territory or in occupied or invaded territory to civilian victims of all acts injurious to health or capacity to work, or to honour, as well as to the surviving dependents of such victims.

(4) Damage caused by any kind of maltreatment of prisoners of war.

(5) As damage caused to the peoples of the Allied and Associated Powers, all pensions and compensation in the nature of pensions to naval and military victims of war (including members of the air force), whether mutilated, wounded, sick or invalided, and to the dependents of such victims, the amount due to the Allied and Associated Governments being calculated for each of them as being the capitalised cost of such pensions and compensation at the date of the coming into force of the present Treaty on the basis of the scales in force in France at such date.

(6) The cost of assistance by the Government of the Allied and Associated Powers to prisoners of war and to their families and dependents.

(7) Allowances by the Governments of the Allied and Associated Powers to the families and dependents of mobilised persons or persons serving with the forces, the amount due to them for each calendar year in which hostilities occurred being calculated for each Government on the basis of the average scale for such payments in force in France during that year.

(8) Damage caused to civilians by being forced by Germany or her allies to labour without just remuneration.

(9) Damage in respect of all property wherever situated belonging to any of the Allied or Associated States or their nationals, with the exception of naval and military works or materials, which has been carried off, seized, injured or destroyed by the acts of Germany or her allies on land, on sea or from the air, or damage directly in consequence of hostilities or of any operations of war.

(10) Damage in the form of levies, fines and other similar exactions imposed by Germany or her allies upon the civilian population.

ANNEX II.

1.

The Commission referred to in Article 233 shall be called "The Reparation Commission" and is hereinafter referred to as "the Commission".

2.

Delegates to this Commission shall be nominated by the United States of America, Great Britain, France, Italy, Japan, Belgium and the Serb-Croat-Slovene State. Each of these Powers will appoint one Delegate and also one Assistant Delegate, who will take his place in case of illness or necessary absence, but at other times will only have the right to be present at proceedings without taking any part therein.

On no occasion shall the Delegates of more than five of the above Powers have the right to take part in the proceedings of the Commission and to record their votes. The Delegates of the United States, Great Britain, France and Italy shall have this right on all occasions. The Delegate of Belgium shall have this right on all occasions other than those referred to below. The Delegate of Japan shall have this right on occasions when questions relating to damage at sea, and questions arising under Article 260 of Part IX (Financial Clauses) in which Japanese interests are concerned, are under consideration. The Delegate of the Serb-Croat-Slovene State shall have this right when questions relating to Austria, Hungary or Bulgaria are under consideration.

Each Government represented on the Commission shall have the right to withdraw therefrom upon twelve months notice filed with the Commission and confirmed in the course of the sixth month after the date of the original notice.

3.

Such of the other Allied and Associated Powers as may be interested shall have the right to appoint a Delegate to be present and act as Assessor only while their respective claims and interests are under examination or discussion, but without the right to vote.

4.

In case of the death, resignation or recall of any Delegate, Assistant Delegate or Assessor, a successor to him shall be nominated as soon as possible.

5.

The Commission will have its principal permanent Bureau in Paris and will hold its first meeting in Paris as soon as practicable after the coming into force of the present Treaty, and thereafter will meet in such place or places and at such time as it may deem convenient and as may be necessary for the most expeditious discharge of its duties.

6.

At its first meeting the Commission shall elect, from among the Delegates referred to above, a Chairman and a Vice-Chairman, who shall hold office for one year and shall be eligible for re-election. If a vacancy in the Chairmanship or Vice-Chairmanship should occur during the annual period, the Commission shall proceed to a new election for the remainder of the said period.

7.

The Commission is authorised to appoint all necessary officers, agents and employees who may be required for the execution of its functions, and to fix their remuneration; to constitute committees, whose members need not necessarily be members of the Commission, and to take all executive steps necessary for the purpose of discharging its duties; and to delegate authority and discretion to officers, agents and committees.

8.

All proceedings of the Commission shall be private, unless, on particular occasions, the Commission shall otherwise determine for special reasons.

9.

The Commission shall be required, if the German Government so desire, to hear, within a period which it will fix from time to time, evidence and arguments on the part of Germany on any question connected with her capacity to pay.

10.

The Commission shall consider the claims and give to the German Government a just opportunity to be heard, but not to take any part whatever in the decisions of the Commission. The Commission shall afford a similar opportunity to the allies of Germany, when it shall consider that their interests are in question.

11.

The Commission shall not be bound by any particular code or rules of law or by any particular rule of evidence or of procedure, but shall be guided by justice, equity and good faith. Its decisions must follow the same principles and rules in all cases where they are applicable. It will establish rules relating to methods of proof of claims. It may act on any trustworthy modes of computation.

12.

The Commission shall have all the powers conferred upon it, and shall exercise all the functions assigned to it, by the present Treaty.

The Commission shall in general have wide latitude as to its control and handling of the whole reparation problem as dealt with in this Part of the present Treaty and shall have authority to interpret its provisions. Subject to the provisions of the present Treaty, the Commission is constituted by the several Allied and Associated Governments referred to in paragraphs 2 and 3 above as the exclusive agency of the said Governments respectively for receiving, selling, holding, and distributing the reparation payments to be made by Germany under this Part of the present Treaty. The Commission must comply with the following conditions and provisions:

a) Whatever part of the full amount of the proved claims is not paid in gold, or in ships, securities and commodities or otherwise, Germany shall be required, under such conditions as the Commission may determine, to cover by way of guarantee by an equivalent issue of bonds, obligations or otherwise, in order to constitute an acknowledgment of the said part of the debt.

(*b*) In periodically estimating Germany's capacity to pay, the Commission shall examine the German system of taxation, first, to the end that the sums for reparation which Germany is required to pay shall become a charge upon all her revenues prior to that for the service or discharge of any domestic loan, and secondly, so as to satisfy itself that, in general, the German scheme of taxation is fully as heavy proportionately as that of any of the Powers represented on the Commission.

(*c*) In order to facilitate and continue the immediate restoration of the economic life of the Allied and Associated countries, the Commission will as provided in Article 235 take from Germany by way of security for and acknowledgment of her debt a first instalment of gold bearer bonds free of all taxes and charges of every description established or to be established by the Government of the German Empire or of the German States, or by any authority subject to them; these bonds will be delivered on account and in three portions, the marks gold being payable in conformity with Article 262 of Part IX (Financial Clauses) of the present Treaty as follows:

(1) To be issued forthwith, 20,000,000,000 Marks gold bearer bonds, payable not later than May 1, 1921, without interest. There shall be specially applied towards the amortisation of these bonds the payments which Germany is pledged to make in conformity with Article 235, after deduction of the sums used for the reimbursement of expenses of the armies of occupation and for payment of foodstuffs and raw materials. Such bonds as have not been redeemed by May 1, 1921, shall then be exchanged or new bonds of the same type as those provided for below (paragraph 12, *c*, (2).

(2) To be issued forthwith, further 40,000,000,000 Marks gold bearer bonds, bearing interest at 2½ per cent. per annum between 1921 and 1926, and thereafter at 5 per cent. per annum with an addi-

tional 1 per cent. for amortisation beginning in 1926 on the whole amount of the issue.

(3) To be delivered forthwith a covering undertaking in writing to issue when, but not until, the Commission is satisfied that Germany can meet such interest and sinking fund obligations, a further instalment of 40,000,000,000 Marks gold 5 per cent. bearer bonds, the time and mode of payment of principal and interest to be determined by the Commission.

The dates for payment of interest, the manner of applying the amortisation fund, and all other questions relating to the issue, management and regulation of the bond issue shall be determined by the Commission from time to time.

Further issues by way of acknowledgment and security may be required as the Commission subsequently determines from time to time.

(d) In the event of bonds, obligations or other evidence of indebtedness issued by Germany by way of security for or acknowledgment of her reparation debt being disposed of outright, not by way of pledge, to persons other than the several Governments in whose favour Germany's original reparation indebtedness was created, an amount of such reparation indebtedness shall be deemed to be extinguished corresponding to the nominal value of the bonds, etc., so disposed of outright, and the obligation of Germany in respect of such bonds shall be confined to her liabilities to the holders of the bonds, as expressed upon their face.

(e) The damage for repairing, reconstructing and rebuilding property in the invaded and devastated districts, including reinstallation of furniture, machinery and other equipment, will be calculated according to the cost at the dates when the work is done.

(f) Decisions of the Commission relating to the total or partial cancellation of the capital or interest of any verified debt of Germany must be accompanied by a statement of its reasons.

13.

As to voting, the Commission will observe the following rules:

When a decision of the Commission is taken, the votes of all the Delegates entitled to vote, or in the absence of any of them, of their Assistant Delegates, shall be recorded. Abstention from voting is to be treated as a vote against the proposal under discussion. Assessors have no vote.

On the following questions unanimity is necessary:

(a) Questions involving the sovereignty of any of the Allied and Associated Powers, or the cancellation of the whole or any part of the debt or obligations of Germany;

(b) Questions of determining the amount and conditions of bonds or other obligations to be issued by the German Government and of fixing the time and manner for selling, negotiating or distributing such bonds;

(c) Any postponement, total or partial, beyond the end of 1930, of the payment of instalments falling due between May 1, 1921, and the end of 1926 inclusive;

(d) Any postponement, total or partial, of any instalment falling due after 1926 for a period exceeding three years;

(*e*) Questions of applying in any particular case a method of measuring damages different from that which has been previously applied in a similar case;

(*f*) Questions of the interpretation of the provisions of this Part of the present Treaty.

· All other questions shall be decided by the vote of a majority.

In case of any difference of opinion among the Delegates, which cannot be solved by reference to their Governments, upon the question whether a given case is one which requires a unanimous vote for its decision or not, such difference shall be referred to the immediate arbitration of some impartial person to be agreed upon by their Governments, whose award the Allied and Associated Governments agree to accept.

14.

Decisions of the Commission, in accordance with the powers conferred upon it, shall forthwith become binding and may be put into immediate execution without further proceedings.

15.

The Commission will issue to each of the interested Powers, in such form as the Commission shall fix:

(1) A certificate stating that it holds for the account of the said Power bonds of the issues mentioned above, the said certificate, on the demand of the Power concerned, being divisible in a number of parts not exceeding five;

(2) From time to time certificates stating the goods delivered by Germany on account of her reparation debt which it holds for the account of the said Power.

The said certificates shall be registered, and upon notice to the Commission, may be transferred by endorsement.

When bonds are issued for sale or negotiation, and when goods are delivered by the Commission, certificates to an equivalent value must be withdrawn.

16.

Interest shall be debited to Germany as from May 1, 1921, in respect of her debt as determined by the Commission, after allowing for sums already covered by cash payments or their equivalent, or by bonds issued to the Commission, or under Article 243. The rate of interest shall be 5 per cent. unless the Commission shall determine at some future time that circumstances justify a variation of this rate.

The Commission, in fixing on May 1, 1921, the total amount of the debt of Germany, may take account of interest due on sums arising out of the reparation of material damage as from November 11, 1918, up to May 1, 1921.

17.

In case of default by Germany in the performance of any obligation under this Part of the present Treaty, the Commission will forthwith give notice of such default to each of the interested Powers and may make such recommendations as to the action to be taken in consequence of such default as it may think necessary.

18.

The measures which the Allied and Associated Powers shall have the right to take, in case of voluntary default by Germany, and which Germany agrees not to regard as acts of war, may include economic and financial prohibitions and reprisals and in general such other measures as the respective Governments may determine to be necessary in the circumstances.

19.

Payments required to be made in gold or its equivalent on account of the proved claims of the Allied and Associated Powers may at any time be accepted by the Commission in the form of chattels, properties, commodities, businesses, rights, concessions, within or without German territory, ships, bonds, shares or securities of any kind, or currencies of Germany or other States, the value of such substitutes for gold being fixed at a fair and just amount by the Commission itself.

20.

The Commission, in fixing or accepting payment in specified properties or rights, shall have due regard for any legal or equitable interests of the Allied and Associated Powers or of neutral Powers or of their nationals therein.

21.

No member of the Commission shall be responsible, except to the Government appointing him, for any action or omission as such member. No one of the Allied or Associated Governments assumes any responsibility in respect of any other Government.

22.

Subject to the provisions of the present Treaty this Annex may be amended by the unanimous decision of the Governments represented from time to time upon the Commission.

23.

When all the amounts due from Germany and her allies under the present Treaty or the decisions of the Commission have been discharged and all sums received, or their equivalents, shall have been distributed to the Powers interested, the Commission shall be dissolved.

ANNEX III.

1.

Germany recognises the right of the Allied and Associated Powers to the replacement, ton for ton (gross tonnage) and class for class, of all merchant ships and fishing boats lost or damaged owing to the war.

Nevertheless, and in spite of the fact that the tonnage of German shipping at present in existence is much less than that lost by the Allied and Associated Powers in consequence of the German aggression, the right thus recognised will be enforced on German ships and boats under the following conditions:

The German Government, on behalf of themselves and so as to bind all other persons interested, cede to the Allied and Associated Governments the property in all the German merchant ships which are of 1,600 tons gross and upwards; in one-half, reckoned in tonnage, of the ships which are between 1,000 tons and 1,600 tons gross; in one-quarter, reckoned in tonnage, of the steam trawlers; and in one-quarter, reckoned in tonnage, of the other fishing boats.

2.

The German Government will, within two months of the coming into force of the present Treaty, deliver to the Reparation Commission all the ships and boats mentioned in paragraph 1.

3.

The ships and boats mentioned in paragraph 1 include all ships and boats which (*a*) fly, or may be entitled to fly, the German merchant flag; or (*b*) are owned by any German national, company or corporation or by any company or corporation belonging to a country other than an Allied or Associated country and under the control or direction of German nationals; or (*c*) are now under construction (1) in Germany, (2) in other than Allied or Associated countries for the account of any German national, company or corporation.

4.

For the purpose of providing documents of title for the ships and boats to be handed over as above mentioned, the German Government will:

(*a*) Deliver to the Reparation Commission in respect of each vessel a bill of sale or other document of title evidencing the transfer to the Commission of the entire property in the vessel, free from all encumbrances, charges and liens of all kinds, as the Commission may require;

(*b*) Take all measures that may be indicated by the Reparation Commission for ensuring that the ships themselves shall be placed at its disposal.

5.

As an additional part of reparation, Germany agrees to cause merchant ships to be built in German yards for the account of the Allied and Associated Governments as follows:

(*a*) Within three months of the coming into force of the present Treaty, the Reparation Commission will notify to the German Government the amount of tonnage to be laid down in German shipyards in each of the two years next succeeding the three months mentioned above.

(*b*) Within two years of the coming into force of the present Treaty, the Reparation Commission will notify to the German Government the amount of tonnage to be laid down in each of the three years following the two years mentioned above.

(*c*) The amount of tonnage to be laid down in each year shall not exceed 200,000 tons, gross tonnage.

(*d*) The specifications of the ships to be built, the conditions under which they are to be built and delivered, the price per ton at which they are to be accounted for by the Reparation Commission, and all other questions relating to the accounting, ordering, building and delivery of the ships, shall be determined by the Commission.

Germany undertakes to restore in kind and in normal condition of upkeep to the Allied and Associated Powers, within two months of the coming into force of the present Treaty, in accordance with procedure to be laid down by the Reparation Commission, any boats and other movable appliances belonging to inland navigation which since August 1, 1914, have by any means whatever come into her possession or into the possession of her nationals, and which can be identified.

With a view to make good the loss in inland navigation tonnage, from whatever cause arising, which has been incurred during the war by the Allied and Associated Powers, and which cannot be made good by means of the restitution prescribed above, Germany agrees to cede to the Reparation Commission a portion of the German river fleet up to the amount of the loss mentioned above, provided that such cession shall not exceed 20 per cent. of the river fleet as it existed on November 11, 1918.

The conditions of this cession shall be settled by the arbitrators referred to in Article 339 of Part XII (Ports, Waterways and Railways) of the present Treaty, who are charged with the settlement of difficulties relating to the apportionment of river tonnage resulting from the new international régime applicable to certain river systems or from the territorial changes affecting those systems.

7.

Germany agrees to take any measures that may be indicated to her by the Reparation Commission for obtaining the full title to the property in all ships which have during the war been transferred, or are in process of transfer, to neutral flags, without the consent of the Allied and Associated Governments.

8.

Germany waives all claims of any description against the Allied and Associated Governments and their nationals in respect of the detention, employment, loss or damage of any German ships or boats, exception being made of payments due in respect of the employment of ships in conformity with the Armistice Agreement of January 13, 1919, and subsequent Agreements.

The handing over of the ships of the German mercantile marine must be continued without interruption in accordance with the said Agreement.

9.

Germany waives all claims to vessels or cargoes sunk by or in consequence of naval action and subsequently salved, in which any of the Allied or Associated Governments or their nationals may have any interest either as owners, charterers, insurers or otherwise, notwithstanding any decree of condemnation which may have been made by a Prize Court of Germany or of her allies.

ANNEX IV.

1.

The Allied and Associated Powers require, and Germany undertakes, that in part satisfaction of her obligations expressed in the present Part she will, as hereinafter provided, devote her economic resources directly to the physical restoration of the invaded areas of the Allied and Associated Powers, to the extent that these Powers may determine.

2.

The Allied and Associated Governments may file with the Reparation Commission lists showing:

(*a*) Animals, machinery, equipment, tools and like articles of a commercial character, which have been seized, consumed or destroyed by Germany or destroyed in direct consequence of military operations, and which such Governments, for the purpose of meeting immediate and urgent needs, desire to have replaced by animals and articles of the same nature which are in being in German territory at the date of the coming into force of the present Treaty;

(*b*) Reconstruction materials (stones, bricks, refractory bricks, tiles, wood, window-glass, steel, lime, cement, etc.), machinery, heating apparatus, furniture and like articles of a commercial character which the said Governments desire to have produced and manufactured in Germany and delivered to them to permit of the restoration of the invaded areas.

3.

The lists relating to the articles mentioned in 2 (*a*) above shall be filed within sixty days after the date of the coming into force of the present Treaty.

The lists relating to the articles in 2 (*b*) above shall be filed on or before December 31, 1919.

The lists shall contain all such details as are customary in commercial contracts dealing with the subject matter, including specifications, dates of delivery (but not extending over more than four years), and places of delivery, but not price or value, which shall be fixed as hereinafter provided by the Commission.

4.

Immediately upon the filing of such lists with the Commission, the Commission shall consider the amount and number of the materials and animals mentioned in the lists provided for above which are to be required of Germany. In reaching a decision on this matter the Commission shall take into account such domestic requirements of Germany as it deems essential for the maintenance of Germany's social and economic life, the prices and dates at which similar articles can be obtained in the Allied and Associated countries as compared with those to be fixed for German articles, and the general interest of the Allied and Associated Governments that the industrial life of Germany be not so disorganised as to affect adversely the ability of Germany to perform the other acts of reparation stipulated for.

Machinery, equipment, tools and like articles of a commercial character in actual industrial use are not, however, to be demanded of Germany unless there is no free stock of such articles respectively which is not in use and is available, and then not in excess of thirty per cent. of the quantity of such articles in use in any one establishment or undertaking.

The Commission shall give representatives of the German Government and opportuny and a time to be heard as to their capacity to furnish the said materials, articles and animals.

The decision of the Commission shall thereupon and at the earliest possible moment be communicated to the German Government and to the several interested Allied and Associated Governments.

The German Government undertakes to deliver the materials, articles and animals as specified in the said communication, and the interested Allied and Associated Governments severally agree to accept the same, provided they conform to the specification given, or are not, in the judgment of the Commission, unfit to be utilized in the work of reparation.

5.

The Commission shall determine the value to be attributed to the materials, articles and animals to be delivered in accordance with the foregoing, and the Allied or Associated Power receiving the same agrees to be charged with such value, and the amount thereof shall be treated as a payment by Germany to be divided in accordance with Article 237 of this Part of the present Treaty.

In cases where the right to require physical restoration as above provided is exercised, the Commission shall ensure that the amount to be credited against the reparation obligation of Germany shall be the fair value of work done or materials supplied by Germany, and that the claim made by the interested Power in respect of the damage so repaired by physical restoration shall be discharged to the extent of the proportion which the damage thus repaired bears to the whole of the damage thus claimed for.

6.

As an immediate advance on account of the animals referred to in paragraph 2 (*a*) above, Germany undertakes to deliver in equal monthly instalments in the three months following the coming into force of the present Treaty the following quantities of live stock:

(1) *To the French Government.*

     500 stallions (3 to 7 years);
  30,000 fillies and mares (18 months to 7 years), type: Ardennais, Boulonnais or Belgian;
   2,000 bulls (18 months to 3 years);
  90,000 milch cows (2 to 6 years);
   1,000 rams;
 100,000 sheep;
  10,000 goats.

(2) *To the Belgian Government.*

   200 stallions (3 to 7 years), large Belgian type;
 5,000 mares (3 to 7 years), large Belgian type;
 5,000 fillies (18 months to 3 years), large Belgian type;
 2,000 bulls (18 months to 3 years);
50,000 milch cows (2 to 6 years);
40,000 heifers;
   200 rams;
20,000 sheep;
15,000 sows.

The animals delivered shall be of average health and condition.

To the extent that animals so delivered cannot be identified as animals taken away or seized, the value of such animals shall be credited against the reparation obligations of Germany in accordance with paragraph 5 of this Annex.

7.

Without waiting for the decisions of the Commission referred to in paragraph 4 of this Annex to be taken, Germany must continue the delivery to France of the agricultural material referred to in Article III of the renewal dated January 16, 1919, of the Armistice.

ANNEX V.

1.

Germany accords the following options for the delivery of coal and derivatives of coal to the undermentioned signatories of the present Treaty.

2.

Germany undertakes to deliver to France seven million tons of coal per year for ten years. In addition, Germany undertakes to deliver to France annually for a period not exceeding ten years an amount of coal equal to the difference between the annual production before the war of the coal mines of the Nord and Pas de Calais, destroyed as a result of the war, and the production of the mines of the same area during the years in question: such delivery not to exceed twenty million tons in any one year of the first five years, and eight million tons in any one year of the succeeding five years.

It is understood that due diligence will be exercised in the restoration of the destroyed mines in the Nord and the Pas de Calais.

3.

Germany undertakes to deliver to Belgium eight million tons of coal annually for ten years.

4.

Germany undertakes to deliver to Italy up to the following quantities of coal:

July 1919 to	June 1920	_____	4½ million tons,
— 1920	— 1921	_____	6	—
— 1921	— 1922	_____	7½	—
— 1922	— 1923	_____	8	—
— 1923	— 1924	_____ }	8½	—
and each of the following five years	_____			

At least two-thirds of the actual deliveries to be land-borne.

5.

Germany further undertakes to deliver annually to Luxemburg, if directed by the Reparation Commission, a quantity of coal equal to the pre-war annual consumption of German coal in Luxemburg.

6.

The prices to be paid for coal delivered under these options shall be as follows:

(a) For overland delivery, including delivery by barge, the German pithead price to German nationals, plus the freight to French, Belgian, Italian or Luxemburg frontiers, provided that the pithead price does not exceed the pithead price of British coal for export. In the case of Belgian bunker coal, the price shall not exceed the Dutch bunker price.

Railroad and barge tariffs shall not be higher than the lowest similar rates paid in Germany.

(b) For sea delivery, the German export price f. o. b. German ports, or the British export price f. o. b. British ports, whichever may be lower.

7.

The Allied and Associated Governments interested may demand the delivery, in place of coal, of metallurgical coke in the proportion of 3 tons of coke to 4 tons of coal.

8.

Germany undertakes to deliver to France, and to transport to the French frontier by rail or by water, the following products, during each of the three years following the coming into force of this Treaty:

Benzol _____ 35,000 tons.
Coal tar_____ 50,000 tons.
Sulphate of ammonia_____ 30,000 tons.

All or part of the coal tar may, at the option of the French Government, be replaced by corresponding quantities of products of distillation, such as light oils, heavy oils, anthracene, napthalene or pitch.

9.

The price paid for coke and for the articles referred to in the preceding paragraph shall be the same as the price paid by German nationals under the same conditions of shipment to the French frontier or to the German ports, and shall be subject to any advantages which may be accorded similar products furnished to German nationals.

10.

The foregoing options shall be exercised through the intervention of the Reparation Commission, which, subject to the specific provisions hereof, shall have power to determine all questions relative to procedure and the qualities and quantities of products, the quantity of coke which may be substituted for coal, and the times and modes of delivery and payment. In giving notice to the German Government of the foregoing options the Commission shall give at least 120 days' notice of deliveries to be made after January 1, 1920, and at least 30 days' notice of deliveries to be made between the coming into force of this Treaty and January 1, 1920. Until Germany has received the demands referred to in this paragraph, the provisions of the Protocol of December 25, 1918, (Execution of Article VI of the Armistice of November 11, 1918) remain in force. The notice to be given to the German Government of the exercise of the right of substitution accorded by paragraphs 7 and 8 shall be such as the Reparation Commission may consider sufficient. If the Commission shall determine that the full exercise of the foregoing options would interfere unduly with the industrial requirements of Germany, the Commission is authorised to postpone or to cancel deliveries, and in so doing to settle all questions of priority; but the coal to replace coal from destroyed mines shall receive priority over other deliveries.

ANNEX VI.

1.

Germany accords to the Reparation Commission an option to require as part of reparation the delivery by Germany of such quantities and kinds of dyestuffs and chemical drugs as the Commission may designate, not exceeding 50 per cent. of the total stock of each and every kind of dyestuff and chemical drug in Germany or under German control at the date of the coming into force of the present Treaty.

This option shall be exercised within sixty days of the receipt by the Commission of such particulars as to stocks as may be considered necessary by the Commission.

2.

Germany further accords to the Reparation Commission an option to require delivery during the period from the date of the coming into force of the present Treaty until January 1, 1920, and during each period of six months thereafter until January 1, 1925, of any specified kind of dyestuff and chemical drug up to an amount not exceeding 25 per cent. of the German production of such dyestuffs and chemical drugs during the previous six months period. If in any case the production during such previous six months was, in the opinion of the Commission, less than normal, the amount required may be 25 per cent. of the normal production.

Such option shall be exercised within four weeks after the receipt of such particulars as to production and in such form as may be considered necessary by the Commission; these particulars shall be furnished by the German Government immediately after the expiration of each six months period.

3.

For dyestuffs and chemical drugs delivered under paragraph 1, the price shall be fixed by the Commission having regard to pre-war net export prices and to subsequent increases of cost.

For dyestuffs and chemical drugs delivered under paragraph 2, the price shall be fixed by the Commission having regard to pre-war net export prices and subsequent variations of cost, or the lowest net selling price of similar dyestuffs and chemical drugs to any other purchaser.

4.

All details, including mode and times of exercising the options, and making delivery, and all other questions arising under this arrangement shall be determined by the Reparation Commission; the German Government will furnish to the Commission all necessary information and other assistance which it may require.

5.

The above expression " dyestuffs and chemical drugs " includes all synthetic dyes and drugs and intermediate or other products used in connection with dyeing, so far as they are manufactured for sale. The present arrangement shall also apply to cinchona bark and salts of quinine.

ANNEX VII.

Germany renounces on her own behalf and on behalf of her nationals in favour of the Principal Allied and Associated Powers all rights, titles or privileges of whatever nature in the submarine cables set out below, or in any portions thereof:

Emden-Vigo: from the Straits of Dover to off Vigo;
Emden-Brest: from off Cherbourg to Brest;
Emden-Teneriffe: from off Dunkirk to off Teneriffe;
Emden-Azores (1): from the Straits of Dover to Fayal;
Emden-Azores (2): from the Straits of Dover to Fayal;
Azores-New-York (1): from Fayal to New York;
Azores-New-York (2): from Fayal to the longitude of Halifax,
Teneriffe-Monrovia: from off Teneriffe to off Monrovia;
Monrovia-Lome:

from about _____	lat.	:2° 30′ N.;
	long.	:7° 40′ W. of Greenwich;
to about _____	lat.	:2° 20′ N.;
	long.	:5° 30′ W. of Greenwich;
and from about _____	lat.	:3° 48′ N.;
	long.	:0° 00′,

to Lome;
Lome-Duala: from Lome to Duala;
Monrovia-Pernambuco: from off Monrovia to off Pernambuco;
Constantinople-Constanza: from Constantinople to Constanza;
Yap-Shanghai, Yap-Guam, and Yap-Menado (Celebes): from Yap Island to Shanghai, from Yap Island to Guam Island, and from Yap Island to Menado.

The value of the above mentioned cables or portions thereof in so far as they are privately owned, calculated on the basis of the original cost less a suitable allowance for depreciation, shall be credited to Germany in the reparation account.

SECTION II.

SPECIAL PROVISIONS.

ARTICLE 245.

Within six months after the coming into force of the present Treaty the German Government must restore to the French Government the trophies, archives, historical souvenirs or works of art carried away from France by the German authorities in the course of the war of 1870–1871 and during this last war, in accordance with a list which will be communicated to it by the French Government; particularly the French flags taken in the course of the war of 1870–1871 and all the political papers taken by the German authorities on October 10, 1870, at the chateau of Cerçay, near Brunoy (Seine-et-Oise) belonging at the time to Mr. Rouher, formerly Minister of State.

ARTICLE 246.

Within six months from the coming into force of the present Treaty, Germany will restore to His Majesty the King of the Hedjaz the original Koraṇ of the Caliph Othman, which was removed from Medīna by the Turkish authorities and is stated to have been presented to the ex-Emperor William II.

Within the same period Germany will hand over to His Britannic Majesty's Government the skull of the Sultan Mkwawa which was removed from the Protectorate of German East Africa and taken to Germany.

The delivery of the articles above referred to will be effected in such place and in such conditions as may be laid down by the Governments to which they are to be restored.

ARTICLE 247.

Germany undertakes to furnish to the University of Louvain, within three months after a request made by it and transmitted through the intervention of the Reparation Commission, manuscripts, incunabula, printed books, maps and objects of collection corresponding in number and value to those destroyed in the burning by Germany of the Library of Louvain. All details regarding such replacement will be determined by the Reparation Commission.

Germany undertakes to deliver to Belgium, through the Reparation Commission, within six months of the coming into force of the present Treaty, in order to enable Belgium to reconstitute two great artistic works:

(1) The leaves of the triptych of the Mystic Lamb painted by the Van Eyck brothers, formerly in the Church of St. Bavon at Ghent, now in the Berlin Museum;

(2) The leaves of the triptych of the Last Supper, painted by Dierick Bouts, formerly in the Church of St. Peter at Louvain, two of which are now in the Berlin Museum and two in the Old Pinakothek at Munich.

PART IX.

FINANCIAL CLAUSES.

ARTICLE 248.

Subject to such exceptions as the Reparation Commission may approve, a first charge upon all the assets and revenues of the German Empire and its constituent States shall be the cost of reparation and all other costs arising under the present Treaty or any treaties or agreements supplemntary thereto or under arrangements concluded between Germany and the Allied and Associated Powers during the Armistice or its extensions.

Up to May 1, 1921, the German Government shall not export or dispose of, and shall forbid the export or disposal of, gold without the previous approval of the Allied and Associated Powers acting through the Reparation Commission.

ARTICLE 249.

There shall be paid by the German Government the total cost of all armies of the Allied and Associated Governments in occupied

German territory from the date of the signature of the Armistice
of November 11, 1918, including the keep of men and beasts, lodging
and billeting, pay and allowances, salaries and wages, bedding, heating, lighting, clothing, equipment, harness and saddlery, armament
and rolling-stock, air services, treatment of sick and wounded, veter-
inary and remount services, transport service of all sorts (such as by
rail, sea or river, motor lorries), communications and correspondence,
and in general the cost of all administrative or technical services the
working of which is necessary for the training of troops and for
keeping their numbers up to strength and preserving their military
efficiency.

The cost of such liabilities under the above heads so far as they
relate to purchases or requisitions by the Allied and Associated Governments in the occupied territories shall be paid by the German
Government to the Allied and Associated Governments in marks
at the current or agreed rate of exchange. All other of the above
costs shall be paid in gold marks.

Article 250.

Germany confirms the surrender of all material handed over to the
Allied and Associated Powers in accordance with the Armistice of
November 11, 1918, and subsequent Armistice Agreements, and recognises the title of the Allied and Associated Powers to such material.

There shall be credited to the German Government, against the
sums due from it to the Allied and Associated Powers for reparation,
the value, as assessed by the Reparation Commission, referred to in
Article 233 of Part VIII (Reparation) of the present Treaty, of
the material handed over in accordance with Article VII of the
Armistice of November 11, 1918, or Article III of the Armistice
Agreement of January 16, 1919, as well as of any other material
handed over in accordance with the Armistice of November 11, 1918,
and of subsequent Armistice Agreements, for which, as having non-
military value, credit should in the judgment of the Reparation Commission be allowed to the German Government.

Property belonging to the Allied and Associated Governments or
their nationals restored or surrendered under the Armistice Agreements in specie shall not be credited to the German Government.

Article 251.

The priority of the charges established by Article 248 shall, subject
to the qualifications made below, be as follows:
  (a) The cost of the armies of occupation as defined under Article
    249 during the Armistice and its extensions;
  (b) The cost of any armies of occupation as defined under Article
    249 after the coming into force of the present Treaty;
  (c) The cost of reparation arising out of the present Treaty or
    any treaties or conventions supplementary thereto;
  (d) The cost of all other obligations incumbent on Germany under
    the Armistice Conventions or under this Treaty or any treaties
    or conventions supplementary thereto.

The payment for such supplies of food and raw material for Germany and such other payments as may be judged by the Allied and Associated Powers to be essential to enable Germany to meet her obligations in respect of reparation will have priority to the extent and upon the conditions which have been or may be determined by the Governments of the said Powers.

ARTICLE 252.

The right of each of the Allied and Associated Powers to dispose of enemy assets and property within its jurisdiction at the date of the coming into force of the present Treaty is not affected by the foregoing provisions.

ARTICLE 253.

Nothing in the foregoing provisions shall prejudice in any manner charges or mortgages lawfully effected in favour of the Allied or Associated Powers or their nationals respectively, before the date at which a state of war existed between Germany and the Allied or Associated Power concerned, by the German Empire or its constituent States, or by German nationals, on assets in their ownership at that date.

ARTICLE 254.

The Powers to which German territory is ceded shall, subject to the qualifications made in Article 255, undertake to pay:

(1) A portion of the debt of the German Empire as it stood on August 1, 1914, calculated on the basis of the ratio between the average for the three financial years 1911, 1912, 1913, of such revenues of the ceded territory, and the average for the same years of such revenues of the whole German Empire as in the judgment of the Reparation Commission are best calculated to represent the relative ability of the respective territories to make payment;

(2) A portion of the debt as it stood on August 1, 1914, of the German State to which the ceded territory belonged, to be determined in accordance with the principle stated above.

Such portions shall be determined by the Reparation Commission. The method of discharging the obligation, both in respect of capital and of interest, so assumed shall be fixed by the Reparation Commission. Such method may take the form, *inter alia*, of the assumption by the Power to which the territory is ceded of Germany's liability for the German debt held by her nationals. But in the event of the method adopted involving any payments to the German Government, such payments shall be transferred to the Reparation Commission on account of the sums due for reparation so long as any balance in respect of such sums remains unpaid.

ARTICLE 255.

(1) As an exception to the above provision and inasmuch as in 1871 Germany refused to undertake any portion of the burden of the French debt, France shall be, in respect of Alsace-Lorraine, exempt from any payment under Article 254.

(2) In the case of Poland that portion of the debt which, in the opinion of the Reparation Commission, is attributable to the measures taken by the German and Prussian Governments for the German colonisation of Poland shall be excluded from the apportionment to be made under Article 254.

(3) In the case of all ceded territories other than Alsace-Lorraine, that portion of the debt of the German Empire or German States which, in the opinion of the Reparation Commission, represents expenditure by the Governments of the German Empire or States upon the Government properties referred to in Article 256 shall be excluded from the apportionment to be made under Article 254.

ARTICLE 256.

Powers to which German territory is ceded shall acquire all property and possessions situated therein belonging to the German Empire or to the German States, and the value of such acquisitions shall be fixed by the Reparation Commission, and paid by the State acquiring the territory to the Reparation Commission for the credit of the German Government on account of the sums due for reparation.

For the purposes of this Article the property and possessions of the German Empire and States shall be deemed to include all the property of the Crown, the Empire or the States, and the private property of the former German Emperor and other Royal personages.

In view of the terms on which Alsace-Lorraine was ceded to Germany in 1871, France shall be exempt in respect thereof from making any payment or credit under this Article for any property or possessions of the German Empire or States situated therein.

Belgium also shall be exempt from making any payment or any credit under this Article for any property or possessions of the German Empire or States situated in German territory ceded to Belgium under the present Treaty.

ARTICLE 257.

In the case of the former German territories, including colonies, protectorates or dependencies, administered by a Mandatory under Article 22 of Part I (League of Nations) of the present Treaty, neither the territory nor the Mandatory Power shall be charged with any portion of the debt of the German Empire or States.

All property and possessions belonging to the German Empire or to the German States situated in such territories shall be transferred with the territories to the Mandatory Power in its capacity as such and no payment shall be made nor any credit given to those Governments in consideration of this transfer.

For the purposes of this Article the property and possessions of the German Empire and of the German States shall be deemed to include all the property of the Crown, the Empire or the States and the private property of the former German Emperor and other Royal personages.

ARTICLE 258.

Germany renounces all rights accorded to her or her nationals by treaties, conventions or agreements, of whatsoever kind, to representation upon or participation in the control or administration of commissions, state banks, agencies or other financial or economic organisations of an international character, exercising powers of control or administration, and operating in any of the Allied or Associated States, or in Austria, Hungary, Bulgaria or Turkey, or in the dependencies of these States, or in the former Russian Empire.

ARTICLE 259.

(1) Germany agrees to deliver within one month from the date of the coming into force of the present Treaty, to such authority as the Principal Allied and Associated Powers may designate, the sum in gold which was to be deposited in the Reichsbank in the name of the Council of the Administration of the Ottoman Public Debt as security for the first issue of Turkish Government currency notes.

(2) Germany recognises her obligation to make annually for the period of twelve years the payments in gold for which provision is made in the German Treasury Bonds deposited by her from time to time in the name of the Council of the Administration of the Ottoman Public Debt as security for the second and subsequent issues of Turkish Government currency notes.

(3) Germany undertakes to deliver, within one month from the coming into force of the present Treaty, to such authority as the Principal Allied and Associated Powers may designate, the gold deposit constituted in the Reichsbank or elsewhere, representing the residue of the advance in gold agreed to on May 5, 1915, by the Council of the Administration of the Ottoman Public Debt to the Imperial Ottoman Government.

(4) Germany agrees to transfer to the Principal Allied and Associated Powers any title that she may have to the sum in gold and silver transmitted by her to the Turkish Ministry of Finance in November, 1918, in anticipation of the payment to be made in May, 1919, for the service of the Turkish Internal Loan.

(5) Germany undertakes to transfer to the Principal Allied and Associated Powers, within a period of one month from the coming into force of the present Treaty, any sums in gold transferred as pledge or as collateral security to the German Government or its nationals in connection with loans made by them to the Austro-Hungarian Government.

(6) Without prejudice to Article 292 of Part X (Economic Clauses) of the present Treaty, Germany confirms the renunciation provided for in Article XV of the Armistice of November 11, 1918, of any benefit disclosed by the Treaties of Bucharest and of Brest-Litovsk and by the treaties supplementary thereto.

Germany undertakes to transfer, either to Roumania or to the Principal Allied and Associated Powers as the case may be, all monetary instruments, specie, securities and negotiable instruments, or goods, which she has received under the aforesaid Treaties.

(7) The sums of money and all securities, instruments and goods

of whatsoever nature, to be delivered, paid and transferred under the provisions of this Article, shall be disposed of by the Principal Allied and Associated Powers in a manner hereafter to be determined by those Powers.

ARTICLE 260.

Without prejudice to the renunciation of any rights by Germany on behalf of herself or of her nationals in the other provisions of the present Treaty, the Reparation Commission may within one year from the coming into force of the present Treaty demand that the German Government become possessed of any rights and intrests of German nationals in any public utility undertaking or in any concession operating in Russia, China, Turkey, Austria, Hungary and Bulgaria, or in the possessions or dependencies of these States or in any territory formerly belonging to Germany or her allies, to be ceded by Germany or her allies to any Power or to be administered by a Mandatory under the present Treaty, and may require that the German Government transfer, within six months of the date of demand, all such rights and interests and any similar rights and interests the German Government may itself possess to the Reparation Commission.

Germany shall be responsible for indemnifying her nationals so dispossessed, and the Reparation Commission shall credit Germany, on account of sums due for reparation, with such sums in respect of the value of the transferred rights and interests as may be assessed by the Reparation Commission, and the German Government shall, within six months from the coming into force of the present Treaty, communicate to the Reparation Commission all such rights and interests, whether already granted, contingent or not yet exercised, and shall renounce on behalf of itself and its nationals in favour of the Allied and Associated Powers all such rights and interests which have not been so communicated.

ARTICLE 261.

Germany undertakes to transfer to the Allied and Associated Powers any claims she may have to payment or repayment by the Governments of Austria, Hungary, Bulgaria or Turkey, and, in particular, any claims which may arise, now or hereafter, from the fulfilment of undertakings made by Germany during the war to those Governments.

ARTICLE 262.

Any monetary obligation due by Germany arising out of the present Treaty and expressed in terms of gold marks shall be payable at the option of the creditors in pounds sterling payable in London; gold dollars of the United States of America payable in New York; gold francs payable in Paris; or gold lire payable in Rome.

For the purpose of this Article the gold coins mentioned above shall be defined as being of the weight and fineness of gold as enacted by law on January 1, 1914.

ARTICLE 263.

Germany gives a guarantee to the Brazilian Government that all sums representing the sale of coffee belonging to the State of Sao Paolo in the ports of Hamburg, Bremen, Antwerp and Trieste, which were deposited with the Bank of Bleichröder at Berlin, shall be reimbursed together with interest at the rate or rates agreed upon. Germany having prevented the transfer of the sums in question to the State of Sao Paolo at the proper time, guarantees also that the reimbursement shall be effected at the rate of exchange of the day of the deposit.

PART X.

ECONOMIC CLAUSES.

SECTION I.

COMMERCIAL RELATIONS.

CHAPTER I.

CUSTOMS REGULATIONS, DUTIES AND RESTRICTIONS.

ARTICLE 264.

Germany undertakes that goods the produce or manufacture of any one of the Allied or Associated States imported into German territory, from whatsoever place arriving, shall not be subjected to other or higher duties or charges (including internal charges) than those to which the like goods the produce or manufacture of any other such State or of any other foreign country are subject.

Germany will not maintain or impose any prohibition or restriction on the importation into German territory of any goods the produce or manufacture of the territories of any one of the Allied or Associated States, from whatsoever place arriving, which shall not equally extend to the importation of the like goods the produce or manufacture of any other such State or of any other foreign country.

ARTICLE 265.

Germany further undertakes that, in the matter of the régime applicable on importation, no discrimination against the commerce of any of the Allied and Associated States as compared with any other of the said States or any other foreign country shall be made, even by indirect means, such as customs regulations or procedure, methods of verification or analysis conditions of payment of duties, tariff classification or interpretation, or the operation of monopolies.

ARTICLE 266.

In all that concerns exportation Germany undertakes that goods, natural products or manufactured articles, exported from German territory to the territories of any one of the Allied or Associated States shall not be subjected to other or higher duties or charges (including internal charges) than those paid on the like goods exported to any other such State or to any other foreign country.

Germany will not maintain or impose any prohibition or restriction on the exportation of any goods sent from her territory to any one of the Allied or Associated States which shall not equally extend to the exportation of the like goods, natural products or manufactured articles, sent to any other such State or to any other foreign country.

ARTICLE 267.

Every favour, immunity or privilege in regard to the importation, exportation or transit of goods granted by Germany to any Allied or Associated State or to any other foreign country whatever shall simultaneously and unconditionally, without request and without compensation, be extended to all the Allied and Associated States.

ARTICLE 268.

The provisions of Articles 264 to 267 inclusive of this Chapter and of Article 323 of Part XII (Ports, Waterways and Railways) of the present Treaty are subject to the following exceptions:

(a) For a period of five years from the coming into force of the present Treaty, natural or manufactured products which both originate in and come from the territories of Alsace and Lorraine reunited to France shall, on importation into German customs territory, be exempt from all customs duty.

The French Government shall fix each year, by decree communicated to the German Government, the nature and amount of the products which shall enjoy this exemption.

The amount of each product which may be thus sent annually into Germany shall not exceed the average of the amounts sent annually in the years 1911–1913.

Further, during the period above mentioned the German Government shall allow the free export from Germany, and the free re-importation into Germany, exempt from all customs duties and other charges (including internal charges), of yarns, tissues, and other textile materials or textile products of any kind and in any condition, sent from Germany into the territories of Alsace or Lorraine, to be subjected there to any finishing process, such as bleaching, dyeing, printing, mercerisation, gassing, twisting or dressing.

(b) During a period of three years from the coming into force of the present Treaty natural or manufactured products which both originate in and come from Polish territories which before the war were part of Germany shall, on importation into German customs territory, be exempt from all customs duty.

The Polish Government shall fix each year, by decree communicated to the German Government, the nature and amount of the products which shall enjoy this exemption.

The amount of each product which may be thus sent annually into Germany shall not exceed the average of the amounts sent annually in the years 1911–1913.

(c) The Allied and Associated Powers reserve the right to require Germany to accord freedom from customs duty, on importation into German customs territory, to natural products and manufactured articles which both originate in and come from the Grand Duchy of Luxemburg, for a period of five years from the coming into force of the present Treaty.

The nature and amount of the products which shall enjoy the benefits of this régime shall be communicated each year to the German Government.

The amount of each product which may be thus sent annually into Germany shall not exceed the average of the amounts sent annually in the years 1911–1913.

ARTICLE 269.

During the first six months after the coming into force of the present Treaty, the duties imposed by Germany on imports from Allied and Associated States shall not be higher than the most favourable duties which were applied to imports into Germany on July 31, 1914.

During a further period of thirty months after the expiration of the first six months, this provision shall continue to be applied exclusively with regard to products which, being comprised in Section A of the First Category of the German Customs Tariff of December 25, 1902, enjoyed at the above-mentioned date (July 31, 1914) rates conventionalised by treaties with the Allied and Associated Powers, with the addition of all kinds of wine and vegetable oils, of artificial silk and of washed or scoured wool, whether or not they were the subject of special conventions before July 31, 1914.

ARTICLE 270.

The Allied and Associated Powers reserve the right to apply to German territory occupied by their troops a special customs régime as regards imports and exports, in the event of such a measure being necessary in their opinion in order to safeguard the economic interests of the population of these territories.

CHAPTER II.

SHIPPING.

ARTICLE 271.

As regards sea fishing, maritime coasting trade, and maritime towage, vessels of the Allied and Associated Powers shall enjoy, in German territorial waters, the treatment accorded to vessels of the most favoured nation.

ARTICLE 272.

Germany agrees that, notwithstanding any stipulation to the contrary contained in the Conventions relating to the North Sea fisheries and liquor traffic, all rights of inspection and police shall, in the case of fishing-boats of the Allied Powers, be exercised solely by ships belonging to those Powers.

ARTICLE 273.

In the case of vessels of the Allied or Associated Powers, all classes of certificates or documents relating to the vessel, which were recognised as valid by Germany before the war, or which may hereafter be recognised as valid by the principal maritime States, shall be recognised by Germany as valid and as equivalent to the corresponding certificates issued to German vessels.

A similar recognition shall be accorded to the certificates and documents issued to their vessels by the Governments of new States, whether they have a sea-coast or not, provided that such certificates and documents shall be issued in conformity with the general practice observed in the principal maritime States.

The High Contracting Parties agree to recognise the flag flown by the vessels of an Allied or Associated Power having no sea-coast which are registered at some one specified place situated in its territory; such place shall serve as the port of registry of such vessels.

CHAPTER III.

UNFAIR COMPETITION.

ARTICLE 274.

Germany undertakes to adopt all the necessary legislative and administrative measures to protect goods the produce or manufacture of any one of the Allied and Associated Powers from all forms of unfair competition in commercial transactions.

Germany undertakes to prohibit and repress by seizure and by other appropriate remedies the importation, exportation, manufacture, distribution, sale or offering for sale in its territory of all goods bearing upon themselves or their usual get-up or wrappings any marks, names, devices, or description whatsoever which are calculated to convey directly or indirectly a false indication of the origin, type, nature, or special characteristics of such goods.

ARTICLE 275.

Germany undertakes on condition that reciprocity is accorded in these matters to respect any law, or any administrative or judicial decision given in conformity with such law, in force in any Allied or Associated State and duly communicated to her by the proper authorities, defining or regulating the right to any regional appellation in respect of wine or spirits produced in the State to which the region belongs, or the conditions under which the use of any such appellation may be permitted; and the importation, exportation, manufacture, distribution, sale or offering for sale of products or articles bearing regional appellations inconsistent with such law or order shall be prohibited by the German Government and repressed by the measures prescribed in the preceding Article.

Chapter IV.

TREATMENT OF NATIONALS OF ALLIED AND ASSOCIATED POWERS.

Article 276.

Germany undertakes:

(*a*) Not to subject the nationals of the Allied and Associated Powers to any prohibition in regard to the exercise of occupations, professions, trade and industry, which shall not be equally applicable to all aliens without exception;

(*b*) Not to subject the nationals of the Allied and Associated Powers in regard to the rights referred to in paragraph (*a*) to any regulation or restriction which might contravene directly or indirectly the stipulations of the said paragraph, or which shall be other or more disadvantageous than those which are applicable to nationals of the most favoured nation;

(*c*) Not to subject the nationals of the Allied and Associated Powers, their property, rights or interests, including companies and associations in which they are interested, to any charge, tax or impost, direct or indirect, other or higher than those which are or may be imposed on her own nationals or their property, rights or interests;

(*d*) Not to subject the nationals of any one of the Allied and Associated Powers to any restriction which was not applicable on July 1, 1914, to the nationals of such Powers unless such restriction is likewise imposed on her own nationals.

Article 277.

The nationals of the Allied and Associated Powers shall enjoy in German territory a constant protection for their persons and for their property, rights and interests, and shall have free access to the courts of law.

Article 278.

Germany undertakes to recognise any new nationality which has been or may be acquired by her nationals under the laws of the Allied and Associated Powers and in accordance with the decisions of the competent authorities of these Powers pursuant to naturalisation laws or under treaty stipulations, and to regard such persons as having, in consequence of the acquisition of such new nationality, in all respects severed their allegiance to their country of origin.

Article 279.

The Allied and Associated Powers may appoint consuls-general, consuls, vice-consuls, and consular agents in German towns and ports. Germany undertakes to approve the designation of the consuls-general, consuls, vice-consuls, and consular agents, whose names shall be notified to her, and to admit them to the exercise of their functions in conformity with the usual rules and customs.

CHAPTER V.

GENERAL ARTICLES.

ARTICLE 280.

The obligations imposed on Germany by Chapter I and by Articles 271 and 272 of Chapter II above shall cease to have effect five years from the date of the coming into force of the present Treaty, unless otherwise provided in the text, or unless the Council of the League of Nations shall, at least twelve months before the expiration of that period, decide that these obligations shall be maintained for a further period with or without amendment.

Article 276 of Chapter IV shall remain in operation, with or without amendment, after the period of five years for such further period, if any, not exceeding five years, as may be determined by a majority of the Council of the League of Nations.

ARTICLE 281.

If the German Government engages in international trade, it shall not in respect thereof have or be deemed to have any rights, privileges or immunities of sovereignty.

SECTION II.

TREATIES.

ARTICLE 282.

From the coming into force of the present Treaty and subject to the provisions thereof the multilateral treaties, conventions and agreements of an economic or technical character enumerated below and in the subsequent Articles shall alone be applied as between Germany and those of the Allied and Associated Powers party thereto:

(1) Conventions of March 14, 1884, December 1, 1886, and March 23, 1887, and Final Protocol of July 7, 1887, regarding the protection of submarine cables.

(2) Convention of October 11, 1909, regarding the international circulation of motor-cars.

(3) Agreement of May 15, 1886, regarding the sealing of railway trucks subject to customs inspection, and Protocol of May 18, 1907.

(4) Agreement of May 15, 1886, regarding the technical standardisation of railways.

(5) Convention of July 5, 1890, regarding the publication of customs tariffs and the organisation of an International Union for the publication of customs tariffs.

(6) Convention of December 31, 1913, regarding the unification of commercial statistics.

(7) Convention of April 25, 1907, regarding the raising of the Turkish customs tariff.

(8) Convention of March 14, 1857, for the redemption of toll dues on the Sound and Belts.

(9) Convention of June 22, 1861, for the redemption of the Stade Toll on the Elbe.

(10) Convention of July 16, 1863, for the redemption of the toll dues on the Scheldt.

(11) Convention of October 29, 1888, regarding the establishment of a definite arrangement guaranteeing the free use of the Suez Canal.

(12) Conventions of September 23, 1910, respecting the unification of certain regulations regarding collisions and salvage at sea.

(13) Convention of December 21, 1904, regarding the exemption of hospital ships from dues and charges in ports.

(14) Convention of February 4, 1898, regarding the tonnage measurement of vessels for inland navigation.

(15) Convention of September 26, 1906, for the suppression of nightwork for women.

(16) Convention of September 26, 1906, for the suppression of the use of white phosphorus in the manufacture of matches.

(17) Conventions of May 18, 1904, and May 4, 1910, regarding the suppression of the White Slave Traffic.

(18) Convention of May 4, 1910, regarding the suppression of obscene publications.

(19) Sanitary Conventions of January 30, 1892, April 15, 1893, April 3, 1894, March 19, 1897, and December 3, 1903.

(20) Convention of May 20, 1875, regarding the unification and improvement of the metric system.

(21) Convention of November 29, 1906, regarding the unification of pharmacopœial formulæ for potent drugs.

(22) Convention of November 16 and 19, 1885, regarding the establishment of a concert pitch.

(23) Convention of June 7, 1905, regarding the creation of an International Agricultural Institute at Rome.

(24) Conventions of November 3, 1881, and April 15, 1889, regarding precautionary measures against phylloxera.

(25) Convention of March 19, 1902, regarding the protection of birds useful to agriculture.

(26) Convention of June 12, 1902, as to the protection of minors.

ARTICLE 283.

From the coming into force of the present Treaty the High Contracting Parties shall apply the conventions and agreements hereinafter mentioned, in so far as concerns them, on condition that the special stipulations contained in this Article are fulfilled by Germany.

Postal Conventions:

Conventions and agreements of the Universal Postal Union concluded at Vienna, July 4, 1891.

Conventions and agreements of the Postal Union signed at Washington, June 15, 1897.

Conventions and agreements of the Postal Union signed at Rome, May 26, 1906.

Telegraphic Conventions:

International Telegraphic Conventions signed at St. Petersburg July 10/22, 1875.

Regulations and Tariffs drawn up by the International Telegraphic Conference, Lisbon, June 11, 1908.

Germany undertakes not to refuse her assent to the conclusion by the new States of the special arrangements referred to in the conventions and agreements relating to the Universal Postal Union and to the International Telegraphic Union, to which the said new States have adhered or may adhere.

ARTICLE 284.

From the coming into force of the present Treaty the High Contracting Parties shall apply, in so far as concerns them, the International Radio-Telegraphic Convention of July 5, 1912, on condition that Germany fulfils the provisional regulations which will be indicated to her by the Allied and Associated Powers.

If within five years after the coming into force of the present Treaty a new convention regulating international radio-telegraphic communications should have been concluded to take the place of the Convention of July 5, 1912, this new convention shall bind Germany, even if Germany should refuse either to take part in drawing up the convention, or to subscribe thereto.

This new convention will likewise replace the provisional regulations in force.

ARTICLE 285.

From the coming into force of the present Treaty, the High Contracting Parties shall apply in so far as concerns them and under the conditions stipulated in Article 272, the conventions hereinafter mentioned:

(1) The Conventions of May 6, 1882, and February 1, 1889, regulating the fisheries in the North Sea outside territorial waters.

(2) The Conventions and Protocols of November 16, 1887, February 14, 1893, and April 11, 1894, regarding the North Sea liquor traffic.

ARTICLE 286.

The International Convention of Paris of March 20, 1883, for the protection of industrial property, revised at Washington on June 2, 1911; and the International Convention of Berne of September 9, 1886, for the protection of literary and artistic works, revised at Berlin on November 13, 1908, and completed by the additional Protocol signed at Berne on March 20, 1914, will again come into effect as from the coming into force of the present Treaty, in so far as they are not affected or modified by the exceptions and restrictions resulting therefrom.

ARTICLE 287.

From the coming into force of the present Treaty the High Contracting Parties shall apply, in so far as concerns them, the Convention of the Hague of July 17, 1905, relating to civil procedure. This renewal, however, will not apply to France, Portugal and Roumania.

ARTICLE 288.

The special rights and privileges granted to Germany by Article 3 of the Convention of December 2, 1899, relating to Samoa shall be considered to have terminated on August 4, 1914.

ARTICLE 289.

Each of the Allied or Associated Powers, being guided by the general principles or special provisions of the present Treaty, shall notify to Germany the bilateral treaties or conventions which such Allied or Associated Power wishes to revive with Germany.

The notification referred to in the present Article shall be made either directly or through the intermediary of another Power. Receipt thereof shall be acknowledged in writing by Germany. The date of the revival shall be that of the notification.

The Allied and Associated Powers undertake among themselves not to revive with Germany any conventions or treaties which are not in accordance with the terms of the present Treaty.

The notification shall mention any provisions of the said conventions and treaties which, not being in accordance with the terms of the present Treaty, shall not be considered as revived.

In case of any difference of opinion, the League of Nations will be called on to decide.

A period of six months from the coming into force of the present Treaty is allowed to the Allied and Associated Powers within which to make the notification.

Only those bilateral treaties and conventions which have been the subject of such a notification shall be revived between the Allied and Associated Powers and Germany; all the others are and shall remain abrogated.

The above regulations apply to all bilateral treaties or conventions existing between all the Allied and Associated Powers signatories to the present Treaty and Germany, even if the said Allied and Associated Powers have not been in a state of war with Germany.

ARTICLE 290.

Germany recognises that all the treaties, conventions or agreements which she has concluded with Austria, Hungary, Bulgaria or Turkey since August 1, 1914, until the coming into force of the present Treaty are and remain abrogated by the present Treaty.

ARTICLE 291.

Germany undertakes to secure to the Allied and Associated Powers, and to the officials and nationals of the said Powers, the enjoyment of all the rights and advantages of any kind which she may have granted to Austria, Hungary, Bulgaria or Turkey, or to the officials and nationals of these States by treaties, conventions or arrangements concluded before August 1, 1914, so long as those treaties, conventions or arrangements remain in force.

The Allied and Associated Powers reserve the right to accept or not the enjoyment of these rights and advantages.

ARTICLE 292.

Germany recognises that all treaties, conventions or arrangements which she concluded with Russia, or with any State or Government of which the territory previously formed a part of Russia, or with Roumania, before August 1, 1914, or after that date until coming into force of the present Treaty, are and remain abrogated.

ARTICLE 293.

Should an Allied or Associated Power, Russia, or a State or Government of which the territory formerly constituted a part of Russia, have been forced since August 1, 1914, by reason of military occupation or by any other means or for any other cause, to grant or to allow to be granted by the act of any public authority, concessions, privileges and favours of any kind to Germany or to a German national, such concessions, privileges and favours are *ipso facto* annulled by the present Treaty.

No claims or indemnities which may result from this annulment shall be charged against the Allied or Associated Powers or the Powers, States, Governments or public authorities which are released from their engagements by the present Article.

ARTICLE 294.

From the coming into force of the present Treaty Germany undertakes to give the Allied and Associated Powers and their nationals the benefit *ipso facto* of the rights and advantages of any kind which she has granted by treaties, conventions, or arrangements to non-belligerent States or their nationals since August 1, 1914, until the coming into force of the present Treaty, so long as those treaties, conventions or arrangements remain in force.

ARTICLE 295.

Those of the High Contracting Parties who have not yet signed, or who have signed but not yet ratified, the Opium Convention signed at The Hague on January 23, 1912, agree to bring the said Convention into force, and for this purpose to enact the necessary legislation without delay and in any case within a period of twelve months from the coming into force of the present Treaty.

Furthermore, they agree that ratification of the present Treaty should in the case of Powers which have not yet ratified the Opium Convention be deemed in all respects equivalent to the ratification of that Convention and to the signature of the Special Protocol which was opened at The Hague in accordance with the resolutions adopted by the Third Opium Conference in 1914 for bringing the said Convention into force.

For this purpose the Government of the French Republic will communicate to the Government of the Netherlands a certified copy of the protocol of the deposit of ratifications of the present Treaty, and will invite the Government of the Netherlands to accept and deposit the said certified copy as if it were a deposit of ratifications of the Opium Convention and a signature of the Additional Protocol of 1914.

SECTION III.

DEBTS.

ARTICLE 296.

There shall be settled through the intervention of clearing offices to be established by each of the High Contracting Parties within three months of the notification referred to in paragraph (e) hereafter the following classes of pecuniary obligations:

(1) Debts payable before the war and due by a national of one of the Contracting Powers, residing within its territory, to a national of an Opposing Power, residing within its territory;

(2) Debts which became payable during the war to nationals of one Contracting Power residing within its territory and arose out of transactions or contracts with the nationals of an Opposing Power, resident within its territory, of which the total or partial execution was suspended on account of the declaration of war;

(3) Interest which has accrued due before and during the war to a national of one of the Contracting Powers in respect of securities issued by an Opposing Power, provided that the payment of interest on such securities to the nationals of that Power or to neutrals has not been suspended during the war;

(4) Capital sums which have become payable before and during the war to nationals of one of the Contracting Powers in respect of securities issued by one of the Opposing Powers, provided that the payment of such capital sums to nationals of that Power or to neutrals has not been suspended during the war.

The proceeds of liquidation of enemy property, rights and interests mentioned in Section IV and in the Annex thereto will be accounted for through the Clearing Offices, in the currency and at the rate of exchange hereinafter provided in paragraph (d), and disposed of by them under the conditions provided by the said Section and Annex.

The settlements provided for in this Article shall be effected according to the following principles and in accordance with the Annex to this Section:

(a) Each of the High Contracting Parties shall prohibit, as from the coming into force of the present Treaty, both the payment and the acceptance of payment of such debts, and also all communications between the interested parties with regard to the settlement of the said debts otherwise than through the Clearing Offices;

(b) Each of the High Contracting Parties shall be respectively responsible for the payment of such debts due by its nationals, except in the cases where before the war the debtor was in a state of bankruptcy or failure, or had given formal indication of insolvency or where the debt was due by a company whose business has been liqui-dated under emergency legislation during the war. Nevertheless, debts due by the inhabitants of territory invaded or occupied by the enemy before the Armistice will not be guaranteed by the States of which those territories form part;

(c) The sums due to the nationals of one of the High Contracting Parties by the nationals of an Opposing State will be debited to the Clearing Office of the country of the debtor, and paid to the creditor by the Clearing Office of the country of the creditor;

(d) Debts shall be paid or credited in the currency of such one of the Allied and Associated Powers, their colonies or protectorates, or the British Dominions or India, as may be concerned. If the debts are payable in some other currency they shall be paid or credited in the currency of the country concerned, whether an Allied or Associated Power, Colony, Protectorate, British Dominion or India, at the pre-war rate of exchange.

For the purpose of this provision the pre-war rate of exchange shall be defined as the average cable transfer rate prevailing in the Allied or Associated country concerned during the month immediately pre-ceding the outbreak of war between the said country concerned and Germany.

If a contract provides for a fixed rate of exchange governing the conversion of the currency in which the debt is stated into the cur-rency of the Allied or Associated country concerned, then the above provisions concerning the rate of exchange shall not apply.

In the case of new States the currency in which and the rate of exchange at which debts shall be paid or credited shall be deter-mined by the Reparation Commission provided for in Part VIII (Reparation);

(e) The provisions of this Article and of the Annex hereto shall not apply as between Germany on the one hand and any one of the Allied and Associated Powers, their colonies or protectorates, or any one of the British Dominions or India on the other hand, unless within a period of one month from the deposit of the ratification of the pres-ent Treaty by the Power in question, or of the ratification on behalf of such Dominion or of India, notice to that effect is given to Germany by the Government of such Allied or Associated Power or of such Dominion or of India as the case may be;

(f) The Allied and Associated Powers who have adopted this Article and the Annex hereto may agree between themselves to apply them to their respective nationals established in their territory so far as regards matters between their nationals and German nationals. In this case the payments made by application of this provision will be subject to arrangements between the Allied and Associated Clear-ing Offices concerned.

ANNEX.

1.

Each of the High Contracting Parties will, within three months from the notification provided for in Article 296, paragraph (e), establish a Clearing Office for the collection and payment of enemy debts.

Local Clearing Offices may be established for any particular portion of the territories of the High Contracting Parties. Such local Clearing Offices may perform all the functions of a central Clearing Office in their respective districts, except that all transactions with the Clearing Office in the Opposing State must be effected through the central Clearing Office.

2.

In this Annex the pecuniary obligations referred to in the first paragraph of Article 296 are described " as enemy debts ", the persons from whom the same are due as " enemy debtors ", the persons to whom they are due as " enemy creditors ", the Clearing Office in the country of the creditor is called the " Creditor Clearing Office ", and the Clearing Office in the country of the debtor is called the " Debtor Clearing Office."

3.

The High Contracting Parties will subject contraventions of paragraph (a) of Article 296 to the same penalties as are at present provided by their legislation for trading with the enemy. They will similarly prohibit within their territory all legal process relating to payment of enemy debts, except in accordance with the provisions of this Annex.

4.

The Government guarantee specified in paragraph (b) of Article 296 shall take effect whenever, for any reason, a debt shall not be recoverable, except in a case where at the date of the outbreak of war the debt was barred by the laws of prescription in force in the country of the debtor, or where the debtor was at that time in a state of bankruptcy or failure or had given formal indication of insolvency, or where the debt was due by a company whose business has been liquidated under emergency legislation during the war. In such case the procedure specified by this Annex shall apply to payment of the dividends.

The terms "bankruptcy" and "failure" refer to the application of legislation providing for such juridical conditions. The expression "formal indication of insolvency" bears the same meaning as it has in English law.

5.

Creditors shall give notice to the Creditor Clearing Office within six months of its establishment of debts due to them, and shall furnish the Clearing Office with any documents and information required of them.

The High Contracting Parties will take all suitable measures to trace and punish collusion between enemy creditors and debtors. The Clearing Offices will communicate to one another any evidence and information which might help the discovery and punishment of such collusion.

The High Contracting Parties will facilitate as much as possible postal and telegraphic communication at the expense of the parties concerned and through the intervention of the Clearing Offices between debtors and creditors desirous of coming to an agreement as to the amount of their debt.

The Creditor Clearing Office will notify the Debtor Clearing Office of all debts declared to it. The Debtor Clearing Office will, in due course, inform the Creditor Clearing Office which debts are admitted and which debts are contested. In the latter case, the Debtor Clearing Office will give the grounds for the non-admission of debt.

6.

When a debt has been admitted, in whole or in part, the Debtor Clearing Office will at once credit the Creditor Clearing Office with the amount admitted, and at the same time notify it of such credit.

7.

The debt shall be deemed to be admitted in full and shall be credited forthwith to the Creditor Clearing Office unless within three months from the receipt of the notification or such longer time as may be agreed to by the Creditor Clearing Office notice has been given by the Debtor Clearing Office that it is not admitted.

8.

When the whole or part of a debt is not admitted the two Clearing Offices will examine into the matter jointly and will endeavour to bring the parties to an agreement.

9.

The Creditor Clearing Office will pay to the individual creditor the sums credited to it out of the funds placed at its disposal by the Government of its country and in accordance with the conditions fixed by the said Government, retaining any sums considered necessary to cover risks, expenses or commissions.

10.

Any person having claimed payment of an enemy debt which is not admitted in whole or in part shall pay to the clearing office, by way of fine, interest at 5 per cent. on the part not admitted. Any person having unduly refused to admit the whole or part of a debt claimed from him shall pay, by way of fine, interest at 5 per cent. on the amount with regard to which his refusal shall be disallowed.

Such interest shall run from the date of expiration of the period provided for in paragraph 7 until the date on which the claim shall have been disallowed or the debt paid.

Each Clearing Office shall in so far as it is concerned take steps to collect the fines above provided for, and will be responsible if such fines cannot be collected.

The fines will be credited to the other Clearing Office, which shall retain them as a contribution towards the cost of carrying out the present provisions.

11.

The balance between the Clearing Offices shall be struck monthly and the credit balance paid in cash by the debtor State within a week.

Nevertheless, any credit balances which may be due by one or more of the Allied and Associated Powers shall be retained until complete payment shall have been effected of the sums due to the Allied or Associated Powers or their nationals on account of the war.

12.

To facilitate discussion between the Clearing Offices each of them shall have a representative at the place where the other is established.

13.

Except for special reasons all discussions in regard to claims will, so far as possible, take place at the Debtor Clearing Office.

14.

In conformity with Article 296, paragraph (*b*), the High Contracting Parties are responsible for the payment of the enemy debts owing by their nationals.

The Debtor Clearing Office will therefore credit the Creditor Clearing Office with all debts admitted, even in case of inability to collect them from the individual debtor. The Governments concerned will, nevertheless, invest their respective Clearing Offices with all necessary powers for the recovery of debts which have been admitted.

As an exception, the admitted debts owing by persons having suffered injury from acts of war shall only be credited to the Creditor Clearing Office when the compensation due to the person concerned in respect of such injury shall have been paid.

15.

Each Government will defray the expenses of the Clearing Office set up in its territory, including the salaries of the staff.

16.

Where the two Clearing Offices are unable to agree whether a debt claimed is due, or in case of a difference between an enemy debtor and an enemy creditor or between the Clearing Offices, the dispute shall either be referred to arbitration if the parties so agree under conditions fixed by agreement between them, or referred to the Mixed Arbitral Tribunal provided for in Section VI hereafter.

At the request of the Creditor Clearing Office the dispute may, however, be submitted to the jurisdiction of the Courts of the place of domicile of the debtor.

17.

Recovery of sums found by the Mixed Arbitral Tribunal, the Court, or the Arbitration Tribunal to be due shall be effected through the Clearing Offices as if these sums were debts admitted by the Debtor Clearing Office.

18.

Each of the Governments concerned shall appoint an agent who will be responsible for the presentation to the Mixed Arbitral Tribunal of the cases conducted on behalf of its Clearing Office. This agent will exercise a general control over the representatives or counsel employed by its nationals.

Decisions will be arrived at on documentary evidence, but it will be open to the Tribunal to hear the parties in person, or according to their preference by their representatives approved by the two Governments, or by the agent referred to above, who shall be competent to intervene along with the party or to re-open and maintain a claim abandoned by the same.

19.

The Clearing Offices concerned will lay before the Mixed Arbitral Tribunal all the information and documents in their possession, so as to enable the Tribunal to decide rapidly on the cases which are brought before it.

20.

Where one of the parties concerned appeals against the joint decision of the two Clearing Offices he shall make a deposit against the costs, which deposit shall only be refunded when the first judgment is modified in favour of the appellant and in proportion to the success he may attain, his opponent in case of such a refund being required to pay an equivalent proportion of the costs and expenses. Security accepted by the Tribunal may be substituted for a deposit.

A fee of 5 per cent. of the amount in dispute shall be charged in respect of all cases brought before the Tribunal. This fee shall, unless the Tribunal directs otherwise, be borne by the unsuccessful party. Such fee shall be added to the deposit referred to. It is also independent of the security.

The Tribunal may award to one of the parties a sum in respect of the expenses of the proceedings.

Any sum payable under this paragraph shall be credited to the Clearing Office of the successful party as a separate item.

21.

With a view to the rapid settlement of claims, due regard shall be paid in the appointment of all persons connected with the Clearing Offices or with the Mixed Arbitral Tribunal to their knowledge of the language of the other country concerned.

Each of the Clearing Offices will be at liberty to correspond with the other and to forward documents in its own language.

22.

Subject to any special agreement to the contrary between the Governments concerned, debts shall carry interest in accordance with the following provisions:

Interest shall not be payable on sums of money due by way of dividend, interest or other periodical payments which themselves represent interest on capital.

The rate of interest shall be 5 per cent. per annum except in cases where, by contract, law or custom, the creditor is entitled to payment of interest at a different rate. In such cases the rate to which he is entitled shall prevail.

Interest shall run from the date of commencement of hostilities (or, if the sum of money to be recovered fell due during the war, from the date at which it fell due) until the sum is credited to the Clearing Office of the creditor.

Sums due by way of interest shall be treated as debts admitted by the Clearing Offices and shall be credited to the Creditor Clearing Office in the same way as such debts.

23.

Where by decision of the Clearing Offices or the Mixed Arbitral Tribunal a claim is held not to fall within Article 296, the creditor shall be at liberty to prosecute the claim before the Courts or to take such other proceedings as may be open to him.

The presentation of a claim to the Clearing Office suspends the operation of any period of prescription.

24.

The High Contracting Parties agree to regard the decisions of the Mixed Arbitral Tribunal as final and conclusive, and to render them binding upon their nationals.

25.

In any case where a Creditor Clearing Office declines to notify a claim to the Debtor Clearing Office, or to take any step provided for in this Annex, intended to make effective in whole or in part a request of which it has received due notice, the enemy creditor shall be entitled to receive from the Clearing Office a certificate setting out the amount of the claim, and shall then be entitled to prosecute the claim before the courts or to take such other proceedings as may be open to him.

SECTION IV.

PROPERTY, RIGHTS AND INTERESTS.

ARTICLE 297.

The question of private property, rights and interests in an enemy country shall be settled according to the principles laid down in this Section and to the provisions of the Annex hereto.

(a) The exceptional war measures and measures of transfer (defined in paragraph 3 of the Annex hereto) taken by Germany with respect to the property, rights and interests of nationals of Allied or Associated Powers, including companies and associations in which they are interested, when liquidation has not been completed, shall be immediately discontinued or stayed and the property, rights and interests concerned restored to their owners, who shall enjoy full rights therein in accordance with the provisions of Article 298.

(b) Subject to any contrary stipulations which may be provided for in the present Treaty, the Allied and Associated Powers reserve the right to retain and liquidate all property, rights and interests belonging at the date of the coming into force of the present Treaty to German nationals, or companies controlled by them, within their territories, colonies, possessions and protectorates, including territories ceded to them by the present Treaty.

The liquidation shall be carried out in accordance with the laws of the Allied or Associated State concerned, and the German owner shall not be able to dispose of such property, rights or interests nor to subject them to any charge without the consent of that State.

German nationals who acquire *ipso facto* the nationality of an Allied or Associated Power in accordance with the provisions of the present Treaty will not be considered as German nationals within the meaning of this paragraph.

(c) The price or the amount of compensation in respect of the exercise of the right referred to in the preceding paragraph (b) will be fixed in accordance with the methods of sale or valuation adopted by the laws of the country in which the property has been retained or liquidated.

(d) As between the Allied and Associated Powers or their nationals on the one hand and Germany or her nationals on the other hand, all the exceptional war measures, or measures of transfer, or acts done or to be done in execution of such measures as defined in paragraphs 1 and 3 of the Annex hereto shall be considered as final and binding upon all persons except as regards the reservations laid down in the present Treaty.

(e) The nationals of Allied and Associated Powers shall be entitled to compensation in respect of damage or injury inflicted upon their property, rights or interests, including any company or association in which they are interested, in German territory as it existed on August 1, 1914, by the application either of the exceptional war measures or measures of transfer mentioned in paragraphs 1 and 3 of the Annex hereto. The claims made in this respect by such nationals shall be investigated, and the total of the compensation shall be determined by the Mixed Arbitral Tribunal provided for in Section

VI or by an Arbitrator appointed by that Tribunai. This compensation shall be borne by Germany, and may be charged upon the property of German nationals within the territory or under the control of the claimant's State. This property may be constituted as a pledge for enemy liabilities under the conditions fixed by paragraph 4 of the Annex hereto. The payment of this compensation may be made by the Allied or Associated State, and the amount will be debited to Germany.

(*f*) Whenever a national of an Allied or Associated Power is entitled to property which has been subjected to a measure of transfer in German territory and expresses a desire for its restitution, his claim for compensation in accordance with paragraph (*e*) shall be satisfied by the restitution of the said property if it still exists in specie.

In such case Germany shall take all necessary steps to restore the evicted owner to the possession of his property, free from all encumbrances or burdens with which it may have been charged after the liquidation, and to indemnify all third parties injured by the restitution.

If the restitution provided for in this paragraph cannot be effected, private agreements arranged by the intermediation of the Powers concerned or the Clearing Offices provided for in the Annex to Section III may be made, in order to secure that the national of the Allied or Associated Power may secure compensation for the injury referred to in paragraph (*e*) by the grant of advantages or equivalents which he agrees to accept in place of the property, rights or interests of which he was deprived.

Through restitution in accordance with this Article, the price or the amount of compensation fixed by the application of paragraph (*e*) will be reduced by the actual value of the property restored, account being taken of compensation in respect of loss of use or deterioration.

(*g*) The rights conferred by paragraph (*f*) are reserved to owners who are nationals of Allied or Associated Powers within whose territory legislative measures prescribing the general liquidation of enemy property, rights or interests were not applied before the signature of the Armistice.

(*h*) Except in cases where, by application of paragraph (*f*), restitutions in specie have been made, the net proceeds of sales of enemy property, rights or interests wherever situated carried out either by virtue of war legislation, or by application of this Article, and in general all cash assets of enemies, shall be dealt with as follows:

(1) As regards Powers adopting Section III and the Annex thereto, the said proceeds and cash assets shall be credited to the Power of which the owner is a national, through the Clearing Office established thereunder; any credit balance in favour of Germany resulting therefrom shall be dealt with as provided in Article 243.

(2) As regards Powers not adopting Section III and the Annex thereto, the proceeds of the property, rights and interests, and the cash assets, of the nationals of Allied or Associated Powers held by Germany shall be paid immediately to the person entitled thereto or to his Government; the proceeds of the property, rights and interests, and the cash assets, of German nationals received by an

Allied or Associated Power shall be subject to disposal by such Power in accordance with its laws and regulations and may be applied in payment of the claims and debts defined by this Article or paragraph 4 of the Annex hereto. Any property, rights and interests or proceeds thereof or cash assets not used as above provided may be retained by the said Allied or Associated Power and if retained the cash value thereof shall be dealt with as provided in Article 243.

In the case of liquidations effected in new States, which are signatories of the present Treaty as Allied and Associated Powers, or in States which are not entitled to share in the reparation payments to be made by Germany, the proceeds of liquidations effected by such States shall, subject to the rights of the Reparation Commission under the present Treaty, particularly under Articles 235 and 260, be paid direct to the owner. If on the application of that owner, the Mixed Arbitral Tribunal, provided for by Section VI of this Part, or an arbitrator appointed by that Tribunal, is satisfied that the conditions of the sale or measures taken by the Government of the State in question outside its general legislation were unfairly prejudicial to the price obtained, they shall have discretion to award to the owner equitable compensation to be paid by that State.

(*i*) Germany undertakes to compensate her nationals in respect of the sale or retention of their property, rights or interests in Allied or Associated States.

(*j*) The amount of all taxes and imposts upon capital levied or to be levied by Germany on the property, rights and interests of the nationals of the Allied or Associated Powers from November 11, 1918, until three months from the coming into force of the present Treaty, or, in the case of property, rights or interests which have been subjected to exceptional measures of war, until restitution in accordance with the present Treaty, shall be restored to the owners.

ARTICLE 298.

Germany undertakes, with regard to the property, rights and interests, including companies and associations in which they were interested, restored to nationals of Allied and Associated Powers in accordance with the provisions of Article 297, paragraph (*a*) or (*f*):

(*a*) to restore and maintain, except as expressly provided in the present Treaty, the property, rights and interests of the nationals of Allied or Associated Powers in the legal position obtaining in respect of the property, rights and interests of German nationals under the laws in force before the war;

(*b*) not to subject the property, rights or interests of the nationals of the Allied or Associated Powers to any measures in derogation of property rights which are not applied equally to the property, rights and interests of German nationals, and to pay adequate compensation in the event of the application of these measures.

ANNEX.

1.

In accordance with the provisions of Article 297, paragraph (d), the validity of vesting orders and of orders for the winding up of businesses or companies, and of any other orders, directions, decisions or instructions of any court or any department of the Government of any of the High Contracting Parties made or given, or purporting to be made or given, in pursuance of war legislation with regard to enemy property, rights and interests is confirmed. The interests of all persons shall be regarded as having been effectively dealt with by any order, direction, decision or instruction dealing with property in which they may be interested, whether or not such interests are specifically mentioned in the order, direction, decision, or instruction. No question shall be raised as to the regularity of a transfer of any property, rights or interests dealt with in pursuance of any such order, direction, decision or instruction. Every action taken with regard to any property, business, or company, whether as regards its investigation, sequestration, compulsory administration, use, requisition, supervision, or winding up, the sale or management of property, rights or interests, the collection or discharge of debts, the payment of costs, charges or expenses, or any other matter whatsoever, in pursuance of orders, directions, decisions, or instructions of any court or of any department of the Government of any of the High Contracting Parties, made or given, or purporting to be made or given, in pursuance of war legislation with regard to enemy property, rights or interests, is confirmed. Provided that the provisions of this paragraph shall not be held to prejudice the titles to property heretofore acquired in good faith and for value and in accordance with the laws of the country in which the property is situated by nationals of the Allied and Associated Powers.

The provisions of this paragraph do not apply to such of the above-mentioned measures as have been taken by the German authorities in invaded or occupied territory, nor to such of the above mentioned measures as have been taken by Germany or the German authorities since November 11, 1918, all of which shall be void.

2.

No claim or action shall be made or brought against any Allied or Associated Power or against any person acting on behalf of or under the direction of any legal authority or Department of the Government of such a Power by Germany or by any German national wherever resident in respect of any act or omission with regard to his property, rights or interests during the war or in preparation for the war. Similarly no claim or action shall be made or brought against any person in respect of any act or omission under or in accordance with the exceptional war measures, laws or regulations of any Allied or Associated Power.

3.

In Article 297 and this Annex the expression "exceptional war measures" includes measures of all kinds, legislative, administrative, judicial or others, that have been taken or will be taken hereafter with regard to enemy property, and which have had or will have the effect of removing from the proprietors the power of disposition over their property, though without affecting the ownership, such as measures of supervision, of compulsory administration, and of sequestration; or measures which have had or will have as an object the seizure of, the use of, or the interference with enemy assets, for whatsoever motive, under whatsoever form or in whatsoever place. Acts in the execution of these measures include all detentions, instructions, orders or decrees of Government departments or courts applying these measures to enemy property, as well as acts performed by any person connected with the administration or the supervision of enemy property, such as the payment of debts, the collecting of credits, the payment of any costs, charges or expenses, or the collecting of fees.

Measures of transfer are those which have affected or will affect the ownership of enemy property by transferring it in whole or in part to a person other than the enemy owner, and without his consent, such as measures directing the sale, liquidation, or devolution of ownership in enemy property, or the cancelling of titles or securities.

4.

All property, rights and interests of German nationals within the territory of any Allied or Associated Power and the net proceeds of their sale, liquidation or other dealing therewith may be charged by that Allied or Associated Power in the first place with payment of amounts due in respect of claims by the nationals of that Allied or Associated Power with regard to their property, rights and interests, including companies and associations in which they are interested, in German territory, or debts owing to them by German nationals, and with payment of claims growing out of acts committed by the German Government or by any German authorities since July 31, 1914, and before that Allied or Associated Power entered into the war. The amount of such claims may be assessed by an arbitrator appointed by Mr. Gustave Ador, if he is willing, or if no such appointment is made by him, by an arbitrator appointed by the Mixed Arbitral Tribunal provided for in Section VI. They may be charged in the second place with payment of the amounts due in respect of claims by the nationals of such Allied or Associated Power with regard to their property, rights and interests in the territory of other enemy Powers, in so far as those claims are otherwise unsatisfied.

5.

Notwithstanding the provisions of Article 297, where immediately before the outbreak of war a company incorporated in an Allied or Associated State had rights in common with a company controlled by it and incorporated in Germany to the use of trade-marks in third countries, or enjoyed the use in common with such company of unique means of reproduction of goods or articles for sale in third countries, the former company shall alone have the right to use these trade-marks in third countries to the exclusion of the German company, and these unique means of reproduction shall be handed over to the former company, notwithstanding any action taken under German war legislation with regard to the latter company or its business, industrial property or shares. Nevertheless, the former company, if requested, shall deliver the latter company derivative copies permitting the continuation of reproduction of articles for use within German territory.

6.

Up to the time when restitution is carried out in accordance with Article 297, Germany is responsible for the conservation of property, rights and interests of the nationals of Allied or Associated Powers, including companies and associations in which they are interested, that have been subjected by her to exceptional war measures.

7.

Within one year from the coming into force of the present Treaty the Allied or Associated Powers will specify the property, rights and interests over which they intend to exercise the right provided in Article 297, paragraph (f).

8.

The restitution provided in Article 297 will be carried out by order of the German Government or of the authorities which have been substituted for it. Detailed accounts of the action of administrators shall be furnished to the interested persons by the German authorities upon request, which may be made at any time after the coming into force of the present Treaty.

9.

Until completion of the liquidation provided for by Article 297, paragraph (b), the property, rights and interests of German nationals will continue to be subject to exceptional war measures that have been or will be taken with regard to them.

10.

Germany will, within six months from the coming into force of the present Treaty, deliver to each Allied or Associated Power all securities, certificates, deeds, or other documents of title held by its nationals and relating to property, rights or interests situated in the territory of that Allied or Associated Power, including any shares, stock, debentures, debenture stock, or other obligations of any company incorporated in accordance with the laws of that Power.

Germany will at any time on demand of any Allied or Associated Power furnish such information as may be required with regard to

the property, rights and interests of German nationals within the
territory of such Allied or Associated Power, or with regard to any
transactions concerning such property, rights or interests effected
since July 1, 1914.

11.

The expression " cash assets " includes all deposits or funds established before or after the declaration of war, as well as all assets
coming from deposits, revenues, or profits collected by administrators, sequestrators, or others from funds placed on deposit or
otherwise, but does not include sums belonging to the Allied or
Associated Powers or to their component States, Provinces, or
Municipalities.

12.

All investments wheresoever effected with the cash assets of
nationals of the High Contracting Parties, including companies
and associations in which such nationals were interested, by persons
responsible for the administration of enemy properties or having
control over such administration, or by order of such persons or
of any authority whatsoever shall be annulled. These cash assets
shall be accounted for irrespective of any such investment.

13.

Within one month from the coming into force of the present
Treaty, or on demand at any time, Germany will deliver to the Allied
and Associated Powers all accounts, vouchers, records, documents
and information of any kind which may be within German territory,
and which concern the property, rights and interests of the nationals
of those Powers, including companies and associations in which they
are interested, that have been subjected to an exceptional war measure, or to a measure of transfer either in German territory or in
territory occupied by Germany or her allies.

The contollers, supervisors, managers, administrators, sequestrators, liquidators and receivers shall be personally responsible under
guarantee of the German Government for the immediate delivery in
full of these accounts and documents, and for their accuracy.

14.

The provisions of Article 297 and this Annex relating to property,
rights and interests in an enemy county, and the proceeds of the
liquidation thereof, apply to debts, credits and accounts, Section III
regulating only the method of payment.

In the settlement of matters provided for in Article 297 between
Germany and the Allied or Associated States, their colonies or protectorates, or any one of the British Dominions or India, in respect
of any of which a declaration shall not have been made that they
adopt Section III, and between their respective nationals, the provisions of Section III respecting the currentcy in which payment
is to be made and the rate of exchange and of interest shall apply
unless the Government of the Allied or Associated Power concerned

shall within six months of the coming into force of the present Treaty notify Germany that the said provisions are not to be applied.

15.

The provisions of Article 297 and this Annex apply to industrial, literary and artistic property which has been or will be dealt with in the liquidation of property, rights, interests, companies or businesses under war legislation by the Allied or Associated Powers, or in accordance with the stipulations of Article 297, paragraph (*b*).

SECTION V.

CONTRACTS, PRESCRIPTIONS, JUDGMENTS.

ARTICLE 299.

(*a*) Any contract concluded between enemies shall be regarded as having been dissolved as from the time when any two of the parties became enemies, except in respect of any debt or other pecuniary obligation arising out of any act done or money paid thereunder, and subject to the exceptions and special rules with regard to particular contracts or classes of contracts contained herein or in the Annex hereto.

(*b*) Any contract of which the execution shall be required in the general interest, within six months from the date of the coming into force of the present Treaty, by the Allied or Associated Governments of which one of the parties is a national, shall be excepted from dissolution under this Article.

When the execution of the contract thus kept alive would, owing to the alteration of trade conditions, cause one of the parties substantial prejudice the Mixed Arbitral Tribunal provided for by Section VI shall be empowered to grant to the prejudiced party equitable compensation.

(*c*) Having regard to the provisions of the constitution and law of the United States of America, of Brazil, and of Japan, neither the present Article, nor Article 300, nor the Annex hereto shall apply to contracts made between nationals of these States and German nationals; nor shall Article 305 apply to the United States of America or its nationals.

(*d*) The present Article and the annex hereto shall not apply to contracts the parties to which became enemies by reason of one of them being an inhabitant of territory of which the sovereignty has been transferred, if such party shall acquire under the present Treaty the nationality of an Allied or Associated Power, nor shall they apply to contracts between nationals of the Allied and Associated Powers between whom trading has been prohibited by reason of one of the parties being in Allied or Associated territory in the occupation of the enemy.

(*e*) Nothing in the present Article or the annex hereto shall be deemed to invalidate a transaction lawfully carried out in accordance with a contract between enemies if it has been carried out with the authority of one of the belligerent Powers.

7405°—20——10

ARTICLE 300.

(*a*) All periods of prescription, or limitation of right of action, whether they began to run before or after the outbreak of war, shall be treated in the territory of the High Contracting Parties, so far as regards relations between enemies, as having been suspended for the duration of the war. They shall begin to run again at earliest three months after the coming into force of the present Treaty. This provision shall apply to the period prescribed for the presentation of interest or dividend coupons or for the presentation for repayment of securities drawn for repayment or, repayable on any other ground.

(*b*) Where, on account of failure to perform any act or comply with any formality during the war, measures of execution have been taken in German territory to the prejudice of a national of an Allied or Associated Power, the claim of such national shall, if the matter does not fall within the competence of the Courts of an Allied or Associated Power, be heard by the Mixed Arbitral Tribunal provided for by Section VI.

(*c*) Upon the application of any interested person who is a national of an Allied or Associated Power the Mixed Arbitral Tribunal shall order the restoration of the rights which have been prejudiced by the measures of execution referred to in paragraph (*b*), wherever, having regard to the particular circumstances of the case, such restoration is equitable and possible.

If such restoration is inequitable or impossible the Mixed Arbitral Tribunal may grant compensation to the prejudiced party to be paid by the German Government.

(*d*) Where a contract between enemies has been dissolved by reason either of failure on the part of either party to carry out its provisions or of the exercise of a right stipulated in the contract itself the party prejudiced may apply to the Mixed Arbitral Tribunal for relief. The Tribunal will have the powers provided for in paragraph (*c*.)

(*e*) The provisions of the preceding paragraphs of this Article shall apply to the nationals of Allied and Associated Powers who have been prejudiced by reason of measures referred to above taken by Germany in invaded or occupied territory, if they have not been otherwise compensated.

(*f*) Germany shall compensate any third party who may be prejudiced by any restitution or restoration ordered by the Mixed Arbitral Tribunal under the provisions of the preceding paragraphs of this Article.

(*g*) As regards negotiable instruments, the period of three months provided under paragraph (*a*) shall commence as from the date on which any exceptional regulations applied in the territories of the interested Power with regard to negotiable instruments shall have definitely ceased to have force.

ARTICLE 301.

As between enemies no negotiable instrument made before the war shall be deemed to have become invalid by reason only of failure within the required time to present the instrument for acceptance or payment or to give notice of non-acceptance or non-payment to drawers or indorsers or to protest the instrument, nor by reason of failure to complete any formality during the war.

Where the period within which a negotiable instrument should have been presented for acceptance or for payment, or within which notice of non-acceptance or non-payment should have been given to the drawer or indorser, or within which the instrument should have been protested, has elapsed during the war, and the party who should have presented or protested the instrument or have given notice of non-acceptance or non-payment has failed to do so during the war, a period of not less than three months from the coming into force of the present Treaty shall be allowed within which presentation, notice of non-acceptance or non-payment or protest may be made.

ARTICLE 302.

Judgments given by the Courts of an Allied or Associated Power in all cases which, under the present Treaty, they are competent to decide, shall be recognised in Germany as final, and shall be enforced without it being necessary to have them declared executory.

If a judgment in respect to any dispute which may have arisen has been given during the war by a German Court against a national of an Allied or Associated State in a case in which he was not able to make his defence, the Allied and Associated national who has suffered prejudice thereby shall be entitled to recover compensation, to be fixed by the Mixed Arbitral Tribunal provided for in Section VI.

At the instance of the national of the Allied or Associated Power the compensation above-mentioned may, upon order to that effect of the Mixed Arbitral Tribunal, be effected where it is possible by replacing the parties in the situation which they occupied before the judgment was given by the German Court.

The above compensation may likewise be obtained before the Mixed Arbitral Tribunal by the nationals of Allied or Associated Powers who have suffered prejudice by judicial measures taken in invaded or occupied territories, if they have not been otherwise compensated.

ARTICLE 303.

For the purpose of Sections III, IV, V and VII, the expression "during the war" means for each Allied or Associated Power the period between the commencement of the state of war between that Power and Germany and the coming into force of the present Treaty.

ANNEX.

I. *General Provisions.*

1.

Within the meaning of Articles 299, 300 and 301, the parties to a contract shall be regarded as enemies when trading between them shall have been prohibited by or otherwise became unlawful under laws, orders or regulations to which one of those parties was subject. They shall be deemed to have become enemies from the date when such trading was prohibited or otherwise became unlawful.

2.

The following classes of contracts are excepted from dissolution by Article 299 and, without prejudice to the rights contained in Article 297 (*b*) of Section IV, remain in force subject to the application of domestic laws, orders or regulations made during the war by the Allied and Associated Powers and subject to the terms of the contracts:

(*a*) Contracts having for their object the transfer of estates or of real or personal property where the property therein had passed or the object had been delivered before the parties became enemies;

(*b*) Leases and agreements for leases of land and houses;

(*c*) Contracts of mortgage, pledge or lien;

(*d*) Concessions concerning mines, quarries or deposits;

(*e*) Contracts between individuals or companies and States, provinces, municipalities, or other similar juridical persons charged with administrative functions, and concessions granted by States, provinces, municipalites, or other similar juridical persons charged with administrative functions.

3.

If the provisions of a contract are in part dissolved under Article 299, the remaining provisions of that contract shall, subject to the same application of domestic laws as is provided for in paragraph 2, continue in force if they are severable, but where they are not severable the contract shall be deemed to have been dissolved in its entirety.

II. *Provisions relating to certain classes of Contracts.*

Stock Exchange and Commercial Exchange Contracts.

4.

(*a*) Rules made during the war by any recognised Exchange or Commercial Association providing for the closure of contracts entered into before the war by an enemy are confirmed by the High Contracting Parties, as also any action taken thereunder, provided:

(1) That the contract was expressed to be made subject to the rules of the Exchange or Association in question;

(2) That the rules applied to all persons concerned;

(3) That the conditions attaching to the closure were fair and reasonable.

(*b*) The preceding paragraph shall not apply to rules made during the occupation by Exchanges or Commercial Associations in the districts occupied by the enemy.

(*c*) The closure of contracts relating to cotton "futures", which were closed as on July 31, 1914, under the decision of the Liverpool Cotton Association, is also confirmed.

Security.

5.

The sale of a security held for an unpaid debt owing by an enemy shall be deemed to have been valid irrespective of notice to the owner if the creditor acted in good faith and with reasonable care and prudence, and no claim by the debtor on the ground of such sale shall be admitted.

This stipulation shall not apply to any sale of securities effected by an enemy during the occupation in regions invaded or occupied by the enemy.

Negotiable Instruments.

6.

As regards Powers which adopt Section III and the Annex thereto the pecuniary obligations existing between enemies and resulting from the issue of negotiable instruments shall be adjusted in conformity with the said Annex by the instrumentality of the Clearing Offices, which shall assume the rights of the holder as regards the various remedies open to him.

7.

If a person has either before or during the war become liable upon a negotiable instrument in accordance with an undertaking given to him by a person who has subsequently become an enemy, the latter shall remain liable to indemnify the former in respect of his liability notwithstanding the outbreak of war.

III. *Contracts of Insurance.*

8.

Contracts of insurance entered into by any person with another person who subsequently became an enemy will be dealt with in accordance with the following paragraphs.

Fire Insurance.

9.

Contracts for the insurance of property against fire entered into by a person interested in such property with another person who subsequently became an enemy shall not be deemed to have been dissolved by the outbreak of war, or by the fact of the person becoming an enemy, or on account of the failure during the war and for a period of three months thereafter to perform his obligations under the contract, but they shall be dissolved at the date when the annual premium becomes payable for the first time after the expiration of a period of three months after the coming into force of the present Treaty.

A settlement shall be effected of unpaid premiums which became due during the war, or of claims for losses which occurred during the war.

10.

Where by administrative or legislative action an insurance against fire effected before the war has been transferred during the war from the original to another insurer, the transfer will be recognised and the liability of the original insurer will be deemed to have ceased as from the date of the transfer. The original insurer will, however, be entitled to receive on demand full information as to the terms of the transfer, and if it should appear that these terms were not equitable they shall be amended so far as may be necessary to render them equitable.

Furthermore, the insured shall, subject to the concurrence of the original insurer, be entitled to retransfer the contract to the original insurer as from the date of the demand.

Life Insurance.

11.

Contracts of life insurance entered into between an insurer and a person who subsequently became an enemy shall not be deemed to have been dissolved by the outbreak of war, or by the fact of the person becoming an enemy.

Any sum which during the war became due upon a contract deemed not to have been dissolved under the preceding provision shall be recoverable after the war with the addition of interest at five per cent. per annum from the date of its becoming due up to the day of payment.

Where the contract has lapsed during the war owing to non-payment of premiums, or has become void from breach of the conditions of the contract, the assured or his representatives or the person entitled shall have the right at any time within twelve months of the coming into force of the present Treaty to claim from the insurer the surrender value of the policy at the date of its lapse or avoidance.

Where the contract has lapsed during the war owing to non-payment of premiums the payment of which has been prevented by the enforcement of measures of war, the assured or his representative or the persons entitled shall have the right to restore the contract on payment of the premiums with interest at five per cent. per annum within three months from the coming into force of the present Treaty.

12.

Any Allied or Associated Power may within three months of the coming into force of the present Treaty cancel all the contracts of insurance running between a German insurance company and its nationals under conditions which shall protect its nationals from any prejudice.

To this end the German insurance company will hand over to the Allied or Associated Government concerned the proportion of its assets attributable to the policies so cancelled and will be relieved from all liability in respect of such policies. The assets to be handed over shall be determined by an actuary appointed by the Mixed Arbitral Tribunal.

13.

Where contracts of life insurance have been entered into by a local branch of an insurance company established in a country which subsequently became an enemy country, the contract shall, in the absence of any stipulation to the contrary in the contract itself, be governed by the local law, but the insurer shall be entitled to demand from the insured or his representatives the refund of sums paid on claims made or enforced under measures taken during the war, if the making or enforcement of such claims was not in accordance with the terms of the contract itself or was not consistent with the laws or treaties existing at the time when it was entered into.

14.

In any case where by the law applicable to the contract the insurer remains bound by the contract notwithstanding the non-payment of premiums until notice is given to the insured of the termination of the contract, he shall be entitled where the giving of such notice was prevented by the war to recover the unpaid premiums with interest at five per cent. per annum from the insured.

15.

Insurance contracts shall be considered as contracts of life assurance for the purpose of paragraphs 11 to 14 when they depend on the probabilities of human life combined with the rate of interest for the calculation of the reciprocal engagements between the two parties.

Marine Insurance.

16.

Contracts of marine insurance including time policies and voyage policies entered into between an insurer and a person who subsequently became an enemy, shall be deemed to have been dissolved on his becoming an enemy, except in cases where the risk undertaken in the contract had attached before he became an enemy.

Where the risk had not attached, money paid by way of premium or otherwise shall be recoverable from the insurer.

Where the risk had attached effect shall be given to the contract notwithstanding the party becoming an enemy, and sums due under the contract either by way of premiums or in respect of losses shall be recoverable after the coming into force of the present Treaty.

In the event of any agreement being come to for the payment of interest on sums due before the war to or by the nationals of States which have been at war and recovered after the war, such interest shall in the case of losses recoverable under contracts of marine insurance run from the expiration of a period of one year from the date of the loss.

17.

No contract of marine insurance with an insured person who subsequently became an enemy shall be deemed to cover losses due to belligerent action by the Power of which the insurer was a national or by the allies or associates of such Power.

18.

Where it is shown that a person who had before the war entered into a contract of marine insurance with an insurer who subsequently became an enemy entered after the outbreak of war into a new contract covering the same risk with an insurer who was not an enemy, the new contract shall be deemed to be substituted for the original contract as from the date when it was entered into, and the premiums payable shall be adjusted on the basis of the original insurer having remained liable on the contract only up till the time when the new contract was entered into.

Other Insurances.

19.

Contracts of insurance entered into before the war between an insurer and a person who subsequently became an enemy, other than contracts dealt with in paragraphs 9 to 18, shall be treated in all respects on the same footing as contracts of fire insurance between the same persons would be dealt with under the said paragraphs.

Re-insurance.

20.

All treaties of re-insurance with a person who became an enemy shall be regarded as having been abrogated by the person becoming an enemy, but without prejudice in the case of life or marine risks which had attached before the war to the right to recover payment after the war for sums due in respect of such risks.

Nevertheless if, owing to invasion, it has been impossible for the re-insured to find another re-insurer, the treaty shall remain in force until three months after the coming into force of the present Treaty.

Where a re-insurance treaty becomes void under this paragraph, there shall be an adjustment of accounts between the parties in respect both of premiums paid and payable and of liabilities for losses in respect of life or marine risks which had attached before the war. In the case of risks other than those mentioned in paragraphs 11 to 18 the adjustment of accounts shall be made as at the date of the parties becoming enemies without regard to claims for losses which may have occurred since that date.

21.

The provisions of the preceding paragraph will extend equally to re-insurances existing at the date of the parties becoming enemies of particular risks undertaken by the insurer in a contract of insurance against any risks other than life or marine risks.

22.

Re-insurance of life risks effected by particular contracts and not under any general treaty remain in force.

The provisions of paragraph 12 apply to treaties of re-insurance of life insurance contracts in which enemy companies are the re-insurers.

23.

In case of a re-insurance effected before the war of a contract of marine insurance, the cession of a risk which had been ceded to the re-insurer shall, if it had attached before the outbreak of war, remain valid and effect be given to the contract notwithstanding the outbreak of war; sums due under the contract of re-insurance in respect either of premiums or of losses shall be recoverable after the war.

24.

The provisions of paragraphs 17 and 18 and the last part of paragraph 16 shall apply to contracts for the re-insurance of marine risks.

Section VI.

MIXED ARBITRAL TRIBUNAL.

Article 304.

(a) Within three months from the date of the coming into force of the present Treaty, a Mixed Arbitral Tribunal shall be established between each of the Allied and Associated Powers on the one hand and Germany on the other hand. Each such Tribunal shall consist of three members. Each of the Governments concerned shall appoint one of these members. The President shall be chosen by agreement between the two Governments concerned.

In case of failure to reach agreement, the President of the Tribunal and two other persons either of whom may in case of need take his place, shall be chosen by the Council of the League of Nations, or, until this is set up, by M. Gustave Ador if he is willing. These persons shall be nationals of Powers that have remained neutral during the war.

If any Government does not proceed within a period of one month in case there is a vacancy to appoint a member of the Tribunal, such member shall be chosen by the other Government from the two persons mentioned above other than the President.

The decision of the majority of the members of the Tribunal shall be the decision of the Tribunal.

(b) The Mixed Arbitral Tribunals established pursuant to paragraph (a), shall decide all questions within their competence under Sections III, IV, V and VII.

In addition, all questions, whatsoever their nature, relating to contracts concluded before the coming into force of the present Treaty between nationals of the Allied and Associated Powers and German nationals shall be decided by the Mixed Arbitral Tribunal, always excepting questions which, under the laws of the Allied, Associated or Neutral Powers, are within the jurisdiction of the National Courts of those Powers. Such questions shall be decided by the National Courts in question, to the exclusion of the Mixed Arbitral Tribunal. The party who is a national of an Allied or Associated Power may nevertheless bring the case before the Mixed Arbitral Tribunal if this is not prohibited by the laws of his country.

(c) If the number of cases justifies it, additional members shall be appointed and each Mixed Arbitral Tribunal shall sit in divisions. Each of these divisions will be constituted as above.

(*d*) Each Mixed Arbitral Tribunal will settle its own procedure except in so far as it is provided in the following Annex, and is empowered to award the sums to be paid by the loser in respect of the costs and expenses of the proceedings.

(*e*) Each Government will pay the remuneration of the member of the Mixed Arbitral Tribunal appointed by it and of any agent whom it may appoint to represent it before the Tribunal. The remuneration of the President will be determined by special agreement between the Governments concerned; and this remuneration and the joint expenses of each Tribunal will be paid by the two Governments in equal moieties.

(*f*) The High Contracting Parties agree that their courts and authorities shall render to the Mixed Arbitral Tribunals direct all the assistance in their power, particularly as regards transmitting notices and collecting evidence.

(*g*) The High Contracting Parties agree to regard the decisions of the Mixed Arbitral Tribunal as final and conclusive, and to render them binding upon their nationals.

ANNEX.

1.

Should one of the members of theTribunal either die, retire, or be unable for any reason whatever to discharge his function, the same procedure will be followed for filling the vacancy as was followed for appointing him.

2.

The Tribunal may adopt such rules of procedure as shall be in accordance with justice and equity and decide the order and time at which each party must conclude its arguments, and may arrange all formalities required for dealing with the evidence.

3.

The agent and counsel of the parties on each side are authorized to present orally and in writing to the Tribunal arguments in support or in defence of each case.

4.

The Tribunal shall keep record of the questions and cases submitted and the proceedings thereon, with the dates of such proceedings.

5.

Each of the Powers concerned may appoint a secretary. These secretaries shall act together as joint secretaries of the Tribunal and shall be subject to its direction. The Tribunal may appoint and employ any other necessary officer or officers to assist in the performance of its duties.

6.

The Tribunal shall decide all questions and matters submitted upon such evidence and information as may be furnished by the parties concerned.

7.

Germany agrees to give the Tribunal all facilities and information required by it for carrying out its investigations.

8.

The language in which the proceedings shall be conducted shall, unless otherwise agreed, be English, French, Italian or Japanese, as may be determined by the Allied or Associated Power concerned.

9.

The place and time for the meetings of each Tribunal shall be determined by the President of the Tribunal.

ARTICLE 305.

Whenever a competent court has given or gives a decision in a case covered by Sections III, IV, V or VII, and such decision is inconsistent with the provisions of such Sections, the party who is prejudiced by the decision shall be entitled to obtain redress which shall be fixed by the Mixed Arbitral Tribunal. At the request of the national of an Allied or Associated Power, the redress may, whenever possible, be effected by the Mixed Arbitral Tribunal directing the replacement of the parties in the position occupied by them before the judgment was given by the German court.

SECTION VII.

INDUSTRIAL PROPERTY.

ARTICLE 306.

Subject to the stipulations of the present Treaty, rights of industrial, literary and artistic property, as such property is defined by the International Conventions of Paris and of Berne, mentioned in Article 286, shall be re-established or restored, as from the coming into force of the present Treaty, in the territories of the High Contracting Parties, in favour of the persons entitled to the benefit of them at the moment when the state of war commenced or their legal representatives. Equally, rights which, except for the war, would have been acquired during the war in consequence of an application made for the protection of industrial property, or the publication of a literary or artistic work, shall be recognised and established in favour of those persons who would have been entitled thereto, from the coming into force of the present Treaty.

Nevertheless, all acts done by virtue of the special measures taken during the war under legislative, executive or administrative authority of any Allied or Associated Power in regard to the rights of German nationals in industrial, literary or artistic property shall remain in force and shall continue to maintain their full effect.

No claim shall be made or action brought by Germany or German nationals in respect of the use during the war by the Government of any Allied or Associated Power, or by any persons acting on behalf or with the assent of such Government, of any rights in industrial, literary or artistic property, nor in respect of the sale, offering for sale, or use of any products, articles or apparatus what-soever to which such rights applied.

Unless the legislation of any one of the Allied or Associated Powers in force at the moment of the signature of the present Treaty otherwise directs, sums due or paid in virtue of any act or operation resulting from the execution of the special measures mentioned in paragraph I of this Article shall be dealt with in the same way as other sums due to German nationals are directed to be dealt with by the present Treaty; and sums produced by any special measures taken by the German Government in respect of rights in industrial, literary or artistic property belonging to the nationals of the Allied or Associated Powers shall be considered and treated in the same way as other debts due from German nationals.

Each of the Allied and Associated Powers reserves to itself the right to impose such limitations, conditions or restrictions on rights of industrial, literary or artistic property (with the exception of trade-marks) acquired before or during the war, or which may be subsequently acquired in accordance with its legislation, by German nationals, whether by granting licences, or by the working, or by preserving control over their exploitation, or in any other way, as may be considered necessary for national defence, or in the public interest, or for assuring the fair treatment by Germany of the rights of industrial, literary and artistic property held in German terri-tory by its nationals, or for securing the due fulfilment of all the obligations undertaken by Germany in the present Treaty. As re-gards rights of industrial, literary and artistic property acquired after the coming into force of the present Treaty, the right so re-served by the Allied and Associated Powers shall only be exercised in cases where these limitations, conditions or restrictions may be considered necessary for national defence or in the public interest.

In the event of the application of the provisions of the preceding paragraph by any Allied or Associated Power, there shall be paid reasonable indemnities or royalties, which shall be dealt with in the same way as other sums due to German nationals are directed to be dealt with by the present Treaty.

Each of the Allied or Associated Powers reserves the right to treat as void and of no effect any transfer in whole or in part of or other dealing with rights of or in respect of industrial, literary or artistic property effected after August 1, 1914, or in the future, which would have the result of defeating the objects of the provisions of this Article.

The provisions of this Article shall not apply to rights in indus-trial, literary or artistic property which have been dealt with in the liquidation of businesses or companies under war legislation by the Allied or Associated Powers, or which may be so dealt with by virtue of Article 297, paragraph (*b*).

ARTICLE 307.

A minimum of one year after the coming into force of the present Treaty shall be accorded to the nationals of the High Contracting Parties, without extension fees or other penalty, in order to enable such persons to accomplish any act, fulfil any formality, pay any fees, and generally satisfy any obligation prescribed by the laws or regulations of the respective States relating to the obtaining, preserving, or opposing rights to, or in respect of, industrial property either acquired before August 1, 1914, or which, except for the war, might have been acquired since that date as a result of an application made before the war or during its continuance, but nothing in this Article shall give any right to reopen interference proceedings in the United States of America where a final hearing has taken place.

All rights in, or in respect of, such property which may have lapsed by reason of any failure to accomplish any act, fulfil any formality, or make any payment, shall revive, but subject in the case of patents and designs to the imposition of such conditions as each Allied or Associated Power may deem reasonably necessary for the protection of persons who have manufactured or made use of the subject matter of such property while the rights had lapsed. Further, where rights to patents or designs belonging to German nationals are revived under this Article, they shall be subject in respect of the grant of licences to the same provisions as would have been applicable to them during the war, as well as to all the provisions of the present Treaty.

The period from August 1, 1914, until the coming into force of the present Treaty shall be excluded in considering the time within which a patent should be worked or a trade mark or design used, and it is further agreed that no patent, registered trade mark or design in force on August 1, 1914, shall be subject to revocation or cancellation by reason only of the failure to work such patent or use such trade mark or design for two years after the coming into force of the present Treaty.

ARTICLE 308.

The rights of priority, provided by Article 4 of the International Convention for the Protection of Industrial Property of Paris, of March 20, 1883, revised at Washington in 1911 or by any other Convention or Statute, for the filing or registration of applications for patents or models of utility, and for the registration of trade marks, designs and models which had not expired on August 1, 1914, and those which have arisen during the war, or would have arisen but for the war, shall be extended by each of the High Contracting Parties in favour of all nationals of the other High Contracting Parties for a period of six months after the coming into force of the present Treaty.

Nevertheless, such extension shall in no way affect the right of any of the High Contracting Parties or of any person who before the coming into force of the present Treaty was *bonâ fide* in possession of any rights of industrial property conflicting with rights applied for by another who claims rights of priority in respect of them, to exercise such rights by itself or himself personally, or by such agents or licensees as derived their rights from it or him before the coming into force of the present Treaty; and such persons shall not be amenable to any action or other process of law in respect of infringement.

ARTICLE 309.

No action shall be brought and no claim made by persons residing or carrying on business within the territories of Germany on the one part and of the Allied or Associated Powers on the other, or persons who are nationals of such Powers respectively, or by any one deriving title during the war from such persons, by reason of any action which has taken place within the territory of the other party between the date of the declaration of war and that of the coming into force of the present Treaty, which might constitute an infringement of the rights of industrial property or rights of literary and artistic property, either existing at any time during the war or revived under the provisions of Articles 307 and 308.

Equally, no action for infringement of industrial, literary or artistic property rights by such persons shall at any time be permissible in respect of the sale or offering for sale for a period of one year after the signature of the present Treaty in the territories of the Allied or Associated Powers on the one hand or Germany on the other, of products or articles manufactured, or of literary or artistic works published, during the period between the declaration of war and the signature of the present Treaty, or against those who have acquired and continue to use them. It is understood, nevertheless, that this provision shall not apply when the possessor of the rights was domiciled or had an industrial or commercial establishment in the districts occupied by Germany during the war.

This Article shall not apply as between the United States of America on the one hand and Germany on the other.

Article 310.

Licences in respect of industrial, literary or artistic property concluded before the war between nationals of the Allied or Associated Powers or persons residing in their territory or carrying on business therein, on the one part, and German nationals, on the other part, shall be considered as cancelled as from the date of the declaration of war between Germany and the Allied or Associated Power. But, in any case, the former beneficiary of a contract of this kind shall have the right, within a period of six months after the coming into force of the present Treaty, to demand from the proprietor of the rights the grant of a new licence, the conditions of which, in default of agreement between the parties, shall be fixed by the duly qualified tribunal in the country under whose legislation the rights had been acquired, except in the case of licences held in respect of rights acquired under German law. In such cases the conditions shall be fixed by the Mixed Arbitral Tribunal referred to in Section VI of this Part. The tribunal may, if necessary, fix also the amount which it may deem just should be paid by reason of the use of the rights during the war.

No licence in respect of industrial, literary or artistic property, granted under the special war legislation of any Allied or Associated Power, shall be affected by the continued existence of any licence entered into before the war, but shall remain valid and of full effect, and a licence so granted to the former beneficiary of a licence entered into before the war shall be considered as substituted for such licence.

Where sums have been paid during the war by virtue of a licence or agreement concluded before the war in respect of rights of industrial property or for the reproduction or the representation of literary, dramatic or artistic works, these sums shall be dealt with in the same manner as other debts or credits of German nationals, as provided by the present Treaty.

This Article shall not apply as between the United States of America on the one hand and Germany on the other.

ARTICLE 311.

The inhabitants of territories separated from Germany by virtue of the present Treaty shall, notwithstanding this separation and the change of nationality consequent thereon, continue to enjoy in Germany all the rights in industrial, literary and artistic property to which they were entitled under German legislation at the time of the separation.

Rights of industrial, literary and artistic property which are in force in the territories separated from Germany under the present Treaty at the moment of the separation of these territories from Gemany, or which will be re-established or restored in accordance with the provisions of Article 306 of the present Treaty, shall be recognized by the State to which the said territory is transferred and shall remain in force in that territory for the same period of time given them under the German law.

SECTION VIII.

SOCIAL AND STATE INSURANCE IN CEDED TERRITORY.

ARTICLE 312.

Without prejudice to the provisions contained in other Articles of the present Treaty, the German Government undertakes to transfer to any Power to which German territory in Europe is ceded, and to any Power administering former German territory as a mandatory under Article 22 of Part I (League of Nations), such portion of the reserves accumulated by the Government of the German Empire or of German States, or by public or private organisations under their control, as is attributable to the carrying on of Social or State Insurance in such territory.

The Powers to which these funds are transferred must apply them to the performance of the obligations arising from such insurances.

The conditions of the transfer will be determined by special conventions to be concluded between the German Government and the Governments concerned.

In case these special conventions are not concluded in accordance with the above paragraph within three months after the coming into force of the present Treaty, the conditions of transfer shall in each case be referred to a Commission of five members, one of whom shall be appointed by the German Government, one by the other interested Government and three by the Governing Body of the International Labour Office from the nationals of other States. This Commission shall by majority vote within three months after appointment adopt recommendations for submission to the Council of the League of Nations, and the decisions of the Council shall forthwith be accepted as final by Germany and the other Government concerned.

PART XI.

AERIAL NAVIGATION.

ARTICLE 313.

The aircraft of the Allied and Associated Powers shall have full liberty of passage and landing over and in the territory and territorial waters of Germany, and shall enjoy the same privileges as German aircraft, particularly in case of distress by land or sea.

ARTICLE 314.

The aircraft of the Allied and Associated Powers shall, while in transit to any foreign country whatever, enjoy the right of flying over the territory and territorial waters of Germany without landing, subject always to any regulations which may be made by Germany, and which shall be applicable equally to the aircraft of Germany and to those of the Allied and Associated countries.

ARTICLE 315.

All aerodromes in Germany open to national public traffic shall be open for the aircraft of the Allied and Associated Powers, and in any such aerodrome such aircraft shall be treated on a footing of equality with German aircraft as regards charges of every description, including charges for landing and accommodation.

ARTICLE 316.

Subject to the present provisions, the rights of passage, transit and landing, provided for in Articles 313, 314 and 315, are subject to the observance of such regulations as Germany may consider it necessary to enact, but such regulations shall be applied without distinction to German aircraft and to those of the Allied and Associated countries.

ARTICLE 317.

Certificates of nationality, airworthiness, or competency, and licences, issued or recognised as valid by any of the Allied or Associated Powers, shall be recognised in Germany as valid and as equivalent to the certificates and licences issued by Germany.

ARTICLE 318.

As regards internal commercial air traffic, the aircraft of the Allied and Associated Powers shall enjoy in Germany most favoured nation treatment.

ARTICLE 319.

Germany undertakes to enforce the necessary measures to ensure that all German aircraft flying over her territory shall comply with the Rules as to lights and signals, Rules of the Air and Rules for Air Traffic on and in the neighbourhood of aerodromes, which have been laid down in the Convention relative to Aerial Navigation concluded between the Allied and Associated Powers.

ARTICLE 320.

The obligations imposed by the preceding provisions shall remain in force until January 1, 1923, unless before that date Germany shall have been admitted into the League of Nations or shall have been authorised, by consent of the Allied and Associated Powers, to adhere to the Convention relative to Aerial Navigation concluded between those Powers.

PART XII.

PORTS, WATERWAYS AND RAILWAYS.

SECTION I.

GENERAL PROVISIONS.

ARTICLE 321.

Germany undertakes to grant freedom of transit through her territories on the routes most convenient for international transit, either by rail, navigable waterway, or canal, to persons, goods, vessels, carriages, wagons and mails coming from or going to the territories of any of the Allied and Associated Powers (whether contiguous or not); for this purpose the crossing of territorial waters shall be allowed. Such persons, goods, vessels, carriages, wagons and mails shall not be subjected to any transit duty or to any undue delays or restrictions, and shall be entitled in Germany to national treatment as regards charges, facilities, and all other matters.

Goods in transit shall be exempt from all Customs or other similar duties.

All charges imposed on transport in transit shall be reasonable, having regard to the conditions of the traffic. No charge, facility or restriction shall depend directly or indirectly on the ownership or on the nationality of the ship or other means of transport on which any part of the through journey has been, or is to be, accomplished.

ARTICLE 322.

Germany undertakes neither to impose nor to maintain any control over transmigration traffic through her territories beyond measures necessary to ensure that passengers are *bonâ fide* in transit; nor to allow any shipping company or any other private body, corporation or person interested in the traffic to take any part whatever in, or to exercise any direct or indirect influence over, any administrative service that may be necessary for this purpose.

ARTICLE 323.

Germany undertakes to make no discrimination or preference, direct or indirect, in the duties, charges and prohibitions relating to importations into or exportations from her territories, or, subject

7405°—20——11

to the special engagements contained in the present Treaty, in the charges and conditions of transport of goods or persons entering or leaving her territories, based on the frontier crossed; or on the kind, ownership or flag of the means of transport (including aircraft) employed; or on the original or immediate place of departure of the vessel, wagon or aircraft or other means of transport employed, or its ultimate or intermediate destination; or on the route of or places of trans-shipment on the journey; or on whether any port through which the goods are imported or exported is a German port or a port belonging to any foreign country or on whether the goods are imported or exported by sea, by land or by air.

Germany particularly undertakes not to establish against the ports and vessels of any of the Allied and Associated Powers any surtax or any direct or indirect bounty for export or import by German ports or vessels, or by those of another Power, for example by means of combined tariffs. She further undertakes that persons or goods passing through a port or using a vessel of any of the Allied and Associated Powers shall not be subjected to any formality or delay whatever to which such persons or goods would not be subjected if they passed through a German port or a port of any other Power, or used a German vessel or a vessel of any other Power.

ARTICLE 324.

All necessary administrative and technical measures shall be taken to shorten, as much as possible, the transmission of goods across the German frontiers and to ensure their forwarding and transport from such frontiers, irrespective of whether such goods are coming from or going to the territories of the Allied and Associated Powers or are in transit from or to those territories, under the same material conditions in such matters as rapidity of carriage and care *en route* as are enjoyed by other goods of the same kind carried on German territory under similar conditions of transport.

In particular, the transport of perishable goods shall be promptly and regularly carried out, and the customs formalities shall be effected in such a way as to allow the goods to be carried straight through by trains which make connection.

ARTICLE 325.

The seaports of the Allied and Associated Powers are entitled to all favours and to all reduced tariffs granted on German railways or navigable waterways for the benefit of German ports or of any port of another Power.

ARTICLE 326.

Germany may not refuse to participate in the tariffs or combinations of tariffs intended to secure for ports of any of the Allied and Associated Powers advantages similar to those granted by Germany to her own ports or the ports of any other Power.

SECTION II.

NAVIGATION.

CHAPTER I.

FREEDOM OF NAVIGATION.

ARTICLE 327.

The nationals of any of the Allied and Associated Powers as well as their vessels and property shall enjoy in all German ports and on the inland navigation routes of Germany the same treatment in all respects as German nationals, vessels and property.

In particular the vessels of any one of the Allied or Associated Powers shall be entitled to transport goods of any description, and passengers, to or from any ports or places in German territory to which German vessels may have access, under conditions which shall not be more onerous than those applied in the case of national vessels; they shall be treated on a footing of equality with national vessels as regards port and harbour facilities and charges of every description, including facilities for stationing, loading and unloading, and duties and charges of tonnage, harbour, pilotage, lighthouse, quarantine, and all analogous duties and charges of whatsoever nature, levied in the name of or for the profit of the Government, public functionaries, private individuals, corporations or establishments of any kind.

In the event of Germany granting a preferential régime to any of the Allied or Associated Powers or to any other foreign Power, this régime shall be extended immediately and unconditionally to all the Allied and Associated Powers.

There shall be no impediment to the movement of persons or vessels other than those arising from prescriptions concerning customs, police, sanitation, emigration and immigration, and those relating to the import and export of prohibited goods. Such regulations must be reasonable and uniform and must not impede traffic unnecessarily.

CHAPTER II.

FREE ZONES IN PORTS.

ARTICLE 328.

The free zones existing in German ports on August 1, 1914, shall be maintained. These free zones, and any other free zones which may be established in German territory by the present Treaty, shall be subject to the régime provided for in the following Articles.

Goods entering or leaving a free zone shall not be subjected to any import or export duty, other than those provided for in Article 330.

Vessels and goods entering a free zone may be subjected to the charges established to cover expenses of administration, upkeep and improvement of the port, as well as to the charges for the use of various installations, provided that these charges shall be reasonable having regard to the expenditure incurred, and shall be levied in the conditions of equality provided for in Article 327.

Goods shall not be subjected to any other charge except a statistical duty which shall not exceed 1 per mille *ad valorem,* and which shall be devoted exclusively to defraying the expenses of compiling state- ments of the traffic in the port.

ARTICLE 329.

The facilities granted for the erection of warehouses, for packing and for unpacking goods, shall be in accordance with trade require- ments for the time being. All goods allowed to be consumed in the free zone shall be exempt from duty, whether of excise or of any other description, apart from the statistical duty provided for in Article 328 above.

There shall be no discrimination in regard to any of the provisions of the present Article between persons belonging to different na- tionalities or between goods of different origin or destination.

ARTICLE 330.

Import duties may be levied on goods leaving the free zone for consumption in the country on the territory of which the port is situated. Conversely, export duties may be levied on goods com- ing from such country and brought into the free zone. These im- port and export duties shall be levied on the same basis and at the same rates as similar duties levied at the other Customs frontiers of the country concerned. On the other hand, Germany shall not levy, under any denomination, any import, export or transit duty on goods carried by land or water across her territory to or from the free zone from or to any other State.

Germany shall draw up the necessary regulations to secure and guarantee such freedom of transit over such railways and waterways in her territory as normally give access to the free zone.

CHAPTER III.

CLAUSES RELATING TO THE ELBE, THE ODER, THE NIEMEN (RUSSSTROM-
MEMEL-NIEMEN) AND THE DANUBE.

(1)—*General Clauses.*

ARTICLE 331.

The following rivers are declared international:

 the Elbe (*Labe*) from its confluence with the Vltava (*Moldau*), and the Vltava (*Moldau*) from Prague;
 the Oder (*Ódra*) from its confluence with the Oppa;
 the Niemen (*Russstrom-Memel-Niemen*) from Grodno;
 the Danube from Ulm;
 and all navigable parts of these river systems which naturally provide more than one State with access to the sea, with or without transhipment from one vessel to another; together with lateral canals and channels constructed either to duplicate or to improve naturally navigable sections of the specified river systems, or to connect two naturally navigable sections of the same river.

The same shall apply to the Rhine-Danube navigable waterway, should such a waterway be constructed under the conditions laid down in Article 353.

ARTICLE 332.

On the waterways declared to be international in the preceding Article, the nationals, property and flags of all Powers shall be treated on a footing of perfect equality, no distinction being made to the detriment of the nationals, property or flag of any Power between them and the nationals, property or flag of the riparian State itself or of the most favoured nation.

Nevertheless, German vessels shall not be entitled to carry passengers or goods by regular services between the ports of any Allied or Associated Power, without special authority from such Power.

ARTICLE 333.

Where such charges are not precluded by any existing conventions, charges varying on different sections of a river may be levied on vessels using the navigable channels or their approaches, provided that they are intended solely to cover equitably the cost of maintaining in a navigable condition, or of improving, the river and its approaches, or to meet expenditure incurred in the interests of navigation. The schedule of such charges shall be calculated on the basis of such expenditure and shall be posted up in the ports. These charges shall be levied in such a manner as to render any detailed examination of cargoes unnecessary, except in cases of suspected fraud or contravention.

ARTICLE 334.

The transit of vessels, passengers and goods on these waterways shall be effected in accordance with the general conditions prescribed for transit in Section I above.

When the two banks of an international river are within the same State goods in transit may be placed under seal or in the custody of customs agents. When the river forms a frontier goods and passengers in transit shall be exempt from all customs formalities; the loading and unloading of goods, and the embarkation and disembarkation of passengers, shall only take place in the ports specified by the riparian State.

ARTICLE 335.

No dues of any kind other than those provided for in the present Part shall be levied along the course or at the mouth of these rivers.

This provision shall not prevent the fixing by the riparian States of customs, local octroi or consumption duties, or the creation of reasonable and uniform charges levied in the ports, in accordance with public tariffs, for the use of cranes, elevators, quays, warehouses, etc.

ARTICLE 336.

In default of any special organisation for carrying out the works connected with the upkeep and improvement of the international portion of a navigable system, each riparian State shall be bound to take suitable measures to remove any obstacle or danger to navigation and to ensure the maintenance of good conditions of navigation.

If a State neglects to comply with this obligation any riparian State, or any State represented on the International Commission, if there is one, may appeal to the tribunal instituted for this purpose by the League of Nations.

ARTICLE 337.

The same procedure shall be followed in the case of a riparian State undertaking any works of a nature to impede navigation in the international section. The tribunal mentioned in the preceding Article shall be entitled to enforce the suspension or suppression of such works, making due allowance in its decisions for all rights in connection with irrigation, water-power, fisheries, and other national interests, which, with the consent of all the riparian States or of all the States represented on the International Commission, if there is one, shall be given priority over the requirements of navigation.

Appeal to the tribunal of the League of Nations does not require the suspension of the works.

ARTICLE 338.

The régime set out in Articles 332 to 337 above shall be superseded by one to be laid down in a General Convention drawn up by the Allied and Associated Powers, and approved by the League of Nations, relating to the waterways recognised in such Convention as having an international character. This Convention shall apply in particular to the whole or part of the above-mentioned river systems of the Elbe (*Labe*), the Oder (*Odra*), the Niemen (*Russstrom-Memel-Niemen*), and the Danube, and such other parts of these river systems as may be covered by a general definition.

Germany undertakes, in accordance with the provisions of Article 379, to adhere to the said General Convention as well as to all projects prepared in accordance with Article 343 below for the revision of existing international agreements and regulations.

ARTICLE 339.

Germany shall cede to the Allied and Associated Powers concerned, within a maximum period of three months from the date on which notification shall be given her, a proportion of the tugs and vessels remaining registered in the ports of the river systems referred to in Article 331 after the deduction of those surrendered by way of restitution or reparation. Germany shall in the same way cede material of all kinds necessary to the Allied and Associated Powers concerned for the utilisation of those river systems.

The number of the tugs and boats, and the amount of the material so ceded, and their distribution, shall be determined by an arbitrator or arbitrators nominated by the United States of America, due regard being had to the legitimate needs of the parties concerned, and particularly to the shipping traffic during the five years preceding the war.

All craft so ceded shall be provided with their fittings and gear, shall be in a good state of repair and in condition to carry goods, and shall be selected from among those most recently built.

The cessions provided for in the present Article shall entail a credit of which the total amount, settled in a lump sum by the arbitrator or arbitrators, shall not in any case exceed the value of the capital expended in the initial establishment of the material ceded, and shall be set off against the total sums due from Germany; in consequence, the indemnification of the proprietors shall be a matter for Germany to deal with.

(2) *Special Clauses relating to the Elbe, the Oder and the Niemen (Russstrom-Memel-Niemen).*

ARTICLE 340.

The Elbe (*Labe*) shall be placed under the administration of an International Commission which shall comprise:
4 representatives of the German States bordering on the river;
2 representatives of the Czecho-Slovak State;
1 representative of Great Britain;
1 representative of France;
1 representative of Italy;
1 representative of Belgium.
Whatever be the number of members present, each delegation shall have the right to record a number of votes equal to the number of representatives allotted to it.

If certain of these representatives cannot be appointed at the time of the coming into force of the present Treaty, the decisions of the Commission shall nevertheless be valid.

ARTICLE 341.

The Oder (*Odra*) shall be placed under the administration of an International Commission, which shall comprise:
1 representative of Poland;
3 representatives of Prussia;
1 representative of the Czecho-Slovak State;
1 representative of Great Britain;
1 representative of France;
1 representative of Denmark;
1 representative of Sweden.
If certain of these representatives cannot be appointed at the time of the coming into force of the present Treaty, the decisions of the Commission shall nevertheless be valid.

ARTICLE 342.

On a request being made to the League of Nations by any riparian State, the Niemen (*Russstrom-Memel-Niemen*) shall be placed under the administration of an International Commission, which shall comprise one representative of each riparian State, and three representatives of other States specified by the League of Nations.

ARTICLE 343.

The International Commissions referred to in Articles 340 and 341 shall meet within three months of the date of the coming into force of the present Treaty. The International Commission referred to in Article 342 shall meet within three months from the date of the request made by a riparian State. Each of these Commissions shall proceed immediately to prepare a project for the revision of the existing international agreements and regulations, drawn up in conformity with the General Convention referred to in Article 338, should such Convention have been already concluded. In the absence of such Convention, the project for revision shall be in conformity with the principles of Articles 332 to 337 above.

ARTICLE 344.

The projects referred to in the preceding Article shall, *inter alia*:

(*a*) designate the headquarters of the International Commission, and prescribe the manner in which its President is to be nominated;

(*b*) specify the extent of the Commission's powers, particularly in regard to the execution of works of maintenance, control, and improvement on the river system, the financial régime, the fixing and collection of charges, and regulations for navigation;

(*c*) define the sections of the river or its tributaries to which the international régime shall be applied.

ARTICLE 345.

The international agreements and regulations at present governing the navigation of the Elbe (*Labe*), the Oder (*Odra*), and the Niemen (*Russstrom-Memel-Niemen*) shall be provisionally maintained in force until the ratification of the above-mentioned projects. Nevertheless, in all cases where such agreements and regulations in force are in conflict with the provisions of Articles 332 to 337 above, or of the General Convention to be concluded, the latter provisions shall prevail.

(3) *Special Clauses relating to the Danube.*

ARTICLE 346.

The European Commission of the Danube reassumes the powers it possessed before the war. Nevertheless, as a provisional measure, only representatives of Great Britain, France, Italy and Roumania shall constitute this Commission.

ARTICLE 347.

From the point where the competence of the European Commission ceases, the Danube system referred to in Article 331 shall be placed under the administration of an International Commission composed as follows:

2 representatives of German riparian States;

1 representative of each other riparian State;

1 representative of each non-riparian State represented in the future on the European Commission of the Danube.

If certain of these representatives cannot be appointed at the time of the coming into force of the present Treaty, the decisions of the Commission shall nevertheless be valid.

Article 348.

The International Commission provided for in the preceding Article shall meet as soon as possible after the coming into force of the present Treaty, and shall undertake provisionally the administration of the river in conformity with the provisions of Articles 332 to 337, until such time as a definitive statute regarding the Danube is concluded by the Powers nominated by the Allied and Associated Powers.

Article 349.

Germany agrees to accept the régime which shall be laid down for the Danube by a Conference of the Powers nominated by the Allied and Associated Powers, which shall meet within one year after the coming into force of the present Treaty, and at which German representatives may be present.

Article 350.

The mandate given by Article 57 of the Treaty of Berlin of July 13, 1878, to Austria-Hungary, and transferred by her to Hungary, to carry out works at the Iron Gates, is abrogated. The Commission entrusted with the administration of this part of the river shall lay down provisions for the settlement of accounts subject to the financial provisions of the present Treaty. Charges which may be necessary shall in no case be levied by Hungary.

Article 351.

Should the Czecho-Slovak State, the Serb-Croat-Slovene State or Roumania, with the authorisation of or under mandate from the International Commission, undertake maintenance, improvement, weir, or other works on a part of the river system which forms a frontier, these States shall enjoy on the opposite bank, and also on the part of the bed which is outside their territory, all necessary facilities for the survey, execution and maintenance of such works.

Article 352.

Germany shall be obliged to make to the European Commission of the Danube all restitutions, reparations and indemnities for damages inflicted on the Commission during the war.

Article 353.

Should a deep-draught Rhine-Danube navigable waterway be constructed, Germany undertakes to apply thereto the régime prescribed in Articles 332 to 338.

Chapter IV.

CLAUSES RELATING TO THE RHINE AND THE MOSELLE.

Article 354.

As from the coming into force of the present Treaty, the Convention of Mannheim of October 17, 1868, together with the Final Protocol thereof, shall continue to govern navigation on the Rhine, subject to the conditions hereinafter laid down.

In the event of any provisions of the said Convention being in conflict with those laid down by the General Convention referred to in Article 338 (which shall apply to the Rhine) the provisions of the General Convention shall prevail.

Within a maximum period of six months from the coming into force of the present Treaty, the Central Commission referred to in Article 355 shall meet to draw up a project of revision of the Convention of Mannheim. This project shall be drawn up in harmony with the provisions of the General Convention referred to above, should this have been concluded by that time, and shall be submitted to the Powers represented on the Central Commission. Germany hereby agrees to adhere to the project so drawn up.

Further, the modifications set out in the following Articles shall immediately be made in the Convention of Mannheim.

The Allied and Associated Powers reserve to themselves the right to arrive at an understanding in this connection with Holland, and Germany hereby agrees to accede if required to any such understanding.

ARTICLE 355.

The Central Commission provided for in the Convention of Mannheim shall consist of nineteen members, viz.:

2 representatives of the Netherlands;
2 representatives of Switzerland;
4 representatives of German riparian States;
4 representatives of France, which in addition shall appoint the President of the Commission;
2 representatives of Great Britain;
2 representatives of Italy;
2 representatives of Belgium.

The headquarters of the Central Commission shall be at Strasburg.

Whatever be the number of members present, each Delegation shall have the right to record a number of votes equal to the number of representatives allotted to it.

If certain of these representatives cannot be appointed at the time of the coming into force of the present Treaty, the decisions of the Commission shall nevertheless be valid.

ARTICLE 356.

Vessels of all nations, and their cargoes, shall have the same rights and privileges as those which are granted to vessels belonging to the Rhine navigation, and to their cargoes.

None of the provisions contained in Articles 15 to 20 and 26 of the above-mentioned Convention of Mannheim, in Article 4 of the Final Protocol thereof, or in later Conventions, shall impede the free navigation of vessels and crews of all nations on the Rhine and on waterways to which such Conventions apply, subject to compliance with the regulations concerning pilotage and other police measures drawn up by the Central Commission.

The provisions of Article 22 of the Convention of Mannheim and of Article 5 of the Final Protocol thereof shall be applied only to vessels registered on the Rhine. The Central Commission shall decide on the steps to be taken to ensure that other vessels satisfy the conditions of the general regulations applying to navigation on the Rhine.

ARTICLE 357.

Within a maximum period of three months from the date on which notification shall be given Germany shall cede to France tugs and vessels, from among those remaining registered in German Rhine ports after the deduction of those surrendered by way of restitution or reparation, or shares in German Rhine navigation companies.

When vessels and tugs are ceded, such vessels and tugs, together with their fittings and gear, shall be in good state of repair, shall be in condition to carry on commercial traffic on the Rhine, and shall be selected from among those most recently built.

The same procedure shall be followed in the matter of the cession by Germany to France of:

(1) the installations, berthing and anchorage accommodation, platforms, docks, warehouses, plant, etc., which German subjects or German companies owned on August 1, 1914, in the port of Rotterdam, and

(2) the shares or interests which Germany or German nationals possessed in such installations at the same date.

The amount and specifications of such cessions shall be determined within one year of the coming into force of the present Treaty by an arbitrator or arbitrators appointed by the United States of America, due regard being had to the legitimate needs of the parties concerned.

The cessions provided for in the present Article shall entail a credit of which the total amount, settled in a lump sum by the arbitrator or arbitrators mentioned above, shall not in any case exceed the value of the capital expended in the initial establishment of the ceded material and installations, and shall be set off against the total sums due from Germany; in consequence, the indemnification of the proprietors shall be a matter for Germany to deal with.

ARTICLE 358.

Subject to the obligation to comply with the provisions of the Convention of Mannheim or of the Convention which may be substituted therefor, and to the stipulations of the present Treaty, France shall have on the whole course of the Rhine included between the two extreme points of the French frontiers:

(a) the right to take water from the Rhine to feed navigation and irrigation canals (constructed or to be constructed) or for any other purpose, and to execute on the German bank all works necessary for the exercise of this right;

(b) the exclusive right to the power derived from works of regulation on the river, subject to the payment to Germany of the value of half the power actually produced, this payment, which will take into account the cost of the works necessary for producing the power, being made either in money or in power and in default of agreement being determined by arbitration. For this purpose France alone shall have the right to carry out in this part of the river all works of regulation (weirs or other works) which she may consider necessary for the production of power. Similarly, the right of taking water from the Rhine is accorded to Belgium to feed the Rhine-Meuse navigable waterway provided for below.

The exercise of the rights mentioned under (*a*) and (*b*) of the present Article shall not interfere with navigability nor reduce the facilities for navigation, either in the bed of the Rhine or in the derivations which may be substituted therefor, nor shall it involve any increase in the tolls formerly levied under the Convention in force. All proposed schemes shall be laid before the Central Commission in order that that Commission may assure itself that these conditions are complied with.

To ensure the proper and faithful execution of the provisions contained in (*a*) and (*b*) above, Germany:

(1) binds herself not to undertake or to allow the construction of any lateral canal or any derivation on the right bank of the river opposite the French frontiers;

(2) recognises the possession by France of the right of support on and the right of way over all lands situated on the right bank which may be required in order to survey, to build, and to operate weirs which France, with the consent of the Central Commission, may subsequently decide to establish. In accordance with such consent, France shall be entitled to decide upon and fix the limits of the necessary sites, and she shall be permitted to occupy such lands after a period of two months after simple notification, subject to the payment by her to Germany of indemnities of which the total amount shall be fixed by the Central Commission. Germany shall make it her business to indemnify the proprietors whose property will be burdened with such servitudes or permanently occupied by the works.

Should Switzerland so demand, and if the Central Commission approves, the same rights shall be accorded to Switzerland for the part of the river forming her frontier with other riparian States;

(3) shall hand over to the French Government, during the month following the coming into force of the present Treaty, all projects, designs, drafts of concessions and of specifications concerning the regulation of the Rhine for any purpose whatever which have been drawn up or received by the Governments of Alsace-Lorraine or of the Grand Duchy of Baden.

Article 359.

Subject to the preceding provisions, no works shall be carried out in the bed or on either bank of the Rhine where it forms the boundary of France and Germany without the previous approval of the Central Commission or of its agents.

Article 360.

France reserves the option of substituting herself as regards the rights and obligations resulting from agreements arrived at between the Government of Alsace-Lorraine and the Grand Duchy of Baden concerning the works to be carried out on the Rhine; she may also denounce such agreements within a term of five years dating from the coming into force of the present Treaty.

France shall also have the option of causing works to be carried out which may be recognised as necessary by the Central Commission for the upkeep or improvement of the navigability of the Rhine above Mannheim.

ARTICLE 361.

Should Belgium within a period of 25 years from the coming into force of the present Treaty decide to create a deep-draught Rhine-Meuse navigable waterway, in the region of Ruhrort, Germany shall be bound to construct, in accordance with plans to be communicated to her by the Belgian Government, after agreement with the Central Commission, the portion of this navigable waterway situated within her territory..

The Belgian Government shall, for this purpose, have the right to carry out on the ground all necessary surveys.

Should Germany fail to carry out all or part of these works, the Central Commission shall be entitled to carry them out instead; and, for this purpose, the Commission may decide upon and fix the limits of the necessary sites and occupy the ground after a period of two months after simple notification, subject to the payment of indemnities to be fixed by it and paid by Germany.

This navigable waterway shall be placed under the same administrative régime as the Rhine itself, and the division of the cost of initial construction, including the above indemnities, among the States crossed thereby shall be made by the Central Commission.

ARTICLE 362.

Germany hereby agrees to offer no objection to any proposals of the Central Rhine Commission for extending its jurisdiction:

(1) to the Moselle below the Franco-Luxemburg frontier down to the Rhine, subject to the consent of Luxemburg;

(2) to the Rhine above Basle up to the Lake of Constance, subject to the consent of Switzerland;

(3) to the lateral canals and channels which may be established either to duplicate or to improve naturally navigable sections of the Rhine or the Moselle, or to connect two naturally navigable sections of these rivers, and also any other parts of the Rhine river system which may be covered by the General Convention provided for in Article 338 above.

CHAPTER V.

CLAUSES GIVING TO THE CZECHO-SLOVAK STATE THE USE OF NORTHERN PORTS.

ARTICLE 363.

In the ports of Hamburg and Stettin Germany shall lease to the Czecho-Slovak State, for a period of 99 years, areas which shall be placed under the general régime of free zones and shall be used for the direct transit of goods coming from or going to that State.

ARTICLE 364.

The delimitation of these areas, and their equipment, their exploitation, and in general all conditions for their utilisation, including the amount of the rental, shall be decided by a Commission consisting of one delegate of Germany, one delegate of the Czecho-Slovak State and one delegate of Great Britain.   These conditions shall be susceptible of revision every ten years in the same manner.

Germany declares in advance that she will adhere to the decisions so taken.

SECTION III.

RAILWAYS.

CHAPTER I.

CLAUSES RELATING TO INTERNATIONAL TRANSPORT.

ARTICLE 365.

Goods coming from the territories of the Allied and Associated Powers, and going to Germany, or in transit through Germany from or to the territories of the Allied and Associated Powers, shall enjoy on the German railways as regards charges to be collected (rebates and drawbacks being taken into account), facilities, and all other matters, the most favourable treatment applied to goods of the same kind carried on any German lines, either in internal traffic, or for export, import or in transit, under similar conditions of transport, for example as regards length of route.   The same rule shall be applied, on the request of one or more of the Allied and Associated Powers, to goods specially designated by such Power or Powers coming from Germany and going to their territories.

International tariffs established in accordance with the rates referred to in the preceding paragraph and involving through waybills shall be established when one of the Allied and Associated Powers shall require it from Germany.

ARTICLE 366.

From the coming into force of the present Treaty the High Contracting Parties shall renew, in so far as concerns them and under the reserves indicated in the second paragraph of the present Article, the conventions and arrangements signed at Berne on October 14, 1890, September 20, 1893, July 16, 1895, June 16, 1898, and September 19, 1906, regarding the transportation of goods by rail.

If within five years from the date of the coming into force of the present Treaty a new convention for the transportation of passengers, luggage and goods by rail shall have been concluded to replace the Berne Convention of October 14, 1890, and the subsequent additions referred to above, this new convention and the supplementary provisions for international transport by rail which may be based on it shall bind Germany, even if she shall have refused to take part in the preparation of the convention or to subscribe to it.   Until a new convention shall have been concluded, Germany shall conform to the provisions of the Berne Convention and the subsequent additions referred to above, and to the current supplementary provisions.

ARTICLE 367.

Germany shall be bound to co-operate in the establishment of through ticket services (for passengers and their luggage) which shall be required by any of the Allied and Associated Powers to ensure their communication by rail with each other and with all other countries by transit across the territories of Germany; in particular Germany shall, for this purpose, accept trains and carriages coming from the territories of the Allied and Associated Powers and shall forward them with a speed at least equal to that of her best long-distance trains on the same lines. The rates applicable to such through services shall not in any case be higher than the rates collected on German internal services for the same distance, under the same conditions of speed and comfort.

The tariffs applicable under the same conditions of speed and comfort to the transportation of emigrants going to or coming from ports of the Allied and Associated Powers and using the German railways shall not be at a higher kilometric rate than the most favourable tariffs (drawbacks and rebates being taken into account) enjoyed on the said railways by emigrants going to or coming from any other ports.

ARTICLE 368.

Germany shall not apply specially to such through services, or to the transportation of emigrants going to or coming from the ports of the Allied and Associated Powers, any technical, fiscal or administrative measures, such as measures of customs examination, general police, sanitary police, and control, the result of which would be to impede or delay such services.

ARTICLE 369.

In case of transport partly by rail and partly by internal navigation, with or without through way-bill, the preceding Articles shall apply to the part of the journey performed by rail.

CHAPTER II.

ROLLING-STOCK.

ARTICLE 370.

Germany undertakes that German wagons shall be fitted with apparatus allowing:

(1) of their inclusion in goods trains on the lines of such of the Allied and Associated Powers as are parties to the Berne Convention of May 15, 1886, as modified on May 18, 1907, without hampering the action of the continuous brake which may be adopted in such countries within ten years of the coming into force of the present Treaty, and

(2) of the acceptance of wagons of such countries in all goods trains on the German lines.

The rolling stock of the Allied and Associated Powers shall enjoy on the German lines the same treatment as German rolling stock as regards movement, upkeep and repairs.

CHAPTER III.

CESSIONS OF RAILWAY LINES.

ARTICLE 371.

Subject to any special provisions concerning the cession of ports, waterways and railways situated in the territories over which Germany abandons her sovereignty, and to the financial conditions relating to the concessionnaires and the pensioning of the personnel, the cession of railways will take place under the following conditions:

(1) The works and installations of all the railroads shall be handed over complete and in good condition.

(2) When a railway system possessing its own rolling-stock is handed over in its entirety by Germany to one of the Allied and Associated Powers, such stock shall be handed over complete, in accordance with the last inventory before November 11, 1918, and in a normal state of upkeep.

(3) As regards lines without any special rolling-stock, Commissions of experts designated by the Allied and Associated Powers, on which Germany shall be represented, shall fix the proportion of the stock existing on the system to which those lines belong to be handed over. These Commissions shall have regard to the amount of the material registered on these lines in the last inventory before November 11, 1918, the length of track (sidings included), and the nature and amount of the traffic. These Commissions shall also specify the locomotives, carriages and wagons to be handed over in each case; they shall decide upon the conditions of their acceptance, and shall make the provisional arrangements necessary to ensure their repair in German workshops.

(4) Stocks of stores, fittings and plant shall be handed over under the same conditions as the rolling-stock.

The provisions of paragraphs 3 and 4 above shall be applied to the lines of former Russian Poland converted by Germany to the German gauge, such lines being regarded as detached from the Prussian State System.

CHAPTER IV.

PROVISIONS RELATING TO CERTAIN RAILWAY LINES.

ARTICLE 372.

When as a result of the fixing of new frontiers a railway connection between two parts of the same country crosses another country, or a branch line from one country has its terminus in another, the conditions of working, if not specifically provided for in the present Treaty, shall be laid down in a convention between the railway administrations concerned. If the administrations cannot come to an agreement as to the terms of such convention, the points of difference shall be decided by commissions of experts composed as provided in the preceding Article.

ARTICLE 373.

Within a period of five years from the coming into force of the present Treaty the Czecho-Slovak State may require the construction of a railway line in German territory between the stations of Schlauney and Nachod. The cost of construction shall be borne by the Czecho-Slovak State.

ARTICLE 374.

Germany undertakes to accept, within ten years of the coming into force of the present Treaty, on request being made by the Swiss Government after agreement with the Italian Government, the denunciation of the International Convention of October 13, 1909, relative to the St. Gothard railway. In the absence of agreement as to the conditions of such denunciation, Germany hereby agrees to accept the decision of an arbitrator designated by the United States of America.

CHAPTER V.

TRANSITORY PROVISIONS.

ARTICLE 375.

Germany shall carry out the instructions given her, in regard to transport, by an authorised body acting on behalf of the Allied and Associated Powers:

(1) For the carriage of troops under the provisions of the present Treaty, and of material, ammunition and supplies for army use;

(2) As a temporary measure, for the transportation of supplies for certain regions, as well as for the restoration, as rapidly as possible, of the normal conditions of transport, and for the organisation of postal and telegraphic services.

SECTION IV.

DISPUTES

AND REVISION OF PERMANENT CLAUSES.

ARTICLE 376.

Disputes which may arise between interested Powers with regard to the interpretation and application of the preceding Articles shall be settled as provided by the League of Nations.

ARTICLE 377.

At any time the League of Nations may recommend the revision of such of these Articles as relate to a permanent administrative régime.

ARTICLE 378.

The stipulations in Articles 321 to 330, 332, 365, and 367 to 369 shall be subject to revision by the Council of the League of Nations at any time after five years from the coming into force of the present Treaty.

Failing such revision, no Allied or Associated Power can claim after the expiration of the above period of five years the benefit of any of the stipulations in the Articles enumerated above on behalf of any portion of its territories in which reciprocity is not accorded in respect of such stipulations. The period of five years during which reciprocity cannot be demanded may be prolonged by the Council of the League of Nations.

Section V.

SPECIAL PROVISION.

Article 379.

Without prejudice to the special obligations imposed on her by the present Treaty for the benefit of the Allied and Associated Powers, Germany undertakes to adhere to any General Conventions regarding the international régime of transit, waterways, ports or railways which may be concluded by the Allied and Associated Powers, with the approval of the League of Nations, within five years of the coming into force of the present Treaty.

Section VI.

CAUSES RELATING TO THE KIEL CANAL.

Article 380.

The Kiel Canal and its approaches shall be maintained free and open to the vessels of commerce and of war of all nations at peace with Germany on terms of entire equality.

Article 381.

The nationals, property and vessels of all Powers shall, in respect of charges, facilities, and in all other respects, be treated on a footing of perfect equality in the use of the Canal, no distinction being made to the detriment of nationals, property and vessels of any Power between them and the nationals, property and vessels of Germany or of the most favoured nation.

No impediment shall be placed on the movement of persons or vessels other than those arising out of police, customs, sanitary, emigration or immigration regulations and those relating to the import or export of prohibited goods. Such regulations must be reasonable and uniform and must not unnecessarily impede traffic.

Article 382.

Only such charges may be levied on vessels using the Canal or its approaches as are intended to cover in an equitable manner the cost of maintaining in a navigable condition, or of improving, the Canal or its approaches, or to meet expenses incurred in the interests of navigation. The schedule of such charges shall be calculated on the basis of such expenses, and shall be posted up in the ports.

These charges shall be levied in such a manner as to render any detailed examination of cargoes unnecessary, except in the case of suspected fraud or contravention.

ARTICLE 383.

Goods in transit may be placed under seal or in the custody of customs agents; the loading and unloading of goods, and the embarkation and disembarkation of passengers, shall only take place in the ports specified by Germany.

ARTICLE 384.

No charges of any kind other than those provided for in the present Treaty shall be levied along the course or at the approaches of the Kiel Canal.

ARTICLE 385.

Germany shall be bound to take suitable measures to remove any obstacle or danger to navigation, and to ensure the maintenance of good conditions of navigation. She shall not undertake any works of a nature to impede navigation on the Canal or its approaches.

ARTICLE 386.

In the event of violation of any of the conditions of Articles 380 to 386, or of disputes as to the interpretation of these Articles, any interested Power can appeal to the jurisdiction instituted for the purpose by the League of Nations.

In order to avoid reference of small questions to the League of Nations, Germany will establish a local authority at Kiel qualified to deal with disputes in the first instance and to give satisfaction so far as possible to complaints which may be presented through the consular representatives of the interested Powers.

PART XIII.

LABOUR.

SECTION I.

ORGANISATION OF LABOUR.

Whereas the League of Nations has for its object the establishment of universal peace, and such a peace can be established only if it is based upon social justice;

And whereas conditions of labour exist involving such injustice, hardship and privation to large numbers of people as to produce unrest so great that the peace and harmony of the world are imperilled; and an improvement of those conditions is urgently required: as, for example, by the regulation of the hours of work, including the establishment of a maximum working day and week, the regulation of the labour supply, the prevention of unemployment, the provision of an adequate living wage, the protection of the worker against sickness, disease and injury arising out of his employment, the protection of children, young persons and women, provision for old age and injury, protection of the interests of workers when employed in countries other than their own, recognition of the principle of freedom of association, the organisation of vocational and technical education and other measures;

Whereas also the failure of any nation to adopt humane conditions of labour is an obstacle in the way of other nations which desire to improve the conditions in their own countries;

The HIGH CONTRACTING PARTIES, moved by sentiments of justice and humanity as well as by the desire to secure the permanent peace of the world, agree to the following:

CHAPTER I.

ORGANISATION.

ARTICLE 387.

A permanent organisation is hereby established for the promotion of the objects set forth in the Preamble.

The original Members of the League of Nations shall be the original Members of this organisation, and hereafter membership of the League of Nations shall carry with it membership of the said organisation.

ARTICLE 388.

The permanent organisation shall consist of:

(1) a General Conference of Representatives of the Members and,

(2) an International Labour Office controlled by the Governing Body described in Article 393.

ARTICLE 389.

The meetings of the General Conference of Representatives of the Members shall be held from time to time as occasion may require, and at least once in every year. It shall be composed of four Representatives of each of the Members, of whom two shall be Government Delegates and the two others shall be Delegates representing respectively the employers and the workpeople of each of the Members.

Each Delegate may be accompanied by advisers, who shall not exceed two in number for each item on the agenda of the meeting. When questions specially affecting women are to be considered by the Conference, one at least of the advisers should be a woman.

The Members undertake to nominate non-Government Delegates and advisers chosen in agreement with the industrial organisations, if such organisations exist, which are most representative of employers or workpeople, as the case may be, in their respective countries.

Advisers shall not speak except on a request made by the Delegate whom they accompany and by the special authorization of the President of the Conference, and may not vote.

A Delegate may by notice in writing addressed to the President appoint one of his advisers to act as his deputy, and the adviser, while so acting, shall be allowed to speak and vote.

The names of the Delegates and their advisers will be communicated to the International Labour Office by the Government of each of the Members.

The credentials of Delegates and their advisers shall be subject to scrutiny by the Conference, which may, by two-thirds of the votes cast by the Delegates present, refuse to admit any Delegate or adviser whom it deems not to have been nominated in accordance with this Article.

ARTICLE 390.

Every Delegate shall be entitled to vote individually on all matters which are taken into consideration by the Conference.

If one of the Members fails to nominate one of the non-Government Delegates whom it is entitled to nominate, the other non-Government Delegate shall be allowed to sit and speak at the Conference, but not to vote.

If in accordance with Article 389 the Conference refuses admission to a Delegate of one of the Members, the provisions of the present Article shall apply as if that Delegate had not been nominated.

ARTICLE 391.

The meetings of the Conference shall be held at the seat of the League of Nations, or at such other place as may be decided by the Conference at a previous meeting by two-thirds of the votes cast by the Delegates present.

ARTICLE 392.

The International Labour Office shall be established at the seat of the League of Nations as part of the organisation of the League.

ARTICLE 393.

The International Labour Office shall be under the control of a Governing Body consisting of twenty-four persons, appointed in accordance with the following provisions:

The Governing Body of the International Labour Office shall be constituted as follows:

Twelve persons representing the Governments;

Six persons elected by the Delegates to the Conference representing the employers;

Six persons elected by the Delegates to the Conference representing the workers.

Of the twelve persons representing the Governments eight shall be nominated by the Members which are of the chief industrial importance, and four shall be nominated by the Members selected for the purpose by the Government Delegates to the Conference, excluding the Delegates of the eight Members mentioned above.

Any question as to which are the Members of the chief industrial importance shall be decided by the Council of the League of Nations.

The period of office of the Members of the Governing Body will be three years. The method of filling vacancies and other similar questions may be determined by the Governing Body subject to the approval of the Conference.

The Governing Body shall, from time to time, elect one of its members to act as its Chairman, shall regulate its own procedure and shall fix its own times of meeting. A special meeting shall be held if a written request to that effect is made by at least ten members of the Governing Body.

ARTICLE 394.

There shall be a Director of the International Labour Office, who shall be appointed by the Governing Body, and, subject to the instructions of the Governing Body, shall be responsible for the efficient conduct of the International Labour Office and for such other duties as may be assigned to him.

The Director or his deputy shall attend all meetings of the Governing Body.

ARTICLE 395.

The staff of the International Labour Office shall be appointed by the Director, who shall, so far as is possible with due regard to the efficiency of the work of the Office, select persons of different nationalities. A certain number of these persons shall be women.

ARTICLE 396.

The functions of the International Labour Office shall include the collection and distribution of information on all subjects relating to the international adjustment of conditions of industrial life and labour, and particularly the examination of subjects which it is proposed to bring before the Conference with a view to the conclusion of international conventions, and the conduct of such special investigations as may be ordered by the Conference.

It will prepare the agenda for the meetings of the Conference.

It will carry out the duties required of it by the provisions of this Part of the present Treaty in connection with international disputes.

It will edit and publish in French and English, and in such other languages as the Governing Body may think desirable, a periodical paper dealing with problems of industry and employment of international interest.

Generally, in addition to the functions set out in this Article, it shall have such other powers and duties as may be assigned to it by the Conference.

ARTICLE 397.

The Government Departments of any of the Members which deal with questions of industry and employment may communicate directly with the Director through the Representative of their Government on the Governing Body of the International Labour Office, or failing any such Representative, through such other qualified official as the Government may nominate for the purpose.

ARTICLE 398.

The International Labour Office shall be entitled to the assistance of the Secretary-General of the League of Nations in any matter in which it can be given.

ARTICLE 399.

Each of the Members will pay the travelling and subsistence expenses of its Delegates and their advisers and of its Representatives attending the meetings of the Conference or Governing Body, as the case may be.

All the other expenses of the International Labour Office and of the meetings of the Conference or Governing Body shall be paid to the Director by the Secretary-General of the League of Nations out of the general funds of the League.

The Director shall be responsible to the Secretary-General of the League for the proper expenditure of all moneys paid to him in pursuance of this Article.

CHAPTER II.

PROCEDURE.

ARTICLE 400.

The agenda for all meetings of the Conference will be settled by the Governing Body, who shall consider any suggestion as to the agenda that may be made by the Government of any of the Members or by any representative organisation recognised for the purpose of Article 389.

ARTICLE 401.

The Director shall act as the Secretary of the Conference, and shall transmit the agenda so as to reach the Members four months before the meeting of the Conference, and, through them, the non-Government Delegates when appointed.

ARTICLE 402.

Any of the Governments of the Members may formally object to the inclusion of any item or items in the agenda. The grounds for such objection shall be set forth in a reasoned statement addressed to the Director, who shall circulate it to all the Members of the Permanent Organisation.

Items to which such objection has been made shall not, however, be excluded from the agenda, if at the Conference a majority of two-thirds of the votes cast by the Delegates present is in favour of considering them.

If the Conference decides (otherwise than under the preceding paragraph) by two-thirds of the votes cast by the Delegates present that any subject shall be considered by the Conference, that subject shall be included in the agenda for the following meeting.

ARTICLE 403.

The Conference shall regulate its own procedure, shall elect its own President, and may appoint committees to consider and report on any matter.

Except as otherwise expressly provided in this Part of the present Treaty, all matters shall be decided by a simple majority of the votes cast by the Delegates present.

The voting is void unless the total number of votes cast is equal to half the number of the Delegates attending the Conference.

ARTICLE 404.

The Conference may add to any committees which it appoints technical experts, who shall be assessors without power to vote.

ARTICLE 405.

When the Conference has decided on the adoption of proposals with regard to an item in the agenda, it will rest with the Conference to determine whether these proposals should take the form: (a) of a recommendation to be submitted to the Members for consideration with a view to effect being given to it by national legislation or otherwise, or (b) of a draft international convention for ratification by the Members.

In either case a majority of two-thirds of the votes cast by the Delegates present shall be necessary on the final vote for the adoption of the recommendation or draft convention, as the case may be, by the Conference.

In framing any recommendation or draft convention of general application the Conference shall have due regard to those countries in which climatic conditions, the imperfect development of industrial organisation or other special circumstances make the industrial conditions substantially different and shall suggest the modifications, if any, which it considers may be required to meet the case of such countries.

A copy of the recommendation or draft convention shall be authenticated by the signature of the President of the Conference and of the Director and shall be deposited with the Secretary-General of the League of Nations. The Secretary-General will communicate a certified copy of the recommendation or draft convention to each of the Members.

Each of the Members undertakes that it will, within the period of one year at most from the closing of the session of the Conference, or if it is impossible owing to exceptional circumstances to do so within the period of one year, then at the earliest practicable moment and in no case later than eighteen months from the closing of the session of the Conference, bring the recommendation or draft convention before the authority or authorities within whose competence the matter lies, for the enactment of legislation or other action.

In the case of a recommendation, the Members will inform the Secretary-General of the action taken.

In the case of a draft convention, the Member will, if it obtains the consent of the authority or authorities within whose competence the matter lies, communicate the formal ratification of the convention to the Secretary-General and will take such action as may be necessary to make effective the provisions of such convention.

If on a recommendation no legislative or other action is taken to make a recommendation effective, or if the draft convention fails to obtain the consent of the authority or authorities within whose competence the matter lies, no further obligation shall rest upon the Member.

In the case of a federal State, the power of which to enter into conventions on labour matters is subject to limitations, it shall be in the discretion of that Government to treat a draft convention to which such limitations apply as a recommendation only, and the provisions of this Article with respect to recommendations shall apply in such case.

The above Article shall be interpreted in accordance with the following principle:

In no case shall any Member be asked or required, as a result of the adoption of any recommendation or draft convention by the Conference, to lessen the protection afforded by its existing legislation to the workers concerned.

ARTICLE 406.

Any convention so ratified shall be registered by the Secretary-General of the League of Nations, but shall only be binding upon the Members which ratify it.

ARTICLE 407.

If any convention coming before the Conference for final consideration fails to secure the support of two-thirds of the votes cast by the Delegates present, it shall nevertheless be within the right of any of the Members of the Permanent Organisation to agree to such convention among themselves.

Any convention so agreed to shall be communicated by the Governments concerned to the Secretary-General of the League of Nations, who shall register it.

ARTICLE 408.

Each of the Members agrees to make an annual report to the International Labour Office on the measures which it has taken to give effect to the provisions of conventions to which it is a party. These reports shall be made in such form and shall contain such particulars as the Governing Body may request. The Director shall lay a summary of these reports before the next meeting of the Conference.

ARTICLE 409.

In the event of any representation being made to the International Labour Office by an industrial association of employers or of workers that any of the Members has failed to secure in any respect the effective observance within its jurisdiction of any convention to which it is a party, the Governing Body may communicate this representation to the Government against which it is made and may invite that Government to make such statement on the subject as it may think fit.

ARTICLE 410.

If no statement is received within a reasonable time from the Government in question, or if the statement when received is not deemed to be satisfactory by the Governing Body, the latter shall have the right to publish the representation and the statement, if any, made in reply to it.

ARTICLE 411.

Any of the Members shall have the right to file a complaint with the International Labour Office if it is not satisfied that any other Member is securing the effective observance of any convention which both have ratified in accordance with the foregoing Articles.

The Governing Body may, if it thinks fit, before referring such a complaint to a Commission of Enquiry, as hereinafter provided for, communicate with the Government in question in the manner described in Article 409.

If the Governing Body does not think it necessary to communicate the complaint to the Government in question, or if, when they have made such communication, no statement in reply has been received within a reasonable time which the Governing Body considers to be satisfactory, the Governing Body may apply for the appointment of a Commission of Enquiry to consider the complaint and to report thereon.

The Governing Body may adopt the same procedure either of its own motion or on receipt of a complaint from a Delegate to the Conference.

When any matter arising out of Articles 410 or 411 is being considered by the Governing Body, the Government in question shall, if not already represented thereon, be entitled to send a representative to take part in the proceedings of the Governing Body while the matter is under consideration. Adequate notice of the date on which the matter will be considered shall be given to the Government in question.

ARTICLE 412.

The Commission of Enquiry shall be constituted in accordance with the following provisions:

Each of the Members agrees to nominate within six months of the date on which the present Treaty comes into force three persons of industrial experience, of whom one shall be a representative of employers, one a representative of workers, and one a person of independent standing, who shall together form a panel from which the Members of the Commission of Enquiry shall be drawn.

The qualifications of the persons so nominated shall be subject to scrutiny by the Governing Body, which may by two-thirds of the votes cast by the representatives present refuse to accept the nomination of any person whose qualifications do not in its opinion comply with the requirements of the present Article.

Upon the application of the Governing Body, the Secretary-General of the League of Nations shall nominate three persons, one from each section of this panel, to constitute the Commission of Enquiry, and shall designate one of them as the President of the Commission. None of these three persons shall be a person nominated to the panel by any Member directly concerned in the complaint.

ARTICLE 413.

The Members agree that, in the event of the reference of a complaint to a Commission of Enquiry under Article 411, they will each, whether directly concerned in the complaint or not, place at the disposal of the Commission all the information in their possession which bears upon the subject-matter of the complaint.

ARTICLE 414.

When the Commission of Enquiry has fully considered the complaint, it shall prepare a report embodying its findings on all questions of fact relevant to determining the issue between the parties and containing such recommendations as it may think proper as to the steps which should be taken to meet the complaint and the time within which they should be taken.

It shall also indicate in this report the measures, if any, of an economic character against a defaulting Governement which it considers to be appropriate, and which it considers other Governments would be justified in adopting.

ARTICLE 415.

The Secretary-General of the League of Nations shall communicate the report of the Commission of Enquiry to each of the Governments concerned in the complaint, and shall cause it to be published.

Each of these Governments shall within one month inform the Secretary-General of the League of Nations whether or not it accepts the recommendations contained in the report of the Commission; and if not, whether it proposes to refer the complaint to the Permanent Court of International Justice of the League of Nations.

ARTICLE 416.

In the event of any Member failing to take the action required by Article 405, with regard to a recommendation or draft Convention, any other Member shall be entitled to refer the matter to the Permanent Court of International Justice.

ARTICLE 417.

The decision of the Permanent Court of International Justice in regard to a complaint or matter which has been referred to it in pursuance of Article 415 or Article 416 shall be final.

ARTICLE 418.

The Permanent Court of International Justice may affirm, vary or reverse any of the findings or recommendations of the Commission of Enquiry, if any, and shall in its decision indicate the measures, if any, of an economic character which it considers to be appropriate, and which other Governments would be justified in adopting against a defaulting Government.

ARTICLE 419.

In the event of any Member failing to carry out within the time specified the recommendations, if any, contained in the report of the Commission of Enquiry, or in the decision of the Permanent Court of International Justice, as the case may be, any other Member may take against that Member the measures of an economic character indicated in the report of the Commission or in the decision of the Court as appropriate to the case.

ARTICLE 420.

The defaulting Government may at any time inform the Governing Body that it has taken the steps necessary to comply with the recommendations of the Commission of Enquiry or with those in the decision of the Permanent Court of International Justice, as the case may be, and may request it to apply to the Secretary-General of the League to constitute a Commission of Enquiry to verify its contention. In this case the provisions of Articles 412, 413, 414, 415, 417 and 418 shall apply, and if the report of the Commission of

Enquiry or the decision of the Permanent Court of International Justice is in favour of the defaulting Government, the other Governments shall forthwith discontinue the measures of an economic character that they have taken against the defaulting Government.

CHAPTER III.

GENERAL.

ARTICLE 421.

The Members engage to apply conventions which they have ratified in accordance with the provisions of this Part of the present Treaty to their colonies, protectorates and possessions which are not fully self-governing:

(1) Except where owing to the local conditions the convention is inapplicable, or

(2) Subject to such modifications as may be necessary to adapt the convention to local conditions.

And each of the Members shall notify to the International Labour Office the action taken in respect of each of its colonies, protectorates and possessions which are not fully self-governing.

ARTICLE 422.

Amendments to this Part of the present Treaty which are adopted by the Conference by a majority of two-thirds of the votes cast by the Delegates present shall take effect when ratified by the States whose representatives compose the Council of the League of Nations and by three-fourths of the Members.

ARTICLE 423.

Any question or dispute relating to the interpretation of this Part of the present Treaty or of any subsequent convention concluded by the Members in pursuance of the provisions of this Part of the present Treaty shall be referred for decision to the Permanent Court of International Justice.

CHAPTER IV.

TRANSITORY PROVISIONS.

ARTICLE 424.

The first meeting of the Conference shall take place in October, 1919. The place and agenda for this meeting shall be as specified in the Annex hereto.

Arrangements for the convening and the organisation of the first meeting of the Conference will be made by the Government designated for the purpose in the said Annex. That Government shall be assisted in the preparation of the documents for submission to the Conference by an International Committee constituted as provided in the said Annex.

The expenses of the first meeting and of all subsequent meetings held before the League of Nations has been able to establish a general fund, other than the expenses of Delegates and their advisers, will be borne by the Members in accordance with the apportionment of the expenses of the International Bureau of the Universal Postal Union.

ARTICLE 425.

Until the League of Nations has been constituted all communications which under the provisions of the foregoing Articles should be addressed to the Secretary-General of the League will be preserved by the Director of the International Labour Office, who will transmit them to the Secretary-General of the League.

ARTICLE 426.

Pending the creation of a Permanent Court of International Justice disputes which in accordance with this Part of the present Treaty would be submitted to it for decision will be referred to a tribunal of three persons appointed by the Council of the League of Nations.

ANNEX.

FIRST MEETING OF ANNUAL LABOUR CONFERENCE, 1919.,

The place of meeting will be Washington.

The Government of the United States of America is requested to convene the Conference.

The International Organising Committee will consist of seven Members, appointed by the United States of America, Great Britain, France, Italy, Japan, Belgium and Switzerland. The Committee may, if it thinks necessary, invite other Members to appoint representatives.

Agenda:

(1) Application of principle of the 8-hours day or of the 48-hours week.

(2) Question of preventing or providing against unemployment.

(3) Women's employment:

    (a) Before and after child-birth, including the question of maternity benefit: •

    (b) During the night;

    (c) In unhealthy processes.

(4) Employment of children:

    (a) Minimum age of employment;

    (b) During the night;

    (c) In unhealthy processes.

(5) Extension and application of the International Conventions adopted at Berne in 1906 on the prohibition of night work for women employed in industry and the prohibition of the use of white phosphorus in the manufacture of matches.

SECTION II.

GENERAL PRINCIPLES.

ARTICLE 427.

The High Contracting Parties, recognising that the well-being, physical, moral and intellectual, of industrial wage-earners is of supreme international importance, have framed, in order to further this great end, the permanent machinery provided for in Section I and associated with that of the League of Nations.

They recognise that differences of climate, habits and customs, of economic opportunity and industrial tradition, make strict uniformity in the conditions of labour difficult of immediate attainment. But, holding as they do, that labour should not be regarded merely as an article of commerce, they think that there are methods and principles for regulating labour conditions which all industrial communities should endeavour to apply, so far as their special circumstances will permit.

Among these methods and principles, the following seem to the High Contracting Parties to be of special and urgent importance:

First.—The guiding principle above enunciated that labour should not be regarded merely as a commodity or article of commerce.

Second.—The right of association for all lawful purposes by the employed as well as by the employers.

Third.—The payment to the employed of a wage adequate to maintain a reasonable standard of life as this is understood in their time and country.

Fourth.—The adoption of an eight hours day or a forty-eight hours week as the standard to be aimed at where it has not already been attained.

Fifth.—The adoption of a weekly rest of at least twenty-four hours, which should include Sunday wherever practicable.

Sixth.—The abolition of child labour and the imposition of such limitations on the labour of young persons as shall permit the continuation of their education and assure their proper physical development.

Seventh.—The principle that men and women should receive equal remuneration for work of equal value.

Eighth.—The standard set by law in each country with respect to the conditions of labour should have due regard to the equitable economic treatment of all workers lawfully resident therein.

Ninth.—Each State should make provision for a system of inspection in which women should take part, in order to ensure the enforcement of the laws and regulations for the protection of the employed.

Without claiming that these methods and principles are either complete or final, the High Contracting Parties are of opinion that they are well fitted to guide the policy of the League of Nations; and that, if adopted by the industrial communities who are members of the League, and safeguarded in practice by an adequate system of such inspection, they will confer lasting benefits upon the wage-earners of the world.

PART XIV.

GUARANTEES.

SECTION 1.

WESTERN EUROPE.

ARTICLE 428.

As a guarantee for the execution of the present Treaty by Germany, the German territory situated to the west of the Rhine, together with the bridgeheads, will be occupied by Allied and Associated troops for a period of fifteen years from the coming into force of the present Treaty.

ARTICLE 429.

If the conditions of the present Treaty are faithfully carried out by Germany, the occupation referred to in Article 428 will be successively restricted as follows:

(1) At the expiration of five years there will be evacuated: the bridgehead of Cologne and the territories north of a line running along the Ruhr, then along the railway Jülich, Duren, Euskirchen, Rheinbach, thence along the road Rheinbach to Sinzig, and reaching the Rhine at the confluence with the Ahr; the roads, railways and places mentioned above being excluded from the area evacuated.

(2) At the expiration of ten years there will be evacuated: the bridgehead of Coblenz and the territories north of a line to be drawn from the intersection between the frontiers of Belgium, Germany and Holland, running about from 4 kilometres south of Aix la-Chapelle, then to and following the crest of Forst Gemünd, then east of the railway of the Urft Valley, then along Blankenheim, Valdorf, Dreis, Ulmen to and following the Moselle from Bremm to Nehren, then passing by Kappel and Simmern, then following the ridge of the heights between Simmern and the Rhine and reaching this river at Bacharach; all the places, valleys, roads and railways mentioned above being excluded from the area evacuated.

(3) At the expiration of fifteen years there will be evacuated: the bridgehead of Mainz, the bridgehead of Kehl and the remainder of the German territory under occupation.

If at that date the guarantees against unprovoked aggression by Germany are not considered sufficient by the Allied and Associated Governments, the evacuation of the occupying troops may be delayed to the extent regarded as necessary for the purpose of obtaining the required guarantees.

ARTICLE 430.

In case either during the occupation or after the expiration of the fifteen years referred to above the Reparation Commission finds that Germany refuses to observe the whole or part of her obligations under the present Treaty with regard to reparation, the whole or part of the areas specified in Article 429 will be re-occupied immediately by the Allied and Associated forces.

ARTICLE 431.

If before the expiration of the period of fifteen years Germany complies with all the undertakings resulting from the present Treaty, the occupying forces will be withdrawn immediately.

ARTICLE 432.

All matters relating to the occupation and not provided for by the present Treaty shall be regulated by subsequent agreements, which Germany hereby undertakes to observe.

SECTION II.

EASTERN EUROPE.

ARTICLE 433.

As a guarantee for the execution of the provisions of the present Treaty, by which Germany accepts definitely the abrogation of the Brest-Litovsk Treaty, and of all treaties, conventions and agreements entered into by her with the Maximalist Government in Russia, and in order to ensure the restoration of peace and good government in the Baltic Provinces and Lithuania, all German troops at present in the said territories shall return to within the frontiers of Germany as soon as the Governments of the Principal Allied and Associated Powers shall think the moment suitable, having regard to the internal situation of these territories. These troops shall abstain from all requisitions and seizures and from any other coercive measures, with a view to obtaining supplies intended for Germany, and shall in no way interfere with such measures for national defence as may be adopted by the Provisional Governments of Esthonia, Latvia and Lithuania.

No other German troops shall, pending the evacuation or after the evacuation is complete, be admitted to the said territories.

PART XV.

MISCELLANEOUS PROVISIONS.

ARTICLE 434.

Germany undertakes to recognise the full force of the Treaties of Peace and Additional Conventions which may be concluded by the Allied and Associated Powers with the Powers who fought on the side of Germany and to recognise whatever dispositions may be made concerning the territories of the former Austro-Hungarian Monarchy, of the Kingdom of Bulgaria and of the Ottoman Empire, and to recognize the new States within their frontiers as there laid down.

ARTICLE 435.

The High Contracting Parties, while they recognize the guarantees stipulated by the Treaties of 1815, and especially by the Act of November 20, 1815, in favour of Switzerland, the said guarantees constituting international obligations for the maintenance of peace, declare nevertheless that the provisions of these treaties, conventions, declarations and other supplementary Acts concerning the neutralized zone of Savoy, as laid down in paragraph 1 of Article 92 of the Final Act of the Congress of Vienna and in paragraph 2 of Article 3 of the Treaty of Paris of November 20, 1815, are no longer consistent with present conditions. For this reason the High Contracting Parties take note of the agreement reached between the French Government and the Swiss Government for the abrogation of the stipulations relating to this zone which are and remain abrogated.

The High Contracting Parties also agree that the stipulations of the Treaties of 1815 and of the other supplementary Acts concerning the free zones of Upper Savoy and the Gex district are no longer consistent with present conditions, and that it is for France and Switzerland to come to an agreement together with a view to settling between themselves the status of these territories under such conditions as shall be considered suitable by both countries.

ANNEX.

I

The Swiss Federal Council has informed the French Government on May 5, 1919, that after examining the provisions of Article 435 in a like spirit of sincere friendship it has happily reached the conclusion that it was possible to acquiesce in it under the following conditions and reservations:

(1) The neutralized zone of Haute-Savoie:

(a) It will be understood that as long as the Federal Chambers have not ratified the agreement come to between the two Governments concerning the abrogation of the stipulations in respect of the neutralized zone of Savoy, nothing will be definitively settled, on one side or the other, in regard to this subject.

(b) The assent given by the Swiss Government to the abrogation of the above mentioned stipulations presupposes, in conformity with the text adopted, the recognition of the guarantees formulated in favour of Switzerland by the Treaties of 1815 and particularly by the Declaration of November 20, 1815.

(c) The agreement between the Governments of France and Switzerland for the abrogation of the above mentioned stipulations will only be considered as valid if the Treaty of Peace contains this Article in its present wording. In addition the Parties to the Treaty of Peace should endeavour to obtain the assent of the signatory Powers of the Treaties of 1815 and of the Declaration of November 20, 1815, which are not signatories of the present Treaty of Peace.

(2) Free zone of Haute-Savoie and the district of Gex:

(a) The Federal Council makes the most express reservations to the interpretation to be given to the statement mentioned in the last paragraph of the above Article for insertion in the Treaty of Peace, which provides that "the stipulations of the Treaties of 1815 and other supplementary acts concerning the free zones of Haute-Savoie and the Gex district are no longer consistent with present conditions". The Federal Council would not wish that its acceptance of the above wording should lead to the conclusion that it would agree to the suppression of a system intended to give neighbouring territory the benefit of a special régime which is appropriate to the geographical and economical situation and which has been well tested.

In the opinion of the Federal Council the question is not the modification of the customs system of the zones as set up by the Treaties mentioned above, but only the regulation in a manner more appropriate to the economic conditions of the present day of the terms of the exchange of goods between the regions in question. The Federal Council has been led to make the preceding observations by the perusal of the draft Convention concerning the future constitution of the zones which was annexed to the note of April 26 from the French Government. While making the above reservations the Federal Council declares its readiness to examine in the most friendly spirit any proposals which the French Government may deem it convenient to make on the subject.

(b) It is conceded that the stipulations of the Treaties of 1815 and other supplementary acts relative to the free zones will remain in force until a new arrangement is come to between France and Switzerland to regulate matters in this territory.

II

The French Government have addressed to the Swiss Government, on May 18, 1919, the following note in reply to the communication set out in the preceding paragraph:

In a note dated May 5 the Swiss Legation in Paris was good enough to inform the Government of the French Republic that the Federal Government adhered to the proposed Article to be inserted in the Treaty of Peace between the Allied and Associated Governments and Germany.

The French Government have taken note with much pleasure of the agreement thus reached, and, at their request, the proposed Article, which had been accepted by the Allied and Associated Governments, has been inserted under No. 435 in the Peace conditions presented to the German Plenipotentiaries.

The Swiss Government, in their note of May 5 on this subject, have expressed various views and reservations.

Concerning the observations relating to the free zones of Haute-Savoie and the Gex district, the French Government have the honour to observe that the provisions of the last paragraph of Article 435 are so clear that their purport cannot be misapprehended, especially where it implies that no other Power but France and Switzerland will in future be interested in that question.

The French Government, on their part, are anxious to protect the interests of the French territories concerned, and, with that object, having their special situation in view, they bear in mind the desirability of assuring them a suitable customs régime and determining, in a manner better suited to present conditions, the methods of exchanges between these territories and the adjacent Swiss territories, while taking into account the reciprocal interests of both regions.

It is understood that this must in no way prejudice the right of France to adjust her customs line in this region in conformity with her political frontier, as is done on the other portions of her territorial boundaries, and as was done by Switzerland long ago on her own boundaries in this region.

The French Government are pleased to note on this subject in what a friendly disposition the Swiss Government take this opportunity of declaring their willingness to consider any French proposal dealing with the system to be substituted for the present régime of the said free zones, which the French Government intend to formulate in the same friendly spirit.

Moreover, the French Government have no doubt that the provisional maintenance of the régime of 1815 as to the free zones referred to in the above mentioned paragraph of the note from the Swiss Legation of May 5, whose object is to provide for the passage from the present régime to the conventional régime, will cause no delay whatsoever in the establishment of the new situation which has been found necessary by the two Governments. This remark applies also to the ratification by the Federal Chambers, dealt with in paragraph 1 (a), of the Swiss note of May 5, under the heading "Neutralized zone of Haute-Savoie".

ARTICLE 436.

The High Contracting Parties declare and place on record that they have taken note of the Treaty signed by the Government of the French Republic on July 17, 1918, with His Serene Highness the Prince of Monaco defining the relations between France and the Principality.

ARTICLE 437.

The High Contracting Parties agree that, in the absence of a subsequent agreement to the contrary, the Chairman of any Commission established by the present Treaty shall in the event of an equality of votes be entitled to a second vote.

ARTICLE 438.

The Allied and Associated Powers agree that where Christian religious missions were being maintained by German societies or persons in territory belonging to them, or of which the government is entrusted to them in accordance with the present Treaty, the property which these missions or missionary societies possessed, including that of trading societies whose profits were devoted to the support of missions, shall continue to be devoted to missionary purposes. In order to ensure the due execution of this undertaking the Allied and Associated Governments will hand over such property to boards of trustees appointed by or approved by the Governments and composed of persons holding the faith of the Mission whose property is involved.

The Allied and Associated Governments, while continuing to maintain full control as to the individuals by whom the Missions are conducted, will safeguard the interests of such Missions.

Germany, taking note of the above undertaking, agrees to accept all arrangements made or to be made by the Allied or Associated Government concerned for carrying on the work of the said missions or trading societies and waives all claims on their behalf.

ARTICLE 439.

Without prejudice to the provisions of the present Treaty, Germany undertakes not to put forward directly or indirectly against any Allied or Associated Power, signatory of the present Treaty, including those which without having declared war, have broken off diplomatic relations with the German Empire, any pecuniary claim based on events which occurred at any time before the coming into force of the present Treaty.

The present stipulation will bar completely and finally all claims of this nature, which will be thenceforward extinguished, whoever may be the parties in interest.

ARTICLE 440.

Germany accepts and recognises as valid and binding all decrees and orders concerning German shops and goods and all orders relating to the payment of costs made by any Prize Court of any of the Allied or Associated Powers, and undertakes not to put forward any claim arising out of such decrees or orders on behalf of any German national.

The Allied and Associated Powers reserve the right to examine in such manner as they may determine all decisions and orders of German Prize Courts, whether affecting the property rights of nationals of those Powers or of neutral Powers. Germany agrees to furnish copies of all the documents constituting the record of the cases, including the decisions and orders made, and to accept and give effect to the recommendations made after such examination of the cases.

THE PRESENT TREATY, of which the French and English texts are both authentic, shall be ratified.

The deposit of ratifications shall be made at Paris as soon as possible.

Powers of which the seat of the Government is outside Europe will be entitled merely to inform the Government of the French Republic through their diplomatic representative at Paris that their ratification has been given; in that case they must transmit the instrument of ratification as soon as possible.

A first procès-verbal of the deposit of ratifications will be drawn up as soon as the Treaty has been ratified by Germany on the one hand, and by three of the Principal Allied and Associated Powers on the other hand.

From the date of this first procès-verbal the Treaty will come into force between the High Contracting Parties who have ratified it. For the determination of all periods of time provided for in the present Treaty this date will be the date of the coming into force of the Treaty.

In all other respects the Treaty will enter into force for each Power at the date of the deposit of its ratification.

The French Government will transmit to all the signatory Powers a certified copy of the procès-verbaux of the deposit of ratifications.

IN FAITH WHEREOF the above-named Plenipotentiaries have signed the present Treaty.

Done at Versailles, the twenty-eighth day of june, one thousand nine hundred and nineteen, in a single copy which will remain deposited in the archives of the French Republic, and of which authenticated copies will be transmitted to each of the Signatory Powers.

INDEX.

Page.

O